GOVERNING RACE

GOVERNING RACE

Policy, Process, and the Politics of Race

NINA M. MOORE

 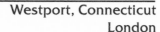

Westport, Connecticut
London

Library of Congress Cataloging-in-Publication Data

Moore, Nina M., 1966–
    Governing race : policy, process, and the politics of race / Nina M. Moore.
        p.   cm.
    Includes bibliographical references and index.
    ISBN 0-275-96761-1 (alk. paper)
    1. Afro-Americans—Civil rights—Government policy.   2. United States—Race
relations—Political aspects.   3. United States—Politics and
government—1945–1989—Decision making.   4. United States—Politics and
government—1989–1993—Decision making.   5. Civil rights—Government policy—United
States—History—20th century.   6. Afro-Americans—Legal status, laws, etc.   I. Title.
E185.61.M786   2000
323.1'196073'09045—dc21   00–022859

British Library Cataloguing in Publication Data is available.

Library of Congress Catalog Card Number: 00–022859
ISBN: 0-275-96761-1

First published in 2000

Praeger Publishers, 88 Post Road West, Westport, CT 06881
An imprint of Greenwood Publishing Group, Inc.
www.praeger.com

Printed in the United States of America

The paper used in this book complies with the
Permanent Paper Standard issued by the National
Information Standards Organization (Z39.48–1984).

10 9 8 7 6 5 4 3 2 1

For My Parents,

Charles and Nora Moore

and for

Dennis

Contents

Illustrations

TABLES

FIGURES

Preface

This book evolved out of my interest in a question that may, in retrospect, be unanswerable in the space of a few hundred pages. That question is perhaps the one most often asked by political scientists: why? Why, I wanted to know, did so many nationally elected lawmakers bother during the sixties with the concerns of a racial minority group that was not only at a numerical disadvantage in an arena of democratic politics, but socially, economically, and politically marginalized as well? Increasingly cognizant of the enormous majoritarian pressures to which legislators are subject, this was and remains an intriguing question to me.

Initially blind to the enormity of the task, I pursued the "why" question and, in the process, stumbled upon yet another, even more probing, inquiry. Perusing the files at several depositories of U.S. senators' personal papers, I found housed under "civil rights" as many and, in some cases, more boxes containing materials on Senate rules and procedures than those pertaining to the actual civil rights bills themselves. This finding was an eye-opener. It forced me to consider the obvious, namely, the special relevance of the infamous Senate filibuster rule for race-related legislative proposals. It seemed plausible to consider also the likelihood that race, in turn, proffered some unique implications for legislative procedure, in light of extensive evidence that the early rules reform efforts in the Senate were driven chiefly by a desire to enact civil rights legislation.

This book explores the relationship between race and institutional structure. It examines the impact that race has upon traditional institutional arrangements and, conversely, the effect of such arrangements upon race. Its basic argument is that race is such a divisive and contentious issue that it cannot be effectively governed. Race-related policy proposals typically have a destabilizing effect upon standard legislative process. And, the alternative process that typically emerges in place of the failed normal process has consistently forced race reform advocates to accept huge policy concessions that, by their nature, far exceed the normal give and take of consensus-building oriented policy negotiations. Driving it all—the abnormal procedural and policy outcomes attendant to racial politics—I argue, is the fact that race presents a challenge too difficult for American governing institutions to meet.

At its broadest level, the analysis concerns governance. It implies, first, that democratic governance yields special consequences in certain kinds of policy areas, namely, those characterized by extreme controversy. A second background theme of the analysis is that American governance is designed to facilitate meaningful resolution of matters about which there is already some measure of consensus in the larger political arena. It is relatively less well equipped to grapple with controversial issues, particularly those that overlap with major, long-standing political cleavages. The third, more central theoretical claim of the book is that issue politics drives institutional process and policy—that is, the politics of the issue "at issue" dictate the structure and substantive outcomes of government decisionmaking. And, as issues vary, so will institutional behavior and decisionmaking. Some are especially difficult and perhaps even impossible to govern through traditional parliamentary channels. Relatedly, some issues lend themselves to meaningful government resolution and some do not. In essence, to fully understand how government operates and what it accomplishes substantively, we must look to the nature of the "governance" challenge inherent in policy issues. The capacity to govern is a function of governability.

To support its basic contention that race is among the ungovernable issues, the book presents, to my knowledge, the most comprehensive, integrative analysis of modern civil rights politics and policymaking to date. It examines in detail nearly forty years of racial politics, civil rights parliamentary procedure, and federal civil rights law. It is this extensive empirical base of the book that, I believe, distinguishes the argument presented from its suspect past and also its potentially fatalistic undercurrent. It is, admittedly, a suspect argument because it is reminiscent of the objections voiced by many southern legislators who vigorously fought passage of civil rights laws. The so-called race problem, they argued, was not a matter of law, but a matter of the heart that the federal government could not and, in their view, should not attempt on its own to correct. The reader will find that normative overtones of this kind (or any other) are largely absent from the book's main discussion.

On its flip side, the incompatibility argument may also appear somewhat fatalistic at first glance. To posit a structural incongruity between race and governance may, to some, suggest the inevitability of weak race reform policies and, thus, the permanence of racial inequality. By illuminating the conditions that produce the misfit between race and governance, however, this book, in the same stroke, hints at the kind of changes that must take place in order for meaningful race reform to occur through governmental channels. The practical implications of this study are these: unless and until the conditions that have led to the outcomes highlighted in this analysis are changed, true socioeconomic and political race reform will remain a laudable, but elusive, goal of government policymakers.

Another aspect of the argument that perhaps deserves some prefatorial remark is its reading of the federal civil rights laws enacted during the sixties. The book departs from the view that these bills, collectively, have engendered monumental reform. There can be little question that these laws are appropriately deemed landmark legislation, if only because they broke a nearly 100-year record of inaction on Congress' part, and/or because they invalidated forced racial segregation in the South, and/or because they, in effect, "institutionalized" the race problem. Nonetheless, the bills' real life import is largely symbolic.

The sixties legislation essentially replicates the mandate of nondiscrimination already contained in the Fourteenth Amendment and entrusts courts with the responsibility of enforcing the constitutionally based right of equal treatment. This amounts to something I refer to as "constitutional redundancy." Added to this is perhaps the most telling fact: the sixties legislative reforms have failed to create tangible socioeconomic race reform. Hard evidence of this can be found in the disproportionate share of impoverishment, poor schooling, unemployment, ghettoization, and so on, to which blacks have had in the past and continue now to lay claim.

In addition to demonstrating the unsuitability of race for government and vice versa, there are also two scholarship objectives I hope to accomplish in the discussion and analysis to follow. The first is to stimulate more thinking about the uniqueness of race as a policy issue, as an issue that is quite distinguishable from most other policy issues in terms of what it brings to the legislative table and, also, as one that is capable of altering existing institutional arrangements. Finally, by way of analyzing the dynamics of governing race, I hope to also help bridge in a meaningful way what are closely related, but as yet insufficiently linked, approaches to the study of American politics, namely, the study of American institutions and the study of race.

During the course of researching and writing this book, I have accumulated a great many debts. Much of the groundwork for it was laid while completing my Ph.D. dissertation at the University of Chicago. Thus, I am especially grateful for the advice and support of my advisors Gary Orfield, Gerald R. Rosenberg, and William J. Wilson. I am thankful also for the last minute, but crucial "stand-in," contribution of Lynn Sanders. My insights at the early phases of this project were enormously enlightened by participation in the 1992–1993 *Race, Ethnicity, Representation and Governance* workshop series at Harvard University, which was funded by a travel grant from the Center for American Political Studies. The field research completed for this book was made possible by a research grant from the University of Minnesota and was greatly aided by the generous help of librarian Dale Johnson of the University of Montana and also John J. Kornacki and his staff at the Dirksen Congressional Leadership Research Center. Jenny Chanley of the Computer Center in the Department of Political Science at the University of Minnesota helped with the compilation of survey data. Hanes Walton, Jr., was instrumental in helping me to think more critically about certain aspects of the book's argument. He allowed me to bend his ear at various times, reviewed chapter drafts, and supplied additional research materials as food for thought. To each of these reviewers I am grateful for the time and energy they extended to this project. Any and all of the weaknesses in the discussion and analysis to follow are entirely my own. Finally, to the editor at Praeger, James T. Sabin, thank you for your confidence and your patience.

A personal thank you is owed to a number of individuals who have at various times indulged me in extensive conversations about race and power or who simply encouraged me to move toward a tangible finish line. Included among these are John Strassburger, Rodney Davis, Robert Seibert, Edwina Beavers, Frances Carter, Yvonne Miller, Anna Davis-Hall, Hugh Calhoun, Tawanna Brown, Luther V. Douthard, Richard D. Henton, Ronald B. Dewberry, the late Joseph R. Lee, and many more too numerous to list here. Finally, to my family, especially Debra, Linda, and Greg, for their constant support and good humor, I owe my biggest thanks. As a special expression of gratitude for their enduring faith and confidence, I dedicate this book to my parents, Charles and Nora Moore, and to my son, Dennis, who is, quite simply, my inspiration.

Introduction

Race cannot be governed. It cannot be accommodated by existing institutional arrangements, nor can those arrangements produce policies sufficient to redress the more entrenched elements of the race problem. In short, race and American governance are incompatible. The driving force behind this strained relationship is the politics of race. Race is among the most divisive, controversial issues in American politics. And, it is this circumstance that renders the race problem unsuitable for governance. The main objective of this book is to illuminate the existence and underlying causes of what it contends is a fundamental misfit between race and governance.

The contention that race is an unworkable policy issue suggests more broadly that there is a dynamic relationship between political issues and governing processes. The manner in which government grapples with certain societal problems and also the extent to which such problems can be adequately resolved by government are variable. These things vary, moreover, largely as a function of the politics of the issue "at issue." Traditional governmental processes are structured to facilitate resolution of matters about which there is some preexisting agreement in principle and/or in practice. There is, in essence, a measure of consensus that undergirds and enables normal government decisionmaking. Certain issues supply the preconditions necessary for normal functioning of the governance process and some do not. As a consequence, some issues are suitable to governance, while others are not. Race is best understood to be among the latter. Thus, while the analytic lens of this book is centered upon race, ultimately, it is a statement about the interplay between issue politics, procedure, and policy.

The dysfunctional relationship between race and governance is most evident in two phenomena. Both are conceptualized here as indicators of governance capacity. The first involves formal procedural outcomes and the second has to do with substantive policy outcomes. What is observed in the first instance is that traditional legislative processes typically break down when race-related proposals are introduced, prompting the emergence of alternative processes. Second, the public policies produced by the ensuing unconventional process are consistently compromised far and above the usual parameters of compromise. These policies, as a result, have failed to bring about meaningful race reform as is unmistakably evident in the persistence of huge racial disparities in American life and society.

That racial politics is the underlying cause of these trends is demonstrated by the following: (1) race has evoked the kind of intense opposition that resorts to seldom-used structural impediments that inhibit passage of race reform proposals, and (2) it often presents formidable challenges to building the amount of consensus required to overcome such impediments and enact strong racial legislative reforms. In other words, the most critical, enduring features of the politics of race are the extreme opposition and constrained bargainability they interpose in legislative proceedings and policy negotiations. It is these components of racial politics that distinguish them from most other policy issues and that produce the abnormal procedures and policy outcomes characteristic of civil rights decisionmaking.

Despite the enormous implications of these concerns for both the study of formal institutions and the study of racial politics, few analyses of legislative process or race deal squarely with the intersection between race and governance as such. Neither the existing literature on congressional decisionmaking nor that on the politics of race offers an integrative framework for understanding the interplay between these two critical facets of American politics. There are, however, a number of important insights regarding the relationship that we can glean from these two otherwise rich areas of research.

The major works on Congress that offer some discussion of civil rights policymaking appropriately detail the inordinate use of parliamentary procedure against civil rights and, thus, shed light on the special relevance of rules, primarily the Senate filibuster rule, for race-related proposals.[1] For the most part, however, such studies tend to offer largely descriptive analyses of congressional civil rights decisionmaking. Even these are fairly limited in scope as most center almost exclusively upon Rule 22, with the exception of Howard Schuman's "Senate Rules and the Civil Rights Bill: A Case Study."[2] Also, the sixties legislative battles consume much of the literature's attention, with almost none devoted to the later proceedings of the seventies, eighties, and nineties. Partly because of this concentration on the sixties, in identifying the immediate impetuses for the excessive filibustering against civil rights, few studies go beyond identification of southern senators as the primary culprits. Seldom offered is an in-depth examination of the broader political dynamics shaping these senators' legislative behavior. In essence, few outline the general causal dynamics driving civil rights legislative process.

Several more important considerations are also missing from the study of legislative process as it pertains to civil rights policymaking. Little explored is the notion that the experience of race-related policies says something about legislative process itself. What has occurred where civil rights proposals are concerned is not simply a matter of what has occurred to civil rights proposals. It is plausible to consider the possibility that their experience stands to inform our thinking about institutional decisionmaking generally. However, much of the research on Congress conceptualizes civil rights policymaking as simply an aberration of the normal model. A related weakness is the tendency to discuss legislative process as if there is only one, with the recognition of occasional deviations.[3] Seldom is there serious consideration of the possibility that, in fact, there are many legislative processes, of which the more frequently observed "normal process" constitutes only one. Even those studies that detail the existence of so-called unconventional lawmaking do not see it as a relatively permanent phenomenon, but instead as one that is produced and sustained by the periodic convergence of certain political factors and, therefore, as one whose existence is temporary and/or tenuous at best.[4] This analysis will shed light on at least one of the many possible alternative processes that regularly attends race-related policy proposals.

The conditions under which alternative policymaking processes will likely emerge receive scant attention as well. When are filibusters and other forms of deviant legislative behavior most likely to occur? Similarly, why do they occur at certain times and not at others? What fundamentally drives the use of abnormal procedure? These questions are important to a more complete understanding of Congress and decisionmaking, yet there are no integrative frameworks that fully address them. Very closely related to this gap in the research on Congress is another: most discussions of normal congressional process take its existence as a given. Left relatively underexplored is the possibility that the standard process is maintained essentially because the issues being "processed" satisfy the preconditions necessary to sustain the process—that is, it is likely the process prevails in the ordinary course of things because the ingredients needed to make it work are there and that, without these conditions undergirding the process, it would fold.

Studies of the substance of policymaking, policy bargaining, and policy compromise are also limited in what they contribute to the discourse about civil rights policymaking. There can be no question but that substantive policy compromise—which affects the actual provisions of legislative proposals—is common. Where major legislation is concerned, it is perhaps the rule of the day. Compromise may indeed be more frequent than logrolling and side payments on controversial legislation. In this regard, the civil rights policy concessions of the sixties are not distinctive. But at least one problematic trend in the literature is the tendency to monotype policy compromise. Policy compromise is conceptualized as a singular phenomenon, as something of which there is only one kind. Given this conceptualization of policy compromise, it is understandable why most discussions of incrementalism are preoccupied with explaining differences in degrees and why they primarily inquire about when there will be more compromise, rather than less.[5] It makes sense, however, to consider not only differences in degrees of policy compromise, but also differences in the kinds of policy compromise reached. It is plausible to consider the likelihood that most compromise takes place within certain parameters, parameters that are structured by broader political and policy constraints. With this reasoning, it is possible to categorize certain policy compromises as "normal" and others as "abnormal," that is, falling outside of the usual parameters. This book suggests that civil rights laws are among the latter and, more generally, that they are only part of a much broader set of policies that define the latter. There is compromise and then there is Compromise.

Perhaps the most important weakness in the existing scholarship is failure to see procedural process and policy output as fundamentally driven by issue politics, broadly writ. This weakness is, of course, largely the prodigy of many of the weaknesses noted above. Without recognizing the existence of a permanent alternative process and of abnormal substantive outcomes, and without explicating the factors that undergird normal process and policy, it would be difficult to assess the conditions under which they will arise, let alone the likelihood that the politics of an issue will play a key role in shaping those conditions. This study attempts to shed some light on these conditions, specifically the role of issue politics. Of course, what would enormously expand our understanding of the interplay between process, policy, and politics is a typology that links the various kinds of processes that emerge to the spectrum of policy proposals and politics that give rise to various processes. This kind of broad analysis, though very needful, is not attempted here. What this analysis does do, however, is explore at least one of these many possible intersections, namely, that of race and governance.

At the other end of the relevant literature spectrum is the scholarship on race. There is an extensive and rich body of research on race that explores its politics from many important angles. A significant portion of this examines the extra-institutional politics of race, that is, racial behaviors and patterns that inhere outside of the walls of government. In particular, political participation, mass movement, racial attitudes and opinion, sociological determinants of the race problem, and so forth have received much attention. A relatively small proportion of the literature on racial politics closely examines the intra-institutional politics of race.

The few studies that do attend to the institutional politics of race offer an extensive look at the pattern of weak laws, weak enforcement, and racially conservative and/or liberal legislative behaviors and coalitions to which these politics have given rise.[6] However, as with congressional analyses, most of these studies tend to be largely descriptive. More specifically, they primarily detail the actions, behaviors, and characteristics of the persons and coalitions immediately involved in various aspects of civil rights decisionmaking. Unlike the period-specific congressional analyses, however, these studies do offer a more complete description of civil rights decisionmaking that extends across time periods, in some cases starting with the post-Reconstruction era and continuing through the sixties and into the nineties.

However, a major weakness of these studies is that they do not highlight the more permanent structural dynamics of civil rights decisionmaking that maintain across time periods and that, more importantly, explain the various racial policies and institutional behaviors observed over time. What are the enduring aspects of civil rights decisionmaking? What similarities and dissimilarities inhere between the various presidential, congressional, and Supreme Court coalitions' treatment of the race problem? Critically, what are the determinants of these institutions' choices and how do they differ or remain the same from one institution to the next? These questions are essential to a deeper understanding of race and governance. Yet, we do not have an integrative framework for addressing them.

The bulk of the literature on race and institutions tends to highlight the inadequacy of civil rights laws and implementation. Much has been said about the ways in which civil rights legislation has fallen short of its stated goals and the more general goal of racial equality. But, most such analyses do not identify the structural causes of the outcomes complained about, with the exception of Hanes Walton, Jr.'s *When the Marching Stopped*.[7] This study recognizes the inherent weakness of the enforcement structures established in civil rights laws and therefore enormously aids our understanding of the forces driving policy output. On the whole, however, careful consideration of the larger institutional decisionmaking processes out of which such structures emerge is missing. That is, there is relatively little discussion in the racial policy literature about the reasons why the observed inadequate implementation apparatuses and policy outcomes are formulated in the first place. Admittedly, this is not the central focus or goal of many of these studies. Still, a relatively complete analysis of civil rights policy and decisionmaking must include some examination of the role of entrenched structural and political factors in generating insufficient outcomes. In many respects, as this study will show, the racial policy outcomes complained about are the byproduct of the politics that racial issues themselves present.

At least one notable study offers a direct assessment of the implications of racial politics for permanent structural arrangements and vice versa. Edward Carmines and James Stimson's *Issue Evolution*[8] offers a detailed study of the extent to which racial politics has transformed American politics. While this study goes a long way toward informing our understanding of the distinctive political significance and influence of race within the American political system, it portrays only half of the story—that is, the study's analytic lens is squarely focused on party politics and, thus, informal institutional arrangements. Needed is an analysis that explores the influence of race upon formal institutions, institutional process, and, above all else, legislative procedure. Inasmuch as government exercises a monopoly on power and its use, understanding the effect of race upon formal governance is a critical step in fully gauging its impact on American politics.

This study attempts to shed some light upon these gaps in the literature on race and institutions. It focuses squarely on the relationship between race and formal governance, toward the broader goal of illuminating the dynamic interplay between issue politics, process, and policy. The analytic lens of the discussion centers upon the modern civil rights period, from the fifties to the present, and assesses the civil rights politics, process, and policy outcomes of the entire period.

Three specific concerns guide the analysis presented in this book. The first has to do with the central dynamics of race within the American political system. What does race bring to the table of American politics and, relatedly, what is its political significance within the overall political landscape? In essence, what are the predominant features of the politics of race, broadly writ? In concrete terms, this is a concern about political behavior(s) tangential to the "race problem," specifically the nature of the problem itself and the political system's response to efforts to redress the problem. In broader terms, this is a concern about the extent to which race generates and/or inhibits broad political and policy consensus.

A second analytic concern of the book is the impact of racial politics upon formal governance. More specifically, what kind of influence does the politics of race have upon the parliamentary aspects of legislative proceedings? Is race conformable to the procedures ordinarily used to enact legislation? Or, does race have the kind of destabilizing effect that forces the use of alternative legislative routes that are far more demanding than conventional avenues of passage? In short, how does race affect the formal policy process? In particular, the analysis examines the effect of racial politics on the parliamentary proceedings in the U.S. Senate on thirteen major federal civil rights laws enacted between 1957 and 1992. Thanks to the Senate's historic civil rights filibusters and debates of the sixties, Senate civil rights proceedings afford what is arguably the clearest example of and, thus, the most accessible form of direct interaction between race and structure over an extended period of time.

The final line of inquiry pursued here probes the impact of racial politics upon the substantive provisions of legislative proposals designed to redress the race problem. At issue here is the extent to which race reform proposals can and do survive procedural processes relatively intact—that is, how and in what way does procedure bear upon substance? Is it possible to enact strong race reform proposals or is there something about racial politics that makes this an unlikely prospect? In essence, what effect does race have upon governmental capacity to redress the race problem? Of course, the flip side of this concern is whether racial inequality can be corrected by way of the kinds of policies that emerge from the typical civil rights process.

The book's main analytic conclusion posits a kind of dialectical materialism in which regional and partisan racial conflicts are the determinative forces and abnormal civil rights policymaking is the product of these forces. Evidence of the abnormalcy that inheres in modern civil rights legislating is most clearly manifest in the persistent use of nontraditional procedural routes and the consistent weakening of civil rights policy provisions beyond recognition. Evidence that the extreme nature of racial politics is the primary culprit is its role in forcing both the use of nontraditional routes and the acceptance of huge policy concessions that reduce civil rights proposals to mere legislative pronouncements and prohibitions.

The argument consists of three parts. First, race drives the most fundamental cleavages in American politics. It has divided the nation and its mass politics regionally, pitting the South against the non-South. Race has been and remains a major fault line undergirding the most central component of American politics, the party system, with Republicans and Democrats intensely at odds—specifically over the race question. What is more, the regional and partisan conflict over race is far above and beyond the run-of-the-mill political differences. Racial discord is among the most significant antagonisms in American politics. It has occupied, and continues in many ways still to occupy, center stage of political competition. In essence, race has proven to be an especially salient issue in American politics.

The most immediate effect of racial polarization is that it enormously inhibits consensus building. It is difficult and, as the discussion in the chapters to follow will show, sometimes impossible to effectively bargain race within the legislative context. Two things are key in this regard. First, race provokes intense legislative opposition of the kind that cannot be dissuaded. Race reform advocates have been unable to persuade southern opponents of civil rights in the Senate and also racially conservative Republican presidents to forgo certain procedural prerogatives. Ordinarily, the cloture rule and veto power are seldom used to thwart congressional legislative proposals. However, their inordinate use against civil rights bills has been virtually unavoidable due to the contentiousness of race that carries over into congressional proceedings.

Furthermore, their use has provoked the emergence of an abnormal procedural process that now regularly attends civil rights proposals. This process has proven to be a virtual logistical conundrum. Making civil rights law is an incredibly demanding feat even in the most rudimentary sense. It requires great physical involvement and energy. It calls for an enormous time investment. It takes great parliamentary skill and coordination. And, perhaps above all else, it often necessitates supermajority votes. In short, legislative process exacts a great deal more from proponents of race-related proposals than it requires from supporters of most other bills. The root cause of this dynamic is the limited utility of bargaining relative to civil rights opponents.

Formidable political challenges have confronted civil rights proponents in their attempts to win the votes of Republican moderates in the Senate, votes critical to overcoming both internal and external obstruction of civil rights proposals on the part of opponents. The essence of the challenges they have faced is this: uncommitted senators have been unwilling to abandon their principles on such a highly visible issue as race. The run-of-the-mill modes of bargaining, namely, logrolling and side payments, have proven ineffective where these senators are concerned. As a condition for their critical support, they have demanded instead that civil rights proposals be brought in line with their racially conservative ideology. In essence, even those legislators who remain on the fence in civil rights policy contests are hesitant to play politics as usual and lend their active support to race reform proposals. With virtually little choice but to concede to Republican moderates' compromise demands, advocates have consistently re-crafted their original policy proposals in ways that spell token legislation. Specifically, stronger administrative enforcement provisions have been consistently scrapped in favor of weaker provisions that provide for court enforcement.

An extensive range of qualitative and quantitative data is employed in the analysis of the interplay between race, procedure, and policy over time. To capture the partisan politics of race, party platforms; presidential rhetoric, stances, and policies; trends in the black presidential vote; and various other sources are used. To gauge the regional division that has lain at the center of racial politics, the analysis looks to the history of race, discrimination, and civil rights opposition in the South; a regional comparison of racial socio-economic and political disparity; and, finally, civil rights advocates' targeting of the race problem in the South versus that in other areas of the country. Census Bureau reports as well as National Election Studies, the General Social Survey, Gallup Poll surveys, and other quantitative sources are used to buttress the regional and partisan focus.

For the procedural and policy focus, the book relies foremost on a virtual page-by-page reading of the *Congressional Record of Debate and Proceedings* for each of the thirteen civil rights laws of concern here. Since the *Record* often depicts only half of the story, information contained in the personal papers of key figures in Senate consideration of civil rights laws, along with roll call votes, coalitional lineups, and other data, is used to complete the review of civil rights policy and process presented here.

The six chapters comprised by the book are organized chronologically to clearly portray the changes over time in the three main factors analyzed, namely, the politics of race, the effect of racial politics upon formal governmental process and policy, and the impact of governmental policy upon the race problem. The discussion in each chapter offers a summary overview of the extent and nature of southern obstruction, but without extensively detailing the who's, what's, and when's. The obstruction is not presumed, however.[9] The more central concern of the book is not the nature of obstruction per se, but rather its consequences for civil rights lawmaking. Thus, the analysis centers squarely upon advocates' strategy—the process and procedures by which the bills were enacted.

Before proceeding to its primary analytic concern—the dynamic interplay between racial politics and governmental decisionmaking—the book begins in chapter 1 with a discussion of its main theoretical concern, that of how and why the politics of a given policy issue matter for legislative procedure and policy outcomes. First, mostly for the sake of establishing a clear frame of reference for the discussion in later chapters, chapter 1 gives a basic description of normal policy process and normal policy outcomes. Next it describes what it conceptualizes as "abnormal" policy processes and abnormal policy outcomes. It then proceeds to explain how the politics of an issue converge to yield unconventional lawmaking.

Chapter 2 provides a discussion of the early years of civil rights politics and policymaking. The review of racial politics in chapter 2 actually begins with a brief overview of the early post-Reconstruction years as a means of tracing the regional and partisan racial demarcations that began to crystallize by the fifties. It then looks at the historical development of the politics of race through the fifties to explain the procedures utilized and policies adopted during the 1957 and 1960 Senate civil rights debates.

Chapter 3 focuses on the most widely studied years of civil rights politics and policymaking, the sixties. It lays out the key changes in the race problem that emerge during the peak years of the modern civil rights era, from the early to mid-sixties. It also details the hardening of the North versus South divide and the Democratic versus Republican divide over how best to grapple with the problem. The chapter's analysis of these central dynamics of racial politics is then used to explain, first, the formal logistics of policymaking in the infamous 1964, 1965, and 1968 congressional civil rights proceedings and, then, the final provisions of the landmark federal civil rights laws adopted in these years.

Chapter 4 turns to the transitional phase of modern civil rights politics and policymaking, the seventies, the time during which the regional differences over race begin to dissipate, while those of a partisan nature began to intensify. Major alterations in the nature of the race problem lay at the heart of these shifts in the fault lines beneath racial politics. Chapter 4 demonstrates that these changes in racial politics led to measurable shifts in how the Senate enacts civil rights laws, but yielded little effect upon the Senate's longstanding propensity to dilute even the modest proposals introduced during the seventies. The Senate civil rights debates of 1970, 1972, and 1975 provide a medium for assessing the politics of race during the seventies and its influence upon formal legislative procedure and policy outcomes.

The contemporary politics of race and its bearing upon current civil rights proceedings and legislative enactments is taken up in chapter 5. The most recent congressional debates that have resulted in passage of national civil rights laws include the following five: the 1982 voting rights restoration debate, the 1988 "Grove City" debate, the 1988 housing debate, the 1991 civil rights restoration debate, and the 1992 voting rights extension debate. The discussion in chapter 5 illustrates the kinds of formal procedures used to enact civil rights legislation during the eighties and nineties. It also assesses the nature of the "policy compromise imperative" during these years and its role in shaping the final substance of recent civil rights laws. Most importantly, chapter 5 demonstrates that each of these legislative trends is consistent with those of previous decades. And they flow from the current nature of racial politics, the most critical aspects of which are the "nationalization" of the race problem and the current party system's embattlement over affirmative action.

The final chapter of the book presents a mostly quantitative summary of the discussion presented in chapters 2 through 5. Statistical measures of civil rights proceedings and "normal" Senate legislative proceedings are used to succinctly depict and compare the former's deviation from the norm throughout the 1957–1992 focus period. Given the near impossibility of quantitatively depicting substantive policy provisions and change, a summary discussion of civil rights compromise as compared to normal give and take in the Senate is presented in chapter 6. Survey data depicting the racial attitudes of the South versus those of the non-South and also the attitudes and policy stance of Democrats versus Republicans are used to illuminate the evolution of critical racial political divisions. Finally, while the first five chapters conclude with only a brief foray into the impact of each of the civil rights laws, a more detailed explication of government's real life impact on race is reserved for this chapter. Longitudinal analyses of various measures of racial equality, including poverty, educational achievement, income, employment status, and housing, are used to substantiate a major claim of the book, namely, that the civil rights laws of the fifties through the nineties, individually and combined, have yielded little meaningful change in the socioeconomic status of black Americans.

1

Process, Policy, and Issue Politics

There is a standard legislative process through which policy proposals are enacted and there is an abnormal policy process as well. Similarly, there are substantive policy outcomes that may be characterized as "normal" and certain outcomes appropriately seen as "abnormal." The politics of a given issue determine whether, and when, normal or abnormal policymaking prevails. As a result, certain political issues are well suited for effective resolution through the standard policy process, while others cannot be redressed by the normal process, but must be resolved instead through an alternative policy process. Thus, in order to fully understand why the normal process is effective in redressing certain problems, but not others, we must look to the nature of the politics of the issue "at issue." Issue politics fundamentally drives process and policy.

The purpose of this chapter is to illuminate the dynamic interplay between the politics of an issue, the formal legislative process that attends to it, and the nature of policies designed to deal with the issue. It offers a theoretical framework for understanding and anticipating the conditions under which nontraditional legislative decisionmaking will arise and, relatedly, why it seldom does. The first section describes the basic features and dynamics of normal and abnormal legislative processes. The role that bargaining and consensus play in structuring procedural and policy outcomes is discussed in the second and third sections. The last section explains how the politics of an issue dictate the kind of legislative process attendant to policy issues and also the substance of laws that are produced by those processes. It asks: why do certain issues encounter the normal process and yield normal policy provisions, while others are confronted by an unconventional process and unusual policy outcomes? In demonstrating the relationship between politics, process, and policy, the discussion draws primarily upon the example of the U.S. Senate.

PROCEDURAL PROCESS

The normal policy process is the legislative process we observe most often. Although some minor variation is occasionally observed in specific policy proceedings, there is a significant enough measure of consistency in the overall process through which most legislative proposals are officially adopted that a standard process emerges. It is one that legislative scholars can and have subjected to analysis. Indeed a striking characteristic of the formal process is that it is relatively stable and predictable. Hence while acknowledging that there are occasional deviations, we can nonetheless identify those elements that surface time and again when policymakers craft formal public policy.

Just as there is a normal policy process, there is also an abnormal process through which legislative proposals are enacted. Although this alternative process emerges rarely and is encountered by only a handful of bills that eventually become laws, its emergence is frequent enough that we can explicate its main features. What we find upon doing so is that many of the features of the unconventional process are strikingly different from those of the normal process. The underlying dynamics of the two processes also differ. Structurally, they are very similar to one another. But, content-wise, they are quite different.

The discussion to follow outlines in more detail the major components and operations of legislative process generally and then of the normal and abnormal processes separately; the overall character of each; the requirements and demands of each; and those factors that most immediately give rise to and sustain each process.

Legislative Process

The structural components and mechanics of legislative process are relatively well known and have been duly analyzed by a number of insightful legislative studies.[1] The most basic mechanics of legislating involve securing a proposed bill's movement through each of the various parliamentary stages that make up the formal policy process. The major stages of this process include the introductory, committee, consideration, and final vote stages. At each of these stages a bill is examined and/or acted upon by all or portions of the Senate membership. First, at the introductory stage, a bill is formally introduced or proposed in the Senate and is then assigned to one or more standing committees.

Next is the committee stage of the process. Here bills are scrutinized by members of the committee to which the bill is referred following its introduction. Committees gather information on proposed policies through public hearings at which witnesses, experts, and interested parties are invited for questioning and to present evidence. Committees also make changes to proposed bills through a process known as "markup," which essentially entails adding, deleting, or revising certain portions of the original bills. Finally, each committee compiles the information gathered and recommendations agreed to in a report it then submits to the floor of the Senate. Alternatively, committees can decide to take no action at all on a bill, in which case the bill effectively "dies." The committee stage of the process is a pivotal point because it is here that most bills are defeated, as only a small percentage of bills emerge from committees. In effect, committees serve as funnels in the legislative process.

Following the committee stage is the "consideration" stage. This is the point at which the Senate decides whether to officially pass upon the bill. A bill that is reported out of committee is placed on the Senate calendar where it remains until and unless the floor—the Senate membership as a whole—decides to formally consider it in its legislative capacity. Once the Senate formally proceeds to a bill, the bill officially enters what is referred to here as the "final vote stage." This stage is the most critical of all because it is here that final decisions are made relative to the bill's content and overall fate. Upon entering the final vote stage, for major bills, the presiding officer opens the bill up to debate and amendment by the membership. Following debate and amendment, the presiding officer asks if any others wish to speak, after which he or she puts the question of passage before the Senate, whereupon a vote on final passage is held.

Importantly, at each of these junctures is a set of requirements that advocates of a proposed bill must satisfy in order to move the bill along in the process and, finally, to passage. At a minimum, support from at least a simple majority of senators at each stage is required. It is also important that advocates have some command of formal parliamentary procedure. They must possess the skill needed to recognize potentially hurtful parliamentary maneuvers and also have some experience at responding quickly and decisively to such maneuvers. In addition to support and skill, each stage requires some active involvement on the part of the bill's advocates—that is, supporters' physical presence and activity at the floor and in committee are often needed to ensure a bill stays afloat and that it progresses along in the process.

Normal Legislative Process

There are ordinary means by which bills succeed through the parliamentary stages of the legislative process just described. There is, in essence, a process that regularly attends most legislative proposals. Technically, it comprises the most commonly used procedures for considering and passing upon legislation at each juncture. However, the most notable feature of the normal process in the Senate is that it is relatively straightforward. Often little is involved in facilitating a bill's movement from one stage of the process to the next. That is not to say that the process is an easy one. However, insofar as the procedural dimensions of the process are concerned, seldom is it a terribly complicated process. The deviations are more the exception than the rule. Both by design and in practice, the stages that make up the normal process function primarily as legislative "checkpoints," geared toward ensuring that policies are subjected to ample scrutiny by interested persons and experts, that they are supported by the requisite majority at each stage, and that they are improved upon, substantively, where and as necessary.

The most important practical feature of the normal process is that the procedural demands it imposes upon policy advocates are not onerous—that is, the level of support, skill, and energy necessary to secure a bill's movement from one stage of the process to the next is ordinarily minimal. Introduction of a bill is usually accomplished by a senator either submitting it to the Senate clerk or personally presenting it at the floor. As a result, most bills progress beyond the introduction stage with little notice as few meaningful demands inhere in the process at this point. In terms of support, a single senator is usually enough to secure introduction and referral. Besides the simple act of presenting the bill to the clerk or at the floor, no significant skill or energy is required of the bill's advocates at this stage.

Despite committees' infamous reputation for being the most difficult point in the policy process, what happens at the committee stage, procedurally, is seldom complicated or burdensome for a bill's supporters. With respect to skill, at most a simple motion for a final committee vote on whether to report the bill may be needed to move the bill to the floor. In terms of support, usually little more than a handful of votes, at most, those of 9 to 12 senators, is needed at the committee juncture. And, committee members' voluntary participation in regularly scheduled markup, hearings, and votes is all that is required in terms of active support. Rarely does the floor have any input at this juncture.

The consideration stage is also relatively straightforward with respect to parliamentary procedure. Most often, the question of whether and/or when to take up a bill is decided in advance in off-floor discussions involving the leadership and interested parties and is subsequently codified in a floor agreement. When there is no such agreement, usually a formal motion to proceed to consideration of a bill is made from the floor by the bill's leading sponsor or one of the Senate leaders, followed by a minimal amount of discussion, and then a floor vote. The typical scenario is for a bill to pass the consideration stage within a matter of minutes and, oftentimes, even less time. It is primarily because much of the work is done pre-floor that the consideration stage is usually a pro forma one and, by far, the least demanding of the four stages. Still even without a pre-floor agreement, very little active input is required of supporters beyond submission of a motion to vote on whether to proceed and a simple majority vote to carry the motion.

As with the preceding stages, procedures at the final vote stage for major bills have also become fairly standardized and are not especially onerous for supporters. Here too, pre-arranged floor agreements typically govern the debate and amendment process. And, other parliamentary matters, such as quorum calls, recesses, and adjournments, may also be governed by such agreements, as is the most critical component of the final vote stage—the final vote on passage. Other items that are not decided upon in advance, as well as minor, noncontroversial bills are often handled by ad hoc agreements hammered out at the floor during debate or as proceedings unfold, in line with the spirit of the agreements. Few significant surprises tend to emerge, largely due to the agreements worked out in advance. The result is that few pressing demands are normally placed on supporters. Skill levels are seldom consequential since the agreements spell out and provide for procedural matters in advance. Endorsement by a simple majority of senators often suffices on amendment and parliamentary votes as well as on passage. And with respect to energy, usually no more than participation in the debate and amendment votes is required of advocates.

That the normal process is relatively straightforward and uncomplicated is due to several factors that serve to essentially undergird and sustain the normal process. Foremost among these is the set of parliamentary rules that officially govern the process.[2] The Senate's standing rules of procedure are the formal, technical guidelines for how bills are to be handled at each stage. They specify the requirements, conditions, and manner in which bills are to progress from one stage of the process to the next. Yet, their major contribution is not that of specifying the requirements for a bill's movement beyond each stage, but rather affording would-be opponents with innumerable opportunities to delay and/or prevent a bill's movement through the process. In fact, the rules provide only minimally sufficient guidelines for Senate handling of proposed bills,[3] partly because they are relatively few in number[4] and consist of very broadly framed language. The loopholes in the rules are ripe mostly for manipulation by opposition camps.

However, even though, in practice, the rules provide only limited guidance and are mostly reservoirs of obstructionist power, they are nonetheless best understood as playing a key role in promoting normalcy within the policy process because they influence legislative behavior in another critical way. Simply by virtue of their existence and structure, the rules create strong disincentives for their use and promote, instead, cooperation among senators. Two facts in particular constrain senators' use of the rules for obstructionist purposes. First, use of the rules is equally available to every senator.

Second, and relatedly, just as one senator can invoke the rules to deprive a policy's supporters of a fair and complete hearing in the Senate, so too can the policy's supporters utilize the rules to do the same against future bills advocated by the obstructing senator. So, in effect, the potential power inherent in the Senate's rules and their availability to all goes a long way toward stabilizing the policy process insofar as they constrain senators from wreaking havoc in the process.

Also key in promoting normalcy in legislative decisionmaking are institutional norms and traditions.[5] Norms are behavioral constructs that induce conformity. Usually included by congressional scholars among these norms are the following: apprenticeship, comity, legislative work, institutional patriotism, specialization, and reciprocity. The latter is especially important with regard to official policymaking because it not only requires that policy favors be reciprocated, but it also begets retaliation for those who are uncooperative or, worse, obstructionist. In regards to use of the rules, it dictates restraint. The force of legislative norms is derived primarily from the benefits that arise from compliance with the norms. On the one hand, punishment for non-compliance has been shown to be relatively ineffective, not to mention a less accessible means of ensuring that senators abide by norms. The rewards that flow from norm abidance, on the other hand, are effective in inducing compliance.[6] Legislators conform to norms because doing so helps to facilitate their own individual legislative and political goals.

Unanimous consent agreements also engender stability in policymaking because they input a measure of control over lawmaking. At the same time, they minimize the level of skill and energy demanded of proponents in order to keep a bill afloat and/or move the bill along. Technically, such agreements represent the unanimous consent of the membership to proceed in the manner specified by the agreement. The agreements typically spell out the manner in which proceedings on a bill are to occur. Things such as whether, when, and/or how to vote on bills and amendments; who will speak on a given measure, when, in what order, for how long, and sometimes for what purpose; whether to take up a legislative proposal, when, and with what stipulations, and so forth are the kinds of things for which consent agreements may and often do provide. They enable the Senate to bypass altogether or ignore one or all of its standing rules and to do so on any parliamentary, legislative, or administrative matter, with very few exceptions.[7] The broader significance of floor agreements is that they regulate formal policymaking by forging an operable consensus among members relative to the procedural handling of measures. They resolve in advance potential objections and resistance to the leadership's floor agenda and, thus, enormously aid in the elimination or reduction of irregularities and surprises.

Abnormal Legislative Process

The normal process just described is the process encountered by most legislative proposals. Occasionally, proposals are disposed of through an alternative, or "abnormal," process. This abnormal process, in essence, consists of seldom-used, alternative procedural routes for securing a bill's passage. Collectively, they constitute the unconventional policy process. In many ways the abnormal process is best understood as not only a deviation from the normal process, but also representative of a breakdown in normal policymaking. This is due to several factors.

Notably absent from the abnormal process are the two factors essential to the regularity and manageability of the standard process, namely, norms and unanimous consent procedures. Their absence enormously contributes to the destabilization and unpredictability of the abnormal process. Indeed the fact that the influence of norms is largely nonexistent in the abnormal process is a critical point to note. The alternative process emerges in part because of the failure of such norms to constrain disadvantageous behaviors.

Whereas norms inhibit use of the rules in the normal process and unanimous consent agreements essentially provide for regular circumvention of the rules, the unconventional process centers largely upon invocation of the rules. It is senators' invocation of the rules that initially stimulates the process. The basic formal structure of the alternative process is, in many respects, a byproduct of rules' usage. Specifically, the rules are used to obstruct a bill's movement so that the various parliamentary stages become obstacles, rather than legislative checkpoints.

As compared to the demands and requirements of the normal process, those of the abnormal process are excessive and this is due ultimately to the minority opposition's use of its procedural prerogatives and, importantly, the impact of that use upon advocates' strategy. Opponents, by using the rules, can engage in what is known as a "filibuster"—or blocking strategy. Much of minority obstructionist power in the Senate is rooted in Rule 22, commonly referred to as the cloture rule and the "filibuster rule." Although the rule does not explicitly grant the right of unlimited debate and parliamentary maneuvering, its existence and language serve to underscore the fact that there are no procedures besides those contained in it that automatically limit the amount of "debate and proceedings" in which senators can engage in connection with a matter pending before the Senate.[8] The Senate's Rule 22 effectively provides a limitless time and parliamentary framework within which opponents may actively block progress on a measure or motion.

Let us look at some of the major ways in which minorities can use the rules to obstruct. At the introduction stage there are relatively few, but substantial, opportunities for opponents to block a bill's progress. While little can be done to prevent formal introduction of a bill, there are several means of blocking committee referral, and this is where the introduction stage differences between the normal and abnormal processes emerge most clearly. More specifically, formal introduction of a bill in the Senate can be delayed for one day, at best, under Rule 14. And, because Rule 7 provides for the introduction of bills during a specific time period, any opposing member can raise a point of order against the introduction of a bill outside of the framework specified by this rule. Moreover, opponents can significantly complicate referral of a bill to committee. Prior to referral, under Rule 14, two readings of a bill are required, each of which is to occur on different days "on demand of any Senator."[9] So, an opponent can insist that the two required readings of a bill occur on two separate days. And, because a motion to refer a bill is open to debate, opponents could subject such a motion to lengthy proceedings. Also, Rule 17 enables opponents to challenge the referral decision of the presiding officer, then submit a debatable appeal to the entire membership should the challenge be overruled, and, therefore, force a floor vote.

The committee stage presents opponents with their most promising chance of defeating a bill. The odds against a bill succeeding in the face of intense opposition within the governing committee are enormous. The floor traditionally defers to committee decisions relative to policy proposals. Beyond this, individual members have at their disposal various means of stalling committee action. For example, they can deliberately absent themselves from meetings that require quorums and, thereby, limit the committee's ability to formally act on a measure. Despite the changes made to the congressional committee chairman appointment process during the seventies,[10] under the old and current rules of the Senate, committee and subcommittee chairmen exercise enormous power over the fate of legislation. They have the widest array of tools to hamper a bill's success at the committee juncture. The chairman's control over much of what the committee does, and when and how, positions him or her in an excellent position to prevent a bill from being voluntarily reported out of committee. Specifically, his or her control of the committee's meeting schedule can be used so that no meetings are called for discussion and action on a bill. His or her control of meeting agendas and power to recognize members and witnesses can be used to buttress the momentum and influence of a bill's opponents. Finally, a chairman's primary control of committee staff resources can be utilized to enforce compliance on the part of committee members generally.

The floor affords the greatest number of obstructionist opportunities in comparison to the stages just discussed. Proceedings that unfold within the context of the consideration and the final vote stages are conceptualized here as floor proceedings. Certain floor obstructions are relevant only at the final vote stage, though many are relevant for both stages. There are several major dilatory tactics available to opponents at the consideration stage. First, opponents can block all action on a measure by objecting to unanimous consent requests to vote. Second, opponents can conduct an extended discussion and essentially tie up the floor. In addition, they can engage in extensive parliamentary maneuvering. For example, an enormous opportunity for obstruction is found in the quorum rules, Rules 4 and 6. Rule 4 requires a quorum, that is, a majority of members, to be present while the Senate is conducting business, and Rule 6 provides that a single senator, at any time, can demand a quorum call, for any reason. Although precedent stipulates that business (e.g., a vote) must intervene between quorum calls, the formal rules do not. And, while quorum calls are normally made to allow senators time to work out issues and concerns that arise unexpectedly during floor proceedings or to alert senators to a change in speakers or to a floor vote, opponents can leverage such calls to frustrate and wear down supporters. Since, under the rules, no debate or any other motion is allowed unless and until a quorum is ascertained, opponents can essentially bring an immediate halt to proceedings.

In addition to those just outlined are certain other delaying tactics specifically relevant once a bill is formally before the Senate. Perhaps the most important of these is excessive amendment activity. Also useful are various motions that can be used to essentially undo what progress is made on a bill. These include, to name a few, motions to recommit a bill to committee, motions to reconsider votes on amendments or passage, and motions to lay aside a bill. Certain floor motions consist of multiple obstructionist opportunities. For example, if a quorum call demanded by opponents fails to produce a majority of senators at the floor, then, under the rules, the Senate must adjourn. And, upon reconvening following an adjournment, the Senate is required, under the rules, to first go through a list of cumbersome procedures before resuming consideration of pending measures. Further, some privileged motions are especially tedious. For example, under the rules, opponents can insist that the previous day's journal (sometimes several hundred pages in length) be read in its entirety, and then propose a motion to amend the journal, which at the start of a new legislative day's proceedings, is a privileged motion.

At each stage of the process, moreover, advocates have at their disposal various means of defeating and/or bypassing the obstructions created by opponents. These means are the alternative routes that make up the abnormal process. In an effort to expedite a bill's movement beyond obstacles to committee referral, supporters can do little besides supplying majority votes when and as necessary to counter opposition appeals, and ensuring continuous and ample floor coverage in order to anticipate and respond to opposition maneuvers. However, supporters do have meaningful ways of dealing with committee obstruction. First, under Rule 26, they can force a committee meeting or reporting of a measure. A second route around a committee block is the discharge procedure. Supporters can remove a bill from a committee's possession by discharging the committee from its consideration of the bill. Doing so requires that a motion to discharge be made at the floor and adopted by a majority vote of the floor. A third route past committee obstruction is instructions. Rule 17 empowers the floor by a majority vote to instruct a committee on how to handle a bill referred to it. This includes instructing the committee to carry out certain direct orders from the floor, namely, reporting a bill to the floor, reporting by a specified deadline, investigating certain issues related to the bill, and so forth. This too requires a formal motion and full vote at the floor.

A fourth approach to counteracting committee obstruction is to essentially "preempt" the committee block, by challenging referral of a bill to a likely hostile committee. Under Rule 17, any senator may challenge whether a bill falls within the jurisdiction of a committee by submitting an appeal to the presiding officer. An unfavorable decision from the chair is subject to an appeal and can be overruled by a simple majority vote. A fifth, similarly "preemptive" method for dealing with obstruction is to bypass the committee juncture altogether through the "direct placement" procedure. Direct placement occurs when a bill is placed directly on the floor's calendar, without ever being formally referred to a committee. Under Rule 14, this method is technically available only on bills first passed by the House (although, in practice, it has been used occasionally on bills that originate in the Senate). After a first and second reading of a bill, any senator can object to referral of the bill and, thereby, secure its direct placement on the calendar. A final means of bypassing obstruction at the committee stage is through the use of a "rider" amendment, also a kind of preemptive strike. Except for appropriations measures, amendments proposed to bills considered in the Senate do not have to be germane to the subject matter of a bill, making it possible to propose entire bills in the form of amendments to bills that have already succeeded to the floor.

Several alternative procedures are available to supporters at the consideration stage as well. First, where Rule 8 provides that any senator can object to consideration of certain bills on the calendar during the morning business call of the calendar, the Senate "on motion, may continue such consideration" despite such objection.[11] A second approach is to attempt to submit the motion to proceed at a time when, under the rules, the motion is nondebatable. Under Rule 8, if the motion is submitted after morning business, but before the close of the morning hour, it is nondebatable. A final strategy is to pursue a House-passed version of the targeted bill. Under Rule 7, it is in order at any time for the presiding officer or any senator to move to lay a bill from the House before the Senate. Any question pending is automatically suspended because it is a privileged motion. And, importantly, a motion to proceed to consider a House bill is nondebatable.

To deal with floor obstruction generally, both in the consideration and final vote stages, advocates can do a number of things. They can insist on a strict observance of the rules in ways that would contain the extent and impact of floor obstruction. For example, there are a number of ways supporters can contain debate, short of invoking cloture. Supporters can insist that the initial speaking senator lose the floor if and when he or she gives consent for another senator to speak. As well, supporters can invoke the two-speech rule under Rule 19, which prohibits senators from speaking twice on the same subject matter on the same legislative day. In addition, advocates can directly counteract obstructionists' use of formal motions. The most effective method for doing so is to move to table such motions. A tabling motion is nondebatable and can immediately end consideration of and/or defeat dilatory motions.

Fewer tools are available to supporters to confront certain other parliamentary maneuvers that do not involve formal motions, such as untimely quorum calls. The most supporters can do to respond to such maneuvers is ensure that a sufficient number of supporters "cover" the floor and that those members are skilled enough in parliamentary procedure that they recognize and respond to such maneuvering in an appropriate and timely fashion. Also available to the leadership is the political authority to impose a "one-track" legislative agenda, which would delay consideration of any other measures besides the obstructed bill and, thus, increase the pressure on opponents to end their filibuster. The leadership also has the prerogative of adjusting the daily session schedule in a way that enables more progress on a measure, rather than less. Schedule adjustments can also be used to wear down filibustering senators, especially where around-the-clock sessions are concerned.

The single most powerful tool Senate policy advocates have at their disposal to defeat an obstructionist coalition is cloture. It is a multistep procedure that requires that advocates first obtain the signatures of at least sixteen senators on a cloture petition. The petition must then be presented to the Senate, whereupon the presiding officer lays the motion before the Senate "one hour after the Senate meets on the following calendar day." The support of at least three-fifths of all senators is needed to invoke cloture.[12] Rule 22 also stipulates the manner in which proceedings are to be conducted once cloture has been invoked. For example, once cloture has been invoked, the reading of amendments and submission of additional and/or nongermane amendments is prohibited. Also, points of order and appeals are nondebatable under cloture. Cloture, in effect, limits what was previously an unlimited time frame within which opponents could work to defeat a measure.

On the whole, the most critical distinction of the alternative policy process is that the costs of obtaining a bill's passage through it are significantly higher than the ordinary costs of legislative success. The preceding discussion has alluded to the fact that unconventional routes of passage require greater skill, greater support, and greater energy investment on the part of a bill's supporters. Normally, a relatively simple act on the part of one senator is all that is required to accomplish introduction and referral of a bill. But, in the abnormal process, much more, including repeated floor votes potentially involving the entire membership as well as their continuous, active involvement is needed to succeed beyond the introduction stage. At the committee stage, too, the alternative process deviates from the normal process in terms of its demands. The latter requires only a handful of votes at this juncture, but the former potentially demands that the entire membership become entangled. Another departure is the degree of familiarity with the rules. Only the most rudimentary motions are involved in traditional committee proceedings, but, in the alternative, advocates must possess a keen understanding of the rules applicable at this juncture and great skill at utilizing those rules.

Also at the consideration and final vote stages, the abnormal process demands are markedly different from those of the standard process. An announcement by the leadership or, at most, a simple motion on the part of one senator is usually sufficient to begin floor proceedings on a bill. And, amendment votes, quorum calls, and other procedural matters, including a final vote on passage, are ordinarily resolved without much ado. But, in the unconventional process, formal proceedings at the floor can be enormously complicated by numerous speeches, votes, and parliamentary maneuvers. This circumstance in turn exacts equal and, in many respects, more input from advocates in order to counteract such maneuvering.

External Procedural Obstruction

Thus far, the discussion has detailed the nature and extent of obstruction made possible through use of the Senate's formal written rules. Such obstruction is, necessarily, internal to the chamber's decisionmaking processes. It is carried out by members of the Senate and within the context of Senate legislating. There is, moreover, another type of obstruction that bills may encounter that is an externally imposed form of obstruction. The U.S. Constitution entrusts the president with certain legislative powers that indirectly involve him or her in congressional decisionmaking. Included among these powers is the power to veto bills adopted by Congress. Except where Congress acts to override presidential vetoes through means made available in the Constitution, a presidential veto spells defeat of a bill. Inasmuch as presidential vetoes effectively block enactment of laws adopted by Congress, they constitute a form of obstruction. They block bills from becoming law in much the same way that use of Senate procedures to obstruct its policy process prevents legislative success. Vetoes also resemble procedural obstruction insofar as they exist for similar purposes. Both are designed ostensibly to safeguard minority interests from unwarranted majoritarian impulses. Finally, like internal procedural obstruction, presidential vetoes are relatively infrequent.

The more important, practical way in which presidential vetoes resemble internal obstruction is by way of the extraordinary support requirements they impose on a bill's supporters. Just as Senate filibusters necessitate the building of supermajorities to ensure success, so too do presidential vetoes. And, moreover, to the extent that vetoes currently require a two-thirds majority, whereas Rule 22 requires a smaller, three-fifths majority, the potential ramifications of presidential obstructionism are even greater than that of internal Senate obstruction.

Abnormalcy of Unconventional Process

It is useful to interject as an aside at this point that what has been characterized here as an "abnormal" process is indeed abnormal in the strict sense, that is, it rarely emerges. The alternative process is not the process that is commonly encountered by successful legislation. Although a number of studies intimate that the unconventional process described above has become more common and, perhaps, closer to the contemporary legislative norm, statistical evidence suggests otherwise.[13] Such data indicate, specifically, that against the backdrop of Senate legislating as a whole, though more frequent, abnormal policymaking remains relatively rare. As proof of the infrequent appearance of abnormal process, consider the enormous number of bills introduced in the Senate as compared to the number of bills subjected to obstructionist tactics. Even recently, when the Senate broke its record for cloture votes taken in a single year, only a small percentage of bills were subject to filibusters. Of the roughly 2,266 public bills introduced in the Senate in 1996, only a fraction, twenty-nine (or 1.3%), were put to a cloture vote. Presidential vetoes are relatively infrequent as well. On average, sixty of the roughly 400 bills annually enacted by the contemporary Congress have been vetoed by presidents.

Uniqueness of Senate Process

Another basic premise of the preceding discussion of normal and abnormal legislative processes is that Senate lawmaking is representative of legislative decisionmaking generally. And, we can, therefore, safely look to Senate process in an attempt to understand institutional decisionmaking more generally, that is, what is true of Senate policymaking is true of policymaking in general. However, a large portion of the literature on Congress notes just the opposite, detailing the uniqueness of the Senate process.[14] Among the many claims of this literature are several particularly notable ones. The first of these is that the Senate is the most deliberative body in the world and its deliberative nature alone sets it apart from most, if not all, other institutions. Another oft-noted characteristic of the Senate is that it accords individual legislators a great deal of power in the governance process, more than that accorded by other institutions, and this, in effect, makes it a uniquely atomistic institution. Finally, the Senate's cloture rule is widely recognized as a rare specimen and, moreover, its existence is seen as underscoring the Senate's departure from the more common legislative processes and structures.

Nonetheless, the suggestion made here, namely, that the Senate is similar to most other legislative institutions, is reasonable in light of several considerations. First, while it is true that the cloture rule is in many ways unique to the Senate, the same is not true of the remaining procedures. Every institution has established and employs a set of rules that not only governs policy processes, but does so in a manner that staves off ostensibly unwarranted majoritarian impulses—much like the Senate's. Second, add to this the fact that, as explained earlier, the cloture rule effectively provides a limitless time and procedural framework within which the remaining procedures may be used, all that remains of the Senate's procedural uniqueness is Rule 22. But, even so, the remaining rules are the ones that actually give teeth to the cloture rule. Third, much of the Senate's structure and many of its traditions are historically rooted in and, thus, mirror that of most state, county, and city legislatures. Most have processes comprising stages. Most have requirements in place at each stage. Most offer opportunities to obstruct and to bypass obstruction at each stage. Similarly, many of the Senate's features are indispensable to the functioning of a legislative body in a representative democracy inasmuch as they facilitate majority rule, but at the same time ensure the virtues of a "republican form of government." The rules of most other U.S. legislative institutions, just like the Senate's, are designed to facilitate deliberation, careful consideration, and, above all, preservation of minority rights.

Even if one were to reject the idea that the Senate is similar to other legislatures and embrace instead the common view that it is in a class all its own, it is still the most plausible place to look in order to understand American policymaking. It is the coordinate chamber of America's national legislature, which, over time, has assumed the bulk of governmental power, resources, and decisionmaking within American governance and politics. And, within Congress, the Senate is where the competition of interests is most fierce because it is where the playing field is most level. It is also where major policy struggles come to fore in clearest view. Thus, arguably, the Senate is where the heart of American policymaking unfolds. To understand American legislative process, then, either because of its comparability to most other legislative decisionmaking apparatuses or, alternatively, because of its central importance in American governance, the dynamics of Senate decisionmaking are a very logical point of focus.

BARGAINING, PROCESS, AND POLICY OUTCOMES

One of the most basic features of Senate decisionmaking, moreover, and of the policy process generally is that both are, in essence, majoritarian; and bargaining is the means by which the majoritarian requirements are satisfied. Bargaining is a necessary condition for either the normal or abnormal policy process to work at all and its necessity arises foremost from the inherent nature of democratic decisionmaking. A sufficient majority must endorse a bill at each stage in order for it to succeed to the next stage. And, in order for a bill to succeed to final enactment, the support of multiple, successive majorities is needed. Without majority support at each stage, a proposed bill will not advance through the process. It follows that bargaining is critical to the functioning of the process because it supplies the majority support demanded by the process. Bargaining delivers the votes necessary to facilitate a bill's movement from one stage of the process to the next and, ultimately, to final passage. It, in effect, enables "legislating"—the act of adopting official governmental policies. Without bargaining, the requisite majority support for proposed bills would be lacking; policy proposals would not succeed through the various stage of the process; and, consequently, neither the normal or abnormal process would produce legislation. Both would, for all practical purposes, cease to function. Bargaining operationalizes legislative process and sustains its functionality. It breathes life into the formal elements comprised by the process and is, therefore, indispensable.

In the context of policymaking, bargaining is best described as an act of persuasion, of convincing others to endorse and/or bolster the efforts of a particular policy coalition. Bargaining is negotiating for the purpose of accomplishing one of two ends, either winning over the needed support of unaligned senators or dissuading opponents from pursuing strategies that threaten the bill's parliamentary viability. In either case, its ultimate goal is to promote passage of a particular policy proposal by prevailing upon others to engage in those behaviors most conducive to a proposed bill's success. Toward this end, policy negotiations usually entail also an exchange of benefits. The exchange of benefits is, in many respects, part and parcel of the persuasion element of bargaining to this extent: policy advocates' bargaining efforts are geared most immediately toward convincing those targeted by such efforts that it is to their own advantage to endorse the policy, that they stand to gain by doing so. In return for his or her endorsement of a proposed policy, an as yet uncommitted legislator, whose vote is needed, may be offered certain incentives by policy supporters. Similarly, opponents may also be proffered certain payoffs or at least spared certain punitive returns, in exchange for agreeing to forgo the use of certain obstructionist parliamentary prerogatives.

Critically, as a practical matter, successful bargaining is why the normal procedural process inheres. It helps to remove obstacles to a bill's movement. Failure to effectively deal with and/or overcome procedural obstructions obviously means the process would not function in its normal mode. Bargaining is a key means by which opponents are persuaded to forgo and/or abandon use of the parliamentary prerogatives that enable them to block legislation. Just as benefits are proffered to win over majorities, they are used also to coax opponents into strategic arrangements that facilitate a bill's procedural progress. Inasmuch as bargaining enables legislating through conventional channels, it most directly structures the procedural format of legislating and accounts for normal process.

Bargaining also drives normal substantive policy outcomes insofar as it structures and "contains" policy compromise. Here is what I mean. There are many kinds of bargaining methods available to policy advocates to build support. The most often utilized include the following: logrolling, side payments, and policy compromise. In each case, the objective is to win additional support and/or dissuade obstructionist opposition. In each case, some form of bartering is involved. However, logrolling and side payments do not affect policy substance. Logrolling amounts to vote trading, a classic "back-scratching" agreement. Senator A agrees to support Senator B's Policy X in return for Senator B's support of his or her own Policy Y or Senator B's agreement to forgo obstruction. With side payments, rather than the promise of future support or cooperation, what is tendered is some form of reward, such as appointment to a desired position (e.g., a committee membership or chairmanship) or preferential consideration relative to the Senate's legislative calendar, and so forth.

Policy compromise, unlike logrolling and side payments, is the only one of the three main modes of bargaining that impacts on the actual substance of the bill for which advocates are attempting to build support, and most often the impact is negative. Put simply, policy compromise typically calls for "compromise." It normally results in policy concessions, wherein advocates, in exchange for the needed support of as-yet-uncommitted senators or the reasonable cooperation of opponents, agree to weakening substantive changes, such as revision or removal of one or more controversial legislative provisions or abandonment of strengthening amendments. Policy compromise usually detracts from supporters' ultimate goal of policy success and limits the extent to which they are able to realize the enactment of strong legislation. So, from the advocates' vantage point, among the range of bargaining modes, policy compromise is the least desirable because it limits their ability to implement substantial policy reform.

Despite its drawbacks, policy compromise is common. It is a staple feature of American governance and politics. Legislators engage in give and take relative to substantive policy provisions all the time. Although no studies detail the frequency with which policy compromise is used as against the other two modes of bargaining described above, we can nonetheless safely say that it is used on a regular basis. The reason policy compromise is common is ultimately due to the nature of American democratic politics and decisionmaking. Policy change in America typically occurs gradually, so that a coalition's ultimate policy goal is not accomplished in the stroke of a single legislative effort and/or proceeding, but instead is realized gradually, through successive efforts.[15]

This tendency to move slowly is itself a product of two forces. On the one hand, it is a built-in feature of formal government structure insofar as the various mechanisms (such as separated powers, checks and balances, and federalism) designed to mitigate democratic pressures function, in effect, to conserve change and to permit it only gradually. On the other hand, it is also a product of the dynamics of grassroots democratic politics. The multiplicity of interests and forces existent within the American democratic polity begets mutual consideration of the varied, pertinent interests, which, in turn, begets a balancing of those competing forces, and, further, engenders conservative political change. Just as conservatism manifests itself within the larger political arena, so too does it emerge within the legislative process. And, it is by way of policy compromise that gradualism, also referred to as "incrementalism," manifests itself within legislative processes. Thus, policy compromise is a byproduct of, a manifestation of, both the structural conservatism and the political conservatism of American governance and politics. Above all, policy compromise is normal and it is normal essentially because incrementalism, of which policy compromise is an embodiment, is normal.

Importantly, just as the act of policy compromise itself fits within the standard mode of American politics and governance, so too does the substance of most policy compromise fall within a certain "normal" range—that is, the extent to which policies are modified during the course of coalition-building negotiations can be understood to fall more or less within a certain "norm." How so? First, as noted earlier, policy compromise typically entails concession(s) on the part of advocates, such that what is offered in return for support is a weakening of the policy provisions initially sought by supporters. The proposal is scaled back in one respect or another. Second, such concessions typically affect the scope and enforcement provisions of a proposed bill, more so than the proclamation portions of the bill. The enforcement provisions address and affect the potential real-life impact of the bill, that is, who will be covered, how, in what manner, and with what penal and/or compensatory consequences. The proclamation provisions, on the other hand, concern the objective(s) of the bill, that is, what is required and/or prohibited by the bill. Obviously, when would-be supporters disagree with the basic goal of a proposed bill, then negotiations would likely be either irrelevant or extraordinarily taxing, as it would prove nearly impossible to win them over to a cause whose very objectives they do not support. Consequently, policy negotiations tend to hinge upon hammering out an agreement relative to how the bill's objectives are to be achieved. The devil is in the details.

Moreover, while policy agreements affecting the enforcement provisions of a bill ordinarily minimize the degree to which the bill is implemented, seldom do bargaining efforts discount meaningful implementation of the bill altogether—that is, rarely does policy compromise virtually defeat the very purposes for which a policy proposal is being adopted. Under normal circumstances, bargaining does not produce gutted bills that contain mere pronouncements, with no real force undergirding them. Instead, even as it reduces how much advocates actually accomplish, it facilitates at least some tangible achievement. Advocates walk away with something of meaning. Legislators typically arrive at policy compromise agreements that hold some promise of measurable reform. And, it is because of effective bargaining that there exists such "normal" policy outcomes.

It follows that, if effective bargaining most directly sustains normal policymaking, then abnormal process and policy outcomes are foremost the products of failed or ineffective bargaining. First, with respect to procedural process, inasmuch as bargaining undergirds the normal process, a breakdown in bargaining engenders a disruption of that process. Whereas use of the rules is the most immediate catalyst for emergence of the abnormal process, the fact that the necessary bargains are not struck with opponents and/or moderates is the underlying stimulus for its formation. In particular, given that the abnormal process is precipitated by the use of procedural obstruction, its emergence is obviously indicative of advocates' failure to convince opponents to forgo the use of obstruction. Let us consider some of the reasons why negotiations between supporting and opposing coalitions sometimes fail and, thus, why abnormal procedures are invoked.

The main reason advocates are unable to dissuade active opposition through bargaining and, by the same token, the reason opposition coalitions resort to procedural tactics as a means of furthering their policy objectives has foremost to do with the political and policy demands with which members of opposition coalitions must contend. Such demands include those arising from the voice of constituencies represented by opposition members, or from the objective interests of constituents, or from the demands inherent in members' individual political and/or partisan ideology. Depending upon the alignment of a proposed policy with any or all of those demands, the policy may become a potential target of intense opposition on the part of interested members. So that, if a bill under consideration stands to negatively impact on a member's key constituent interests, or to be perceived by his or her constituents as especially onerous and/or undesirable, or if, alternatively, it is substantially at odds with the member's own central political beliefs about what is fair and or acceptable, then the bill will most likely become a victim of parliamentary jockeying on his or her part. Note that not all targeted interests provoke such intense opposition, but only those interests that are a high priority to a legislator and/or his or her constituents.

There is still another reason why certain attempts to bargain with opponents are ineffective. Because it is an effort that is geared toward building support and/or warding off active opposition, bargaining entails an exchange of benefits for the purpose of achieving these particular ends, as explained earlier. In addition to benefits, however, bargaining also involves sacrifice. There are costs involved in bargaining. By the same token that a legislator accepts a side payment or endorses a logrolling agreement in the spirit of negotiation, he or she also gives something up. There is some measure of relinquishment on the part of the legislator whose cooperation is desired and targeted by the exchange of benefits. This sacrifice is typically that of yielding one's policy stance, abandoning one's own individual ideological or political predisposition relative to a particular policy proposal, in return for the rewards of "going along." Such sacrifice, in turn, involves still further risks and potential costs as voters may not forgive (or find justifiable) a legislator's abandonment of principle or political stance. Further, there exist political circumstances in which the potential rewards of policy negotiations are undercut, that is, those in which the ordinary payoffs of various bargains, such as the benefits of logrolling, side payments, and policy compromise, are superseded by what constitutes the costs of conceding. In short, sometimes the costs of bargaining outweigh the benefits. And, when this occurs, bargaining with opponents will most likely fail and alternative procedures will result.

Abnormal policy outcomes, moreover, are the product of advocates' limited success in bargaining with uncommitted legislators. In many ways, uncommitteds remain the only real hope of a policy effort confronted by intense opposition and obstruction. This is true especially where advocates fall short of the requisite majority (or supermajority), which is often the case. Supporters' bargaining objective, then, becomes that of winning over the votes of uncommitteds in order to overcome obstruction. The options available to advocates in their attempts to win over moderates may sometimes be significantly reduced and it is this circumstance that explains the weak policies characteristically produced by nontraditional legislative processes—that is, the reason the substantive outcomes of the abnormal process are also "abnormal" has to do with the constraints advocates face in their dealings with moderate legislators. Under certain conditions, side payment and logrolling agreements may not be viable means of winning over these legislators, leaving only policy compromise as an effective enticement. When supporters are restricted to policy concessions as a means of winning over needed additional votes, abnormal policy outcomes typically attend abnormal procedural processes.

CONSENSUS, PROCESS, AND POLICY

The preceding discussion has outlined the role that bargaining plays in shaping process and policy. Bargaining itself, moreover, is enabled by consensus. Consensus, in effect, drives advocates' bargaining efforts. It is the basis upon which policy negotiations take place and yield some meaningful resolution. Without consensus, successful bargaining would not be possible. The flip side of this argument is that normal policymaking is possible and takes place ultimately because it is underlain by a measure of consensus. Without it, the normal process would not function, nor for that matter would "normal" policy outcomes be possible.

Simple logic dictates that consensus is an indispensable condition for bargaining. Bargaining is possible only because there is some degree of shared consensus among legislators, some middle road upon which opposing legislators can settle their differences. It would be impossible, as a practical matter, for members of separate policy coalitions to engage in bargaining, let alone reach any form of an agreement, except and unless there is some common ground upon which the various sides can coalesce and then attempt to develop a more specific policy agenda. A "meeting of minds" would be inconceivable in situations where legislators are worlds apart, where there are no shared interests of any kind. Conversely, bargaining regularly occurs because this is not the case. Instead, there are some common-enough interests among legislators that the various sides of a proceeding can and often do come together and reason with one another; thus, there can be, and regularly is, a meeting of minds. In short, successful policy negotiation is possible because the parties to negotiations operate upon the basis of some consensus.

The specific nature of the consensus that undergirds policy bargaining may vary, but most often it pertains to either the substantive or procedural elements of a policy proceeding—that is, the "understanding" among legislators has to do with either the content of the proposed bill and/or how the legislature as a whole should proceed in considering and passing upon the bill. Either the object or the rules of the game are agreed upon. In the first instance, legislators may share similar views regarding the nature, legitimacy, and/or seriousness of the problem addressed in a proposal, the broad contours of the proposal's solution to the problem, and/or the specific provisions of the proposal geared to redress the problem, among other things. This is best understood as "policy consensus." Policy consensus is the kind of agreement that ordinarily exists between advocates of a bill and would-be supporters. Here both sides are "on the same page" with regard to substance. A second form of consensus, which I will refer to as "procedural consensus," has to do with the parliamentary dimensions of a proceeding. At issue here is the official handling of a bill, or what procedural rules and mechanisms will be employed, how the bill will be brought before the legislature, who the primary participants in the proceedings will be, and so forth. And, while such issues may and often do concern all parties in a proceeding, they are especially pertinent to negotiations involving advocates and opponents in particular. At issue here, basically, is not so much whether there is a fight between the two sides, but rather how best to ensure the fight is waged in a fair and productive manner.

In sum, however minimal, the various sides of the standard policy proceeding operate upon the basis of some agreement, whether in principle or in practice. They are in accord, either with respect to the provisions to be contained in a legislative proposal or in regard to the procedures that will govern the proposal's formal consideration. Advocates, moderates, and opponents, in each of their respective efforts, proceed upon some common ground. Critically, because of this, the standard process works; majorities are delivered; obstructions are diffused; bills succeed through the stages of the process; and normal policy outcomes are produced.

Consensus, the cohesive element of policymaking insofar as it enables the "meeting of minds" that is indispensable to bargaining, is noticeably absent in the abnormal process. The process rests not upon common agreement relative to procedure and/or provisions, but instead upon deep divisions. Whereas consensus undergirds the normal process, it is extreme conflict that operationalizes and sustains the abnormal process and its tendency toward weak policy output. Such conflict exists either between advocates and opponents or between supporters and moderates.

In the first instance, there are such deep divisions between advocates and opponents that the latter not only object to, but vehemently oppose, a targeted policy to the extent that they are unwilling (or unable) to even consider agreeing to any arrangements that are conducive to the policy's careful consideration. They are so divided, in fact, that there is little to no agreement relative to how to formally proceed on a given bill. All bets are off. The ordinary rules of the game no longer apply. With respect to advocates versus moderates, moreover, there can exist sharp enough differences with regard to the provisions of a given proposal that there is little agreement concerning even the ends of the policy in question, let alone the most appropriate means of achieving those ends. Where there is severe conflict between advocates and opponents with regard to procedure and/or between advocates and moderates relative to policy content, then bargaining will be substantially inhibited.

ISSUE POLITICS, PROCESS, AND POLICY

Ultimately, the politics of an issue is what determines whether the normal procedural process or the abnormal process will prevail and also whether the policies enacted are strong enough to accomplish reform objectives. Process and policy are, in essence, a function of issue politics. Some issues will provoke normal policymaking, while others will provoke abnormal decision-making. The reason issue politics determines the type of decisionmaking that prevails has to do with the effect of certain political issues on the level of policy and procedural consensus among legislators. When an issue stimulates little division among legislators, a consensus of opinion regarding what to do and how, relative to that issue, will likely formulate. Such consensus, in turn, enables bargaining, which is critical to the functionality of the normal process, as explained earlier. When, on the other hand, an issue proves to be divisive, then substantial disagreement among legislators relative to bills addressing the issue will likely emerge. A lack of consensus means bargaining efforts will be seriously hampered. This limited "bargainability," in turn, increases the likelihood of a breakdown in normal policymaking. Fundamentally, more than just a difference of opinion yields consequences. Also important is the extent to which those differences are politically salient, so that divisive proposals addressing high profile issues will prove much more difficult to negotiate than will those addressing low profile issues.

This section examines the means by which the politics of an issue come to bear upon process and policy. More specifically, it asks, first, what are the conditions under which policy consensus on an issue will emerge? And, what impact does issue politics have on advocates' ability to successfully negotiate a proposed policy, that is, what is its impact on an issue's bargainability? Finally, precisely how are the effects of issue politics on process and policy transmitted through bargaining capacity? The basic conclusion reached is that the unconventional policy process is the making of contentious issues, while the normal process is best suited for consensual issues.

Issue Politics and Consensus

Consensus is largely a function of issue politics. The manner in which an issue is championed, moreover, is the aspect of issue politics that directly shapes the amount of consensus that is existent among legislators. Advocacy of an issue has to do with the political strategies, propaganda, and policy agenda utilized to advance reform on the issue. Some reform strategies will evoke greater consensus than will others. Policy consensus on a given issue will most likely exist when one or more of three conditions are produced by the politics surrounding the issue, namely, when the issue's advocacy is in line with the prevailing principles of the broader polity; when its advocacy corresponds with legislators' individual legislative goals; and/or when its advancement has little to no relevance for most legislators. In the first instance, when advocacy of an issue comports with widely accepted political ideals and principles, then a meaningful measure of policy consensus will emerge. As an example, consider foreign policy. Public opinion polls and legislative roll call data consistently show higher levels of support for foreign policies than domestic policies. This is due to the strength of American beliefs relative to patriotism and the democratic ideal.

The second circumstance under which policy consensus will occur is when an issue's advocacy corresponds to legislators' constituent demands and/or special interests—that is, when the press behind a given issue is in close alignment with legislators' own policy agendas. Of course, lurking behind this line of reasoning is the well-established premise that the preeminent goal of legislators is reelection and that the most critical steppingstone toward achievement of that goal is pursuance of constituent concerns.[16] In this light, a legislator is in agreement with an issue's advocates primarily because such a stance is conducive to his or her ultimate goal of reelection. Pork barrel politics are a prime example of how electoral self-interest stimulates policy consensus. Here, legislators support what could be construed as questionable budget policies largely out of self-interest. A third condition fostering policy consensus is that in which advocacy of an issue has minimal to no political value to many of the remaining legislators, that is, the issue's advocacy is of relatively little importance to legislators' constituent demands and/or interests. For example, agricultural issues generally have little meaning or effect upon urban communities; consequently, representatives of such communities would not likely actively oppose agricultural policies.

When none of the above-described conditions engendering policy consensus prevail, that is, when there is substantial conflict in relation to principles and/or constituent-electoral interests due to the manner in which an issue is advocated within a political arena, then substantial disagreement among legislators with regard to legislative proposals dealing with the issue will likely come to fruition. More specifically, when an issue's advocacy is at odds with the established political principles of a given polity, then policymakers will likely part ways once the issue is formulated into a legislative proposal. Similarly, when an issue is pressed in a manner that goes against the grain of the high priority demands or interests of one or more legislators' constituents, then the policymaking body will likely divide over the question of how best to approach the issue legislatively. In essence, the politics of an issue, especially issue advocacy, drives the level of policy consensus attendant to proposals addressing the issue.

Issue Politics and "Bargainability"

The more practical significance of an issue's politics, beyond its impact on policy consensus, is its effect on bargaining efforts within policy proceedings addressing the issue. The bargainability of an issue plays a direct role in shaping the procedural and policy outcomes observed in a given proceeding, as intimated earlier. "Bargainability," as used here, is the extent to which the issue is amenable to agreement formation within the legislative context. It concerns policy issue advocates' ability to successfully negotiate with other legislators, both with regard to the procedural dimensions and the substantive outcomes of a proceeding. It is the political leverage at their disposal to utilize on the issue's behalf. The bargainability of issues varies. Certain issues are more "bargainable" than others.

There are two factors that mainly shape the bargainability of an issue: the degree of political division and the level of saliency attendant to the issue. First and foremost, divisiveness matters. Divisive issues, that is, issues on which there is relatively little consensus, will prove more difficult to negotiate in policy arenas than will issues on which there is little disagreement. Less consensus means less policy agreement, which, in turn, means less of an ability to bargain. There is little common ground. More than just the divisiveness of an issue matters, however. The division stimulated by the issue must also have some real-life ramifications. Division does not always lead to policy conflict. It is conceivable that legislators may disagree, but, in essence, agree to disagree, that is, their difference of opinion does not affect their behavior toward related policy proposals, most importantly their willingness to bargain. If the clash of opinion fails to produce a "clash" in the legislative arena, then the disagreement does not really matter, for all practical purposes.

Whether or not the policy division sparked by an issue yields meaningful consequences is determined by the issue's broader political saliency. Issue saliency dictates whether differences of opinion will actually affect legislative behavior. It has to do with the overall political significance of an issue within a given political context. It is the degree to which the issue is regarded as more or less controversial and also the amount of attention it receives from political actors within that context. Political context can be the political boundary within which an individual legislator operates, or it can consist of the entire polity and, thus, all legislators' sphere of political operation. In essence, the saliency of an issue within a given political context essentially structures the policy consequences of the divisions surrounding a particular issue division.

Issue saliency impacts legislative behavior by structuring the "worth" of an issue to legislators. Some issues are necessarily deemed more "worthy" of legislators' attention than others. All issues are not equal, that is, worthy of the investment of time and energy involved in active opposition and/or advocacy within a policy proceeding. Both of these activities entail the expenditure of valuable, limited resources. Given the virtually limitless range of policy subjects from which legislators can choose in constructing a suitable individual legislative agenda, some choice is exercised relative to the allocation of such resources. Indeed, due to limited resources, legislators must exercise some selective judgment as to which course of action will prove most useful, which issues deserve more input, which deserve less. Active pursuit of political differences within a policy proceeding, then, will be more or less likely depending upon how important the issue is from the legislator's vantage point. When an issue matters little to a legislator, then he or she is more likely to defer his or her own judgment to that of other policymakers and to engage in cooperative behavior, including policy negotiations. When, on the other hand, it matters a great deal, then he or she is likely to not defer, but instead to exercise his or her own independent judgment.

Because high issue saliency results in more attention from political actors in a given context, it necessarily entails high visibility and, thus, more political value—that is, the greater attention attached to an issue invariably means the issue is in the spotlight more than most other issues. It is this aspect of issue saliency that is especially critical. Issues with greater visibility typically have more at stake for individual legislators than issues with less visibility. More voters care, more pay active attention, and, thus, more may react in the voting booth to a legislator's treatment of the policy issue. Consequently, high profile issues are likely to be perceived by legislators as issues on which there is a great deal at stake, whereas low profile issues are not likely to be regarded as such.

What is most often at stake—in particular, relative to high visibility issues—is greater costs.[17] Legislators think of political value primarily in terms of potential loss—that is, their first concern is the degree of risk. It is because of the greater costs associated with high stakes issues that such issues are more difficult to bargain over. Bargaining, in addition to the proffering of tangible and/or intangible benefits to the parties of a negotiation, also involves certain costs, as explained earlier. What is the greater risk inherent in high profile issues? It is the potentially large number of votes that could be lost due to a fairly large public's negative perceptions of a "bargaining" legislator's political wheeling and dealing. More voters are tuned in to proceedings on high profile issues. Therefore, more are privy when a legislator, in their view, abandons principles and ethics for the sake of political gain. Thus, more are likely to be unforgiving and, critically, unwilling to vote on behalf of the legislator in the next election. In essence, controversial issues diminish the prospects for reaching a workable policy agreement because there can potentially be greater voter backlash on such issues.

At least one tangible legislative outcome of an issue having relatively limited bargainability due to high visibility is that there are fewer viable bargaining modes available to policy advocates, and sometimes none at all. Although there are three common modes of bargaining typically available, namely, policy compromise, logrolling, and side payments, on salient issues the feasibility of the latter two is substantially diminished. Because, again, such issues are attended by greater visibility, on these, legislators are far less likely to openly compromise their principles in return for any advantages that may inhere in side payment and logrolling arrangements. Here the cost of "going along" will far outweigh the benefits of a back-scratching agreement or the securing of some future leadership post. Instead, legislators are more likely to insist upon policy compromise as a way of remaining true to their principles, not to mention making less of a sacrifice. Still, some issues involve such great costs that they, in effect, eliminate the viability of certain bargaining modes altogether because they involve too great a cost risk for legislators. There are instances in which none of the common modes of negotiation will suffice—as legislators will be unwilling to bend at all.

Although divisive, salient issues come in a variety of shapes and colors, we can nonetheless construct a quasi typology of salient issues—that is, we can say something about the profile of controversial issues. Such issues typically have one or more of several characteristics. First, they tend to be those that overlap with strongly held or controversial political ideologies. Some ideologies are held to more dearly than others and, on these, legislators are likely to exhibit more of a vested interest. Second, contentious issues may overlap with a legislator's key constituent demands and/or interests. Some interests are more critical to constituents because they converge with the predominant social, political, and/or economic circumstances of the voters and/or district represented by the legislator. In other words, the issue is "close to home," in a manner of speaking, and thus, more electorally significant for the legislator than for others. As a result, these issues will likely matter more to the legislator. Third, these issues may overlap with major partisan cleavages, so that a legislator's loyalty to party may be in question and, thus, his or her ability to leverage party membership for financial and political support. Finally, divisive, salient issues may overlap with existing regional cleavages.

On the whole, issues that prove to be both divisive and salient within a given polity will also prove to be issues on which the costs of bargaining far outweigh the benefits of bargaining. For these issues, "politics-as-usual" entails high risks, and this fact undercuts the bargainability of such issues.

Dynamic Interplay: Issue Politics, Process, and Policy

Just how does an issue's limited bargainability drive process and policy? More specifically, what are the mechanisms through which the effects of issue politics are brought to bear upon government policymaking—primarily where abnormal policymaking is concerned? It is through one or both of two ways that the influence of issue politics on process and policy is mediated through limited bargainability: either by provoking intense enough opposition so as to trigger use of the rules or by prompting moderate demands for substantive policy concessions as a condition for vote exchanges.

First, by provoking intense legislative opposition, an issue's politics can stimulate abnormal process. Intense opposition comes to fore when the goals and objectives of an issue's advocacy are at such great odds with one or more legislators' constituent demands and/or interests that these legislators are all but compelled to actively seek defeat of related proposals. More than just the lack of policy consensus between supporters and opponents is pertinent, however. The added ingredient of the issue's political significance for the legislator(s)' constituents is also critical. It is when an issue's advocacy threatens a political position to which a district holds more dear than others that representatives of that district will likely undertake whatever steps are necessary to preserve (or at least appear to preserve) the district's interests in the matter. Here, because the district's priority interests are negatively targeted, the district is essentially on the defensive.

As a result, the electoral stakes involved are much higher for the district's representatives—so high that no logrolling or side payment arrangement is likely to be worth the risk of electoral defeat for these legislators. They, instead, will intensely oppose policy proposals that threaten their district's priority interests and, moreover, will do so at all costs. Conformance to norms dictating non-use of the rules is no longer in these legislators' best interest. Legislative productivity, under these circumstances, takes on new meaning. In particular, use of the rules could prove more profitable than non-use. Parliamentary obstruction is the pathway to productivity, rather than abidance by the norms. The likelihood of opponents resorting to procedural obstruction as a means of furthering their objectives is significantly greater than usual. Here, bargaining will almost certainly fail. Thus, intense opposition is the primary trigger for unconventional lawmaking.

In addition to prompting the kind of intense opposition that triggers unusual parliamentary procedures, a second way in which an issue's politics comes to bear directly upon lawmaking is by raising the stakes involved for as-yet-uncommitted legislators whose votes are needed to defeat obstruction. Importantly, it is the effect of issue politics upon these uncommitted legislators' disposition that shapes the substantive policy outcomes produced by the abnormal procedures forced by opponents. Policymakers who remain on the fence with regard to a proposed bill, explicitly aligned with neither advocates nor opponents, are typically those whose support is sought by advocates when necessary (i.e., when advocates number less than the requisite majority). When, moreover, there is some agreement between these legislators and advocates with respect to the general goals of the bill, but there are differences regarding the most appropriate means of achieving these goals, then the bargaining leverage inherent in the issue will likely be affected. The degree to which they regard the issue as a politically significant one, moreover, is what ultimately ensures whether and to what extent moderates' differences will impact on policy outcomes. On high saliency issues, these legislators will be less willing to sacrifice their ideological stance under such great scrutiny, but will instead insist upon compromise as a condition for their votes. And, depending upon the nature and extent of their differences, such compromise could dilute the provisions of the proposed policy significantly or minimally.

CHAPTER SUMMARY

In essence, when legislators on different sides of a proceeding share some consensus on an issue and, as a result, are able to engage in productive negotiations, either with regard to procedure and/or substance, then the normal policy process will likely prevail. Consensus is the foundation of normal policymaking. When, however, legislators encounter issues on which there is little or no political consensus and, on which there is great controversy, then (1) intense obstructionist opposition will likely emerge, stimulating the abnormal policy process, and (2) moderates' interest will be "peaked," most likely resulting in the forced inclusion of weakening policy changes. Abnormal policymaking is the product of divisive and salient politics.

In the remaining chapters of this book, an analysis is presented that demonstrates that race is among the set of issues that is ill suited to normal policymaking. Lacking meaningful political consensus as a basis for civil rights decisionmaking, advocates of racial progressivism have, as a result, encountered abnormal process and have achieved, at best, abnormally weak policy reforms.

2

Governing Race in the Early Years

Race emerged as one of the more pressing issues confronting the nation's dominant political institutions from the post-Reconstruction era through the fifties. The major cleavages existent in American politics during these early years were defined to a great extent in racial terms. The states were divided along racial lines. The two major national political parties were as well. Also, the dissension caused by race was itself of considerable importance within the larger political arena—that is, the regional and partisan political differences concerning race were among the most significant disagreements driving American politics. The outcomes yielded by the politics of race during the early civil rights years were enormous. Specifically, the fact that race was a hot political issue at the time had a major carry-over effect into formal governance at the national level, structuring in uniquely different ways the how's of federal policymaking. The racial antagonisms prevalent during the time also shaped the what's of civil rights policymaking.

The civil rights policy goals of the early years were modest in comparison to later aims. The rights to vote and engage in protest activities were the two main concerns of the 1957 and 1960 congressional civil rights proceedings. It was believed that achieving these aims would lead to the realization of greater minority opportunities in other areas, such as employment, housing, and education. With regard to political strategy, it was also believed that, given the nature of the times and the political context, securing equal political rights was an easy goal, at least when compared to the more controversial, socioeconomic goals that leftist civil rights advocates had in mind.

Few would seriously challenge blacks' right to vote on a nondiscriminatory basis. Winning in 1957 and 1960 would at least be a start toward other nonpolitical goals. In the end, however, even these modest early policy goals proved elusive.

The politics of race during the early portion of the modern civil rights period and the two most prominent institutional consequences of these early politics are the focus of this chapter. Through an examination of congressional proceedings on the Civil Rights Acts of 1957 and 1960, this chapter demonstrates how congressional legislative process and policy outcomes were affected by the dynamics of racial politics. It illuminates the interplay of institutional processes and racial politics during the early period of civil rights politics.

The basic point of the discussion is that the politics of race during the early modern civil rights period proved too explosive for the predominant institutional process and led to major breakdowns in it and that the most civil rights reformers could obtain from the altered process that emerged were laws that were long on promises, but short on change. In this light, the rare procedures and unusual policy concessions of the 1957 and 1960 congressional civil rights proceedings are best understood as byproducts of the political dissension attendant to racial issues during this period. The analysis begins by presenting a portrait of racial politics during these early years. It then proceeds to demonstrate how the politics of race came to bear, first, upon the parliamentary components of civil rights process and, second, upon the viability of the laws that eventually emerged from that process.

THE POLITICS OF RACE DURING THE EARLY YEARS

There is little question but that racial issues were propelled to the center stage of American politics by the late fifties, as evidenced partly by the nation's preoccupation with the events surrounding the Supreme Court's 1954 *Brown* decision and by the extensive news coverage of the 1955 Montgomery Bus Boycott and other movement events and demonstrations. These phenomena underscored at least one of the major divisions sparked by race, namely, the South versus the North divide. Still another major race-related division presented itself in the larger political arena, namely, the growing gulf between the Republican and Democratic parties relative to civil rights. Not only did race underlie these fundamental political cleavages, but more, these divisions occupied the spotlight of American politics. They were politically significant differences.

Let us now examine in greater detail, first, the two great divides relative to race during the early years and, then, the political salience of these divisions within their respective spheres.

RACIAL DIVISIONS OF THE EARLY YEARS

Regional Division

Perhaps the most well known line of demarcation relative to racial issues is that falling along regional lines, specifically that between the former Confederate South and the remaining non-South states. Historically, race reform was so inextricably tied to regional cleavages as to distinguish the "South" from the rest of the country, chiefly in terms of its racial affairs. This was reflected in three ways. First, as a matter of stance, the South stood out as the region most vehemently opposed to the objectives of race reform. Second, given the nature of these objectives, the South also stood to "lose" the most. Finally, the strategies employed by advocates of civil rights explicitly targeted the South in ways that made the region's defensiveness virtually inevitable.

In the first instance, the long history of racial segregation and discrimination in the South served as an embodiment of the region's oppositional stance in the decades preceding the late fifties. Discrimination against blacks had long been a tradition of the region's social, economic, and political structure. An elaborate system of laws designed to relegate and restrict blacks to second-class citizenship was implemented in the wake of the Civil War. Enabled foremost by the North's acquiescence in the struggle for black equality and also by the removal of federal troops from the South in connection with the Compromise of 1877, southern states brought to an early end Reconstruction efforts geared toward securing certain legal, social, and economic rights to newly freed blacks.

Several developments were key in ensuring the permanency of the southern states' anti-Reconstruction campaign. "Jim Crow" laws were adopted by southern state legislatures and they provided the historical and legal bases for the racial caste system that would gradually permeate virtually every aspect of life in the South. These laws drew explicit racial distinctions that served to deprive blacks of the rights and privileges enjoyed by whites. By 1901, their reach affected almost everything, including churches, schools, restaurants, amusement parks, cemeteries and, even, curfews.[1]

Vigorous disenfranchisement efforts further demonstrated the South's predisposition toward race reform during these early years. Disenfranchisement took on a variety of forms. A host of devices were used to prevent, dilute, and/or eliminate black voting. Most took the form of complicated registration, procedures, elections laws, and practices that yielded a racially discriminatory impact.[2] Among the most noted were the Grandfather Clause, exempting from literacy requirements those persons who themselves or whose father or grandfather were eligible to vote in 1867; the white primary, which had the effect of excluding blacks from participation in the

Table 2.1
Estimated Black Voter Registration Rate in Eleven Southern States, 1940–1958, Selected Years (in percentages)

	1940	1947	1952	1956	1958
Alabama	0.4	1.2	5.0	11.0	15.0
Arkansas	1.5	17.3	27.0	36.0	33.0
Florida	5.7	15.4	33.0	32.0	31.0
Georgia	3.0	18.8	23.0	27.0	26.0
Louisiana	0.5	2.6	25.0	31.0	26.0
Mississippi	0.4	0.9	4.0	5.0	5.0
N. Carolina	7.1	15.2	18.0	24.0	32.0
S. Carolina	0.8	13.0	20.0	27.0	15.0
Tennessee	6.5	25.8	27.0	29.0	48.0
Texas	5.6	18.5	31.0	37.0	39.0
Virginia	4.1	13.2	16.0	19.0	21.0
SOUTH	3.0	12.0	20.0	24.9	25.0

Source: Garrow (1978)

South's ruling Democratic party; and poll tax and literacy requirements, both of which were relaxed for whites and stringently applied against blacks.

Adding to the South's distinction during the early years, beyond its long history of anti-black racial preferences, was the fact that race reform, as a practical matter, meant reforming the South in particular. Because the racial inequalities and injustices in existence there far exceeded those in other regions, the South was, in effect, the reluctant primary "beneficiary" of racial progressivism. One of the main objectives of early civil rights advocates was to secure equal voting rights for blacks and it was in the South that they found the most glaring voting inequality. Thanks to the success of the region's disenfranchisement campaign, southern blacks participated in elections at a substantially lower rate than their white counterparts. Specifically, the proportion of blacks registered to vote in the South was much lower than the proportion of blacks who were eligible to vote. Shown in Table 2.1 are estimated figures on black voter registration in the South between 1940 and 1958. These data reflect serious underrepresentation of blacks throughout the years shown. A second major objective of reformers during the early years was to eliminate the excessive use of violence and intimidation against blacks in the South; and, here too, in comparison to other regions, the South's use of violence against blacks stood out. Southern violence served a critical role in establishing and maintaining the region's racial caste

Table 2.2
Lynching by Race for Eleven Southern States, South, and Non-South, 1882–1962

STATE	Black	White	TOTAL
Alabama	299	48	347
Arkansas	226	58	284
Florida	257	25	282
Georgia	491	39	530
Louisiana	335	56	391
Mississippi	538	40	578
N. Carolina	85	15	100
S. Carolina	156	4	160
Tennessee	204	47	251
Texas	352	141	493
Virginia	83	17	100
SOUTH	3026	490	3516
NON-SOUTH	416	804	1220
U.S. TOTAL	3442	1294	4736

Source: Ploski and Williams (1983)

system. Victimization of southern blacks took on a host of forms, the most egregious of which were bombings and lynchings. In virtually every decade following the Civil War through the early sixties, the homes, churches, and schools of many southern blacks and/or their southern white sympathizers were bombed, burned, or vandalized.[3] Unlike bombings, typically reserved for the more prominent civil rights activists, lynching was used on a much wider scale and with much less calculation. Data shown in Table 2.2 demonstrate a number of things. First, the South lynched blacks at a substantially higher rate than did regions outside the South. Of the 4,736 lynchings recorded over an eighty-year period (1882–1962), three-quarters occurred in the South. A full 3,026, or 85 percent, of the South's lynchings involved black victims, while only 34 percent outside the South involved black victims.

In addition to the region's history of active discrimination against blacks and the resulting racial inequalities, the South was also explicitly targeted by civil rights advocates, thus further deepening the regional chasm concerning race. Proponents of black rights focused much of their energies upon the South. Many of the major activities of the civil rights movement either unfolded in southern states and/or were designed to effect changes in that region. The first widely publicized, large-scale coordinated civil rights

movement event occurred in the South, namely, the Montgomery Bus Boycott of 1955–1956, and it was followed by bus boycotts in Florida and
Alabama in 1956.[4] A variety of other pressure tactics were also used primarily
in the South, most notably a series of sit-ins that, between 1958 and 1961,
affected virtually every southern and border state, including some 100 communities. The main formal organizational centers of the civil rights movement, too, focused much of their efforts on the South. The National
Association for the Advancement of Colored People (NAACP) waged virtually all of its early legal battles against certain discriminatory practices of
southern states. Black churches conducted many of their major voter registration drives in large southern cities.

Partisan Division

Not only were the North and South divided over race as evidenced by
these trends, but, in addition, the two major national parties were in disagreement over the question of how best to approach the issue. In order to
gauge the nature of partisan differences concerning race, we can look to the
actions of U.S. presidents. Presidential administrations best reflect the national parties' respective stances inasmuch as presidents are regarded as the
traditional leaders of their party and the embodiment of the principles, policies, agenda, and so forth for which the party stands. What we find in
reviewing the actions of presidents during the early civil rights period is that
the Republican and Democratic parties slowly assumed positions on race
that diverge from one another. More to the point, Republican presidents,
starting in 1877 and continuing through the Eisenhower administration,
exhibited the degree to which the Republican party had become less the
party of Lincoln. It was less willing to advance civil rights, and more cautious
in addressing the race problem. Conversely, starting with the Roosevelt administration in 1941, we find that the Democratic party slowly became more
racially liberal.

Let us look at the specifics of how party racial differences began to crystallize during the early-modern civil rights years. It was Republican Ruth-
erford B. Hayes's succession to the presidency by way of the Compromise
of 1877 that led to the withdrawal of Union troops from the South and
abandonment of the Reconstruction program. Historian Richard Bardolph
writes in *The Civil Rights Record* that Republican Benjamin Harrison's administration (1889–1893) and also William McKinley's (1897–1901) continued with much the same strategy of turning a blind eye to the
mistreatment of southern blacks. Republican Theodore Roosevelt's administration (1901–1909) also made clear his party's willingness to remain the
"do nothing" party where blacks were concerned. It was under his leadership that black delegates from the South were refused seats at the Republican
National Convention and the party rejected an equal rights plan drafted by

W.E.B. Du Bois.[5] William Taft's Republican administration (1909–1913) adopted a policy of not appointing to federal offices anyone whom the local community found objectionable, which, as a practical matter, meant blacks would not be appointed to federal posts in the South. Bardolph adds that the Republican presidents who followed, including Warren G. Harding (1921–1923), Calvin Coolidge (1923–1929), and Herbert Hoover (1929–1933), essentially reassured the South that the federal government, under their administrations, would not become entangled in the region's racial problems and/or simply ignored or downplayed the problems.

The Eisenhower administration approached race with the same timidity as did previous Republican administrations. Although the congressional civil rights proposals discussed below were formally introduced on behalf of his administration, Eisenhower was a weak supporter of civil rights. Elected in 1952, it was not until 1956 that he recommended civil rights legislation to Congress. And, he actually endorsed only two parts of what would eventually become a four-part program, thanks to the efforts of Attorney General Herbert Brownell.[6] Eisenhower dealt a strong blow to the 1957 civil rights proposal when he indicated in a news conference that he did not understand all that was in it, even though it was sponsored by his own administration.[7] Again, in a 1960 news conference, Eisenhower said of the voting rights proposal recommended by the Commission on Civil Rights, "I don't even know whether it is constitutional."[8]

In essence, the first half of the twentieth century witnessed the slow emergence of a Republican party that was decidedly less progressive and more conservative on racial issues. This period marked the beginning of a permanent shift by the party to the right in the field of civil rights. In contrast to the Republican party's emerging racial conservatism was the Democratic party's gradual evolution into a pro–civil rights party. The latter's transformation, nonetheless, evolved out of a historically anti-black posture. Heavily influenced by its southern wing until the thirties, the silence of the Democratic party's national platforms on civil rights from 1884 to 1940 aptly reflected its historical anti–civil rights bent. A champion of the South's right to home rule, the party was for years regarded as an enemy of black rights. During the tenure of Franklin D. Roosevelt's administration, however, it began to be perceived in a much different light.

Various policy initiatives were undertaken by Roosevelt as well as subsequent Democratic presidents that were designed to improve the lot of blacks. Roosevelt issued Executive Order 8802 in 1941 barring discrimination in defense industries or government. Harry Truman followed suit, recommending anti-lynching legislation to Congress and also issuing Executive Order 9809 in 1946, which established the President's Commission on Civil Rights to investigate the status of civil rights. In 1948, on the recommendation of this same commission, Truman was the first president since Ulysses Grant (1869–1877) to present a comprehensive civil rights package to Congress. Roosevelt's and Truman's nondiscrimination executive orders together formed the historical basis of what would later become the country's most aggressive, results-oriented policy in the field of civil rights, namely, affirmative action.

On the whole, the early years of civil rights racial politics were characterized by a lack of consensus. The parties were divided partly along racial lines, and so were the North and the South.

SALIENCE OF RACE DURING THE EARLY YEARS

Of fundamental importance for understanding racial politics during the early years is recognizing not only that there was deep regional and partisan discord surrounding race, but also that this division was itself politically significant. The divergence concerning race during this period figured largely into the broader scheme of American politics. It mattered a great deal. Race was a salient political issue. As far as the national party system and the South were concerned, race was a priority issue.

That race was of central concern particularly in southern politics during the early civil rights years is a fact that is often noted by political scholars. Gunnar Myrdal's 1944 landmark study of race relations offers the following: "The elementary determinant in Southern politics is an intense Negro phobia which has scarcely abated since Reconstruction. The issue of white supremacy vs. Negro domination . . . has for more than a hundred years . . . affected all other civil rights and liberties of both Negroes and whites in the South."[9] Myrdal added that "[i]n the North, on the contrary, the Negro has nowhere and never been a political issue of primary and lasting importance—except insofar as he has constituted an issue in national politics."[10]

Buttressing the South's cognitive preoccupation with its racial affairs was the residential pattern of blacks. The pattern served to further increase the importance of race within the region. The black population in the former Confederate states was large enough to ensure that whatever national efforts were undertaken to affect black rights would be especially relevant to and for the South. It was there that most blacks in the United States lived. As of the 1800s, nearly nine-tenths of the nation's black population resided in the South. And, although over 4 million blacks migrated out of the South to the North between 1910 and 1960, at least 60 percent[11] continued to reside in the eleven-state South as of 1950 and 52 percent did as of 1960.[12]

Whereas the dynamics of race in the South tell us a great deal about the issue's regional implications, the dynamics of race within the party system speak to its broader significance. To the extent that party politics are an embodiment of the many competing viewpoints, stances, and agendas in American politics generally, race's significance within the party system is arguably representative of its national significance. And, what we observe in this regard is that race had become situated near the epicenter of party politics by the late fifties. It was not only a subject on which the two parties disagreed, but it was in the early stages of becoming one of the handful of issues by which the parties distinguished themselves from one another.

Various historical developments had pushed race to the forefront of partisan politics. First, shifts in the black vote made it open game for both parties. During much of the time between Reconstruction and the late fifties, the black vote was not locked up by either major party and, as a result, both saw in it some potential for boosting their national electoral prospects. Prior to 1936, the Republican party's lukewarm post–Civil War record on civil rights was enough to maintain the loyalty of many black voters, even as the party was becoming decidedly less sympathetic. In 1936, however, a large number of blacks abandoned the Republican party to vote for the Democratic nominee of that year, Franklin D. Roosevelt, mostly because they profited, even if unintentionally, from the economic benefits of New Deal programs.[13] Thus, election year 1936 marked a substantial departure from the previous pro-Republican trend in black voting. Twenty years later, just when the Democratic party appeared to be the obvious choice for black voters, a large number, roughly 40 percent,[14] supported the Republican candidate in the 1956 presidential election, Dwight D. Eisenhower. In effect, the dynamics of black voting behavior made civil rights a marketable issue during these early years.

A second factor boosting the value of race within the party system by the late fifties was that both parties were "up to bat" where race was concerned. Both undertook initiatives geared toward winning the black vote. In 1940, for the first time since 1884, Democrats and Republicans included civil rights planks in their national party platforms. Each condemned discriminatory practices and reaffirmed the constitutional right to nonracially discriminatory treatment.[15] The Republican party had done so consistently since 1876, except in the 1912 and 1916 presidential elections. The Democratic party platform, however, had remained silent on the issue for over a half century—since 1884—indicating that race had yet to become an important issue for the party system generally. As such, election year 1940 signaled a boost in the partisan importance of race. Beginning in 1940 and in every year to follow, both parties would include a civil rights plank in their national platforms. Race had become a permanent part of the national party political landscape.

A third development elevating the partisan importance of race was the migration of large numbers of blacks to northern states. As Doug McAdam points out in *Political Process and the Development of Black Insurgency*, it was not simply the movement of large numbers of blacks out of the South to states where voting discrimination was less of an obstacle to blacks' electoral participation that increased black political clout. Instead, it was their relocation to key Electoral College states, including Pennsylvania, New York, Illinois, New Jersey, Michigan, Ohio, and California. Their selective migration pattern enhanced the potential impact of the black vote in presidential contests, especially in states where majority constituencies were evenly split. In these areas, blacks could exercise a critical, decisive swing vote and, thereby, enormously influence national presidential election outcomes.

In summary, race was rapidly moving toward its peak political weight by the late fifties. Even the modest race reform objectives of the period evoked very intense opposition from the South. What is more, the politics of race in the South overshadowed virtually every other brand of politics in the region. Both of the major parties had begun to transform their stance on race in the years leading up to the late fifties and did so in ways that signified a growing rift between the two. And, like the regional differences, the ideological disagreement within the party system concerning race also occupied center stage against the backdrop of partisan politics. In the end, the regional and partisan politics of race together made it a much more challenging issue for the nation and its legislators to grapple with.

CIVIL RIGHTS PROCESS AND PROCEDURES DURING THE EARLY YEARS

Because of the heated nature of racial politics during the early years, racial legislative reforms were non-negotiable as far as southerners were concerned. Civil rights advocates were severely limited in terms of the effectiveness with which they could employ the usual stick-and-carrot approach for influencing legislative behavior. The politics of race in the South altered southern legislators' cost calculations with regard to the pros and cons of conformance to legislative norms, of playing by the conventional rules. Accordingly, the manipulation of Senate rules by civil rights opponents was a virtual inevitability. The obstructions created by the opposition caused a breakdown in the normal process. The result was the emergence of formal legislative proceedings that represented a drastic departure from traditional proceedings in terms of the demands and burdens they placed upon civil rights policy advocates.

The discussion to follow examines the makeup of the opposition coalition in the early years of civil rights policymaking; the legislative strategy the coalition used; and, importantly, the kinds of alternative procedures upon which advocates were forced to rely in order to defeat the opposition.

Civil Rights Opposition in the Early Years

Because the nature of racial politics in the South supplied the region's Senate representatives with ample reason to intensely oppose early civil rights bills, the coalition fighting against the bills was comprised almost exclusively of senators from the South. Likewise, much of the South's Senate representation took part in obstructing the bills. Senator Strom Thurmond remarked during the 1960 debate: "When the South has its back against the wall, we have to rely on the rules to protect ourselves."[16] This statement captures much of the driving force behind the obstruction of early civil rights proceedings.

The 1957 obstructionist group included seventeen senators, all of whom were from southern states. The group represented 77 percent of the eleven-state South's Senate representation. Among its members were Harry Flood Byrd (D-Virginia), James Eastland (D-Mississippi), Allen Ellender (D-Louisiana), Sam Ervin, Jr. (D-North Carolina), J. W. Fulbright (D-Arkansas), Lister Hill (D-Alabama), Spessard Holland (D-Florida), Olin Johnston (D-South Carolina), Russell B. Long (D-Louisiana), John McClellan (D-Arkansas), A. Willis Robertson (D-Virginia), Richard Russell (D-Georgia), W. Kerr Scott (D-North Carolina), John Sparkman (D-Alabama), John Stennis (D-Mississippi), Herman Talmadge (D-Georgia), and Strom Thurmond (D-South Carolina). The 1960 group comprised the same members as the 1957 group, with the addition of George Smathers (D-Florida), who did not take part in the 1957 filibuster effort, and B. Everett Jordan (D-North Carolina), who replaced W. Kerr Scott. Smathers' inclusion brought to eighteen the total number of members opposing the 1960 bill. All were from the South and constituted fully 82 percent of the region's Senate representation.

Obstruction of Civil Rights in the Early Years

Southern opponents used the rules to create obstructions throughout the early civil rights proceedings. The 1957 bill was blocked at each major stage of the process, including the committee consideration and final vote stages, and the 1960 bill was blocked at the committee and final vote stages. The committee juncture proved an especially formidable obstacle. It had bottled up every civil rights proposal referred to it since Reconstruction, according to the *Congressional Quarterly Almanac*.[17] In 1957, the committee was headed by long-standing opponent James Eastland of Mississippi, who boasted during his 1954 reelection campaign that, as chair, he "saw to it that no anti-lynching, anti-poll tax, FEPC or anti-segregation legislation ever reached the Senate floor."[18] Eastland successfully used his powers as chair to prevent any of the Senate versions of the 1957 and 1960 proposals from reaching the floor. At the floor, opponents utilized a wide range of tactics to prevent action on the House versions of the early legislation. Such tactics included refusals to vote, lengthy speechmaking, excessive amendment activity, various other dilatory motions and points of order, numerous quorum call demands, and so forth. During the 1957 debate, Senator Strom Thurmond set a record, speaking against the measure for over twenty-four consecutive hours.

Routes of Passage During the Early Years

In place of the normal process that was obstructed by southerners emerged an alternative process. Opponents' obstruction of the 1957 and 1960 civil rights proposals forced supporters to turn to unusual routes in order to bypass the obstruction. This, in the end, resulted in a set of proceedings that were distinctive in a number of ways. Satisfying the formal requirements of each parliamentary stage entailed a very difficult fight on the part of advocates. Precisely how did advocates respond? And, more to the point, given the obstruction and use of special routes to bypass the obstruction, what was the nature of demands inherent in the early civil rights proceedings and how did they compare to the normal demands of legislative process? I turn now to these questions.

Committee Stage

Whereas a handful of votes and the chairman's input are ordinarily all that is required to get a majority-supported bill beyond the committee juncture, much more was involved in getting the 1957 and 1960 proposals beyond this point in the process. In both cases, advocates were forced to turn to alternative, more costly routes. During the 1957 proceedings, supporters on the Judiciary Committee made repeated, unsuccessful attempts to work on behalf of the bill from inside the committee. In addition, the discharge procedure was considered,[19] but rejected due to the fact that a filibuster could occur at several different junctures of the procedure.

The seldom-used direct placement procedure was the means supporters eventually used to get the bill beyond the committee stage. The House had passed its version of the 1957 administration bill on June 18 and sent it to the Senate. The first reading of the bill was had on June 19, 1960. Following a second reading the next day, Minority Leader William Knowland stated: "I desire to object to any further proceedings on House Bill 6127 at the present time . . . pursuant to rule XIV, subsection 4, of the Rules of the Senate."[20] This statement effectively secured the bill's direct placement on the calendar. Its placement on the calendar, in this manner, however, was challenged by opponents, forcing advocates to do even more. Opposition leader Richard Russell raised a point of order against Knowland's objection, on the grounds that Rule 14 was being improperly used to bypass the most crucial checkpoint in the legislative process. Vice President Richard Nixon, who was presiding, unofficially held that committee referral was not mandatory. Nixon presented Russell's point of order to the floor, where it was voted down in a 45 to 39 vote. Next, supporters had to defeat a motion to refer the bill to Judiciary with instructions that had been submitted by Senator Wayne Morse, a co-sponsor of the bill, who argued that bypassing the committee left even supporters ill-equipped to pass upon the legislation. It too was rejected by a vote of 54 to 35.

Securing the 1960 bill's movement beyond committee obstruction proved equally demanding. Several things were tried. First, a discharge resolution was submitted by Jacob Javits on August 26, 1959, but abandoned as well because of the many filibuster opportunities inherent in the procedure. Also, multiple referral was used. In addition to Judiciary, parts of the bill were referred to the Rules and Administration Committee, chaired by supporter Thomas Hennings. Having received the bill late in 1959, however, the Rules Committee did not have enough time to meet the leadership's deadline for taking up the bill at the floor. Beyond this, amendments containing civil rights provisions were proposed to several bills sponsored by southerners, but subsequently abandoned at the leadership's request.[21]

Additionally, two committee strategies were actually pursued at length by supporters; both were tied to floor motions. The first involved use of a rider amendment to a House bill authorizing the leasing of federal military property to a state school district. On February 15, 1960, Majority Leader Lyndon Johnson obtained unanimous consent that the Senate proceed to consider the House school bill H.R. 8315. He then stated that "[b]ecause there is, as yet, no civil rights legislation on the Senate Calendar, this bill has been selected as the one on which . . . to begin the discussion of civil rights proposal in this Chamber."[22] A package amendment bill containing the same provisions as the administration bill that was blocked in committee was presented two days later by Senator Everett Dirksen. A fight against this rider amendment version ensued, imposing still more burdens on advocates. Richard Russell submitted a motion to postpone consideration of the school bill for one week, but was defeated in a 61 to 28 floor vote. Following this, Morse again argued that bypassing the committee left the membership without the benefit of committee scrutiny and submitted a motion to discharge the Judiciary Committee from consideration of the civil rights proposals in its possession. The motion was defeated in a 68 to 4 roll call vote. A subsequent motion by Morse to discharge the Rules Committee was also defeated at the floor in a voice vote.

The second committee strategy employed by advocates in 1960 was use of committee instructions. Advocates eventually abandoned the rider amendment bill in favor of a House-passed bill due to several considerations. Among these were (1) the potential inviability of the rider amendment under cloture since, technically, it was a nongermane amendment, and (2) the possibility that a conference between the House and Senate on a bill affecting military property would be headed by Armed Services Committee chairperson and opposition leader, Richard Russell. This instructions strategy was also fought by opponents. Russell attempted to undermine the strategy by objecting to Johnson's request for unanimous consent that the House bill (H.R. 8601) be read twice on the same day it arrived in the Senate,

March 24, 1960. The intended effect of Russell's objection was to delay action on the bill until the next day. However, Johnson immediately moved to adjourn for three minutes. The motion was agreed to and the bill was then read a second time, whereupon Johnson moved that it be referred with instructions. Eastland presented a countermotion to have the bill referred without instructions and, thus, there were no time limitations on committee consideration or any stipulations that the bill be reported back to the floor. Eastland's motion was defeated in a floor vote. The Senate on March 24, 1960, adopted instead Johnson's motion to refer the bill with instructions to report the bill back within five days. On March 29, 1960, the bill was reported back to the floor, along with a one-page committee report containing a statement of when the committee had met (two days) and the names of the three witnesses it had questioned.

Consideration Stage

Success at the consideration stage of the 1957 proceedings was costly, but this was not the case in 1960. The first strategy advocates pursued in an attempt to deal with the 1960 committee block, the rider amendment strategy, effectively made movement beyond the consideration stage a *fait accompli*. With regard to the second strategy, the leadership arranged an agreement with opponents that the bill would go through committee, in exchange for the opponents allowing the bill to proceed to the floor without obstruction. As a result, Johnson encountered no opposition when he moved that the Senate formally proceed to consideration of the 1960 bill on March 30, 1960, one day after it had been reported out of committee. The motion to proceed was agreed to in a 71 to 17 vote.[23]

Once the 1957 bill entered the consideration stage, however, floor proceedings were much more complicated. What is ordinarily a pro forma checkpoint at which almost no demands inhere became, in 1957, a roadblock that exacted a great deal from supporters. A floor coverage plan had to be devised that divided supporters into teams with rotating responsibilities. Supporters were warned to be "readily available" to respond to surprise opposition maneuvers. Briefing memos and sessions were used to instruct supporters about parliamentary procedure. Stressed in particular was the need to counter points of order, to submit tabling motions as a way to quash dilatory motions, and to anticipate and respond to numerous live quorum calls in a timely fashion.[24]

Alongside these precautions, still other tactics were employed. Daily sessions were lengthened, ending as late as 10:30 P.M.—well beyond the Senate's usual closing time. Extended sessions were intended to increase the burdens of continuing the filibuster by forcing opponents to remain active at the floor for long periods of time and to minimize the number of days consumed by the filibuster. Also, a one-track system was put in place that blocked all other legislation from being considered, except emergency measures. Its adoption was forced by Knowland, who announced the day he submitted the motion to consider that he and other supporters would object to all motions to consider other measures, except minor and emergency measures. They believed that by doing so they would increase the pressure on opponents to abandon their efforts insofar as it would prevent action on other proposals in which they were especially interested.

Final Vote Stage

Securing a final vote on passage of the 1957 and 1960 bills was also much more complex than usual. Typically, unanimous consent agreements, arranged in advance by a handful of senators, enable the floor to pass upon legislation with relatively little active energy or procedural maneuvering on the part of the bill's supporters—little beyond debating and amending the bill as necessary. The floor fight surrounding the 1957 bill was expected to be contentious enough that supporters had attempted to, in essence, change the rules of the game well before the official start of the civil rights proceedings. The plan to revise Rule 22 at the beginning of the session was announced in October 1956. A letter to members soliciting support for civil rights legislation from Senators Douglas and Humphrey characterized the Senate as the graveyard of civil rights and Rule 22 as its grave digger. It offered this argument:"majority rule in the Senate is a prerequisite to obtaining any civil rights legislation."[25] Senator Jacob Javits added in a letter that "[t]he principal sufferer from the failure of cloture has been civil rights bills."[26] And, as spokesperson of a specially appointed subcommittee for review of rule change proposals, he noted: "[t]he Special Subcommittee . . . could largely determine whether we accomplish civil rights legislation in this session of Congress or not."

Supporters poured enormous energy into the rules change, but it was eventually defeated. The strategy had called for Humphrey and Douglas to submit a motion to proceed to consideration of new rules immediately after the Senate convened in January 1957.[27] In order to prevent the motion from being tabled, the movers would have to have the motion coupled with a ruling from the chair that the motion was in order. Johnson, however, leveraged his leadership position to prevent coupling of the two motions. Senate tradition provides that the majority leader be recognized before other senators. Johnson, as a result, was able to submit a motion to table Douglas' motion before it could be ruled in order. The floor endorsed Johnson's motion to table the motion in a 55 to 38 vote. Some did so because they feared it would open a "parliamentary jungle"[28]; others were acting on the leadership's promise to address Rule 22 later; and still others simply valued the principle of unlimited debate.

The floor strategy pursued once the 1957 floor proceedings were officially underway was itself very demanding. It involved many components, including floor team coverage, briefings on procedure, extended daily sessions, and a one-track system. Also, rather than ending each calendar day by adjourning, daily sessions were ended on a motion to recess. Although some twenty-one calendar days passed between July 17, 1957, and August 7, 1957, the day the bill was adopted, the Senate remained in the same legislative day the entire time period. The purpose of doing so was to spare the floor from having to proceed through a series of time-consuming agenda items required by the rules following an adjournment. Finally, there was also serious consideration given to filing a cloture petition, although one was never filed.[29] The bill advanced to a final vote when opponents voluntarily ended their filibuster, convinced at that point they had accomplished all they could. On August 7, 1957, the Civil Rights Act of 1957 was adopted in a 72 to 18 vote and sent to the House where it was modified and then passed on August 19, 1957. The bill was signed into law by President Eisenhower on September 9, 1957.

Like the 1957 bill, final passage of the 1960 bill at the floor was also secured through the use of abnormal routes. In keeping the rider amendment bill afloat, advocates had to do a great deal. Teams with rotating responsibilities for floor coverage were devised. Also, starting on March 1, 1960, the leadership began to regularly have the sergeant-at-arms of the Senate "request" the attendance of senators who did not respond to quorum calls, especially southerners who were primarily responsible for the repeated quorum calls. Doing so was intended to prevent a failed quorum call that would, in turn, force an adjournment. Also, a strict application of the rules was followed. Morse stated at the beginning of debate on the rider package amendment: "I serve notice now that I intend to apply the rules of the Senate in every way that I can to bring an end to (the) filibuster."[30] These efforts included demanding that opposition speakers speak continuously, permitting them to yield only for the purpose of entertaining a question; raising points of order against various dilatory motions and other opposition actions; and blocking several attempts by opponents to introduce other business in an attempt to displace the civil rights measure. Certain of these tactics were designed to increase the difficulty of maintaining the blockade against the bill, while others were simply geared toward maintaining the bill's procedural viability. Finally, tabling motions were used to quash many of the opponents' speech-enabling amendments.

The most distinguishing feature of the 1960 floor strategy was use of around-the-clock sessions. Johnson announced on February 23 that, beginning February 29, the Senate would remain in session on a twenty-four-hour basis until votes could be obtained on the rider amendment package. The sessions lasted from February 29 through March 8. As a test of support for the sessions, he submitted a motion to adjourn on February 29, which was rejected in a 67 to 23 vote, and another on March 1, also rejected by a vote of 55 to 6.[31] The twenty-four-hour sessions were intended to wear down filibustering senators by forcing them to remain continuously active at the floor throughout the day and night.

Finally, a cloture attempt was made on the 1960 bill, but it failed. Senator Paul Douglas, on March 8, 1960, submitted a cloture petition, signed by thirty-one senators. The leadership was against it. Minority Leader Dirksen, who authored the rider amendment bill, opposed the petition and argued that he thought it premature, given the amount of disagreement among supporters themselves concerning the bill. Majority Leader Johnson stated he also considered the petition premature and would be "reluctant ever to vote cloture."[32] The cloture motion was rejected on March 10, 1960, in a 52 to 42 vote.

In comparison to floor proceedings on the rider amendment version of the 1960 bill, proceedings on the House version of the 1960 bill more closely paralleled the normal process, although it too diverged in notable ways. Much of the complicated strategy advocates employed to advance the rider amendment version of the bill dissipated following the March 30, 1960, vote to take up the House version of the bill. Remember, there was little active floor opposition to this version of the bill. Consequently, the team coverage, strict application of the rules, cloture consideration, and other components of supporters' initial floor strategy in 1960 were abandoned. Gone too was the around-the-clock schedule. What did remain were the one-track system, the recess schedule, and constant floor coverage. The House bill was adopted at the floor of the Senate on April 8, 1960—in a 71 to 18 vote, when opponents again ended their filibuster voluntarily. The House agreed to the Senate amendments in a 288 to 95 vote. The Civil Rights Act of 1960 was signed into law by President Eisenhower on May 6, 1960.

On the whole, the early civil rights congressional proceedings were anything but normal, thanks to the controversial nature of racial politics. Senate representatives of the South, virtually compelled to stave off the passage of civil rights policy proposals by any means necessary, including excessive use of the rules, forced the use of alternative routes. The end result was that the 1957 and 1960 proceedings were punctuated throughout by extraordinary input on the part of advocates. Their input assumed a great variety of forms, from the rules change efforts, to schedule manipulation, to rotating team coverage of the floor, to simultaneous pursuit of several versions of the same bill, and more. In effect, the process was transformed into something very much unlike that confronted by most bills.

CIVIL RIGHTS POLICY OUTCOMES IN THE EARLY YEARS

In addition to altered procedural processes, there was a second major consequence of racial politics during the early civil rights years: its impact on the substance of civil rights legislative proposals. Race's contentiousness during this time period functioned as a severe limitation upon advocates' bargaining leverage with opponents as well as their bargaining leverage with would-be supporters whose votes were sorely needed to overcome obstruction and enact civil rights legislation. As with opponents, advocates did not have at their disposal the full array of bargaining tools ordinarily useful in building support for a measure. Instead, policy concessions proved the only effective means of acquiring the votes required to secure passage of the 1957 and 1960 bills. Consequently, what emerged at the other end of the altered process was a set of laws with more symbolic meaning than real-life impact.

What advocates had hoped to accomplish during the earlier civil rights proceedings was federal enforcement of the Fifteenth Amendment voting rights guarantee and of the Supreme Court's *Brown* decision and its off-spring. It was believed that what was most needed was a means of bypassing the many obstacles to black political participation that had been carefully constructed and maintained in the South. Direct involvement of federal enforcement officials was considered the surest route to accomplishing this objective. Thus, advocates sought to empower the president to deploy federal officials and the U.S. attorney general to southern states to enforce equal protection.

The discussion to follow details the challenges Senate advocates faced in negotiating the additional votes needed to succeed in the altered process. It also outlines the conditions that structured how these challenges were met and, more importantly, how these conditions eventually shaped the extent to which advocates were able to accomplish their policy objectives.

Negotiating Race in the Early Years

Senate uncommitteds played the central role in shaping the actual provisions of early civil rights laws, and, critically, they were also key in ensuring that these laws, as enacted, were far weaker than their original versions. The explanation for uncommitteds' major influence is tied to three factors. First, advocates needed to obtain supermajority support in order to effectively deal with opponents' obstruction. At the outset of the 1957 and 1960 proceedings, only a simple majority of senators actively supported the bills. Hence, to win, which ultimately meant being able to invoke cloture, proponents needed more votes. Though clearly the strategy of choice, there were not enough senators already on board to invoke cloture. At the outset of the 1957 proceedings, advocates had only mustered the support of fifty-three senators, and, with respect to the 1960 proceedings, they initially laid claim to forty-nine votes.[33] Opponents, on the other hand, claimed seventeen members in 1957 and eighteen in 1960. Given the requirements of Rule 22, which in 1957 called for two-thirds of the votes of all ninety-six Senate members in order to invoke cloture and, in 1960, two-thirds of those members present and voting at the floor, advocates were short at least eleven votes in 1957 and at least eighteen in 1960. These additional votes would necessarily have to come from the group of senators who were as yet unaligned with either the opposition and/or supporting coalitions. Uncommitteds in 1957 numbered twenty-six members and, in 1960, thirty-three. These members' votes were needed to enact any form of civil rights legislation during these years. This is a key reason why the uncommitteds' role loomed so large in the final policy outcomes of the early civil rights efforts.

A second crucial factor that further explains the moderating influence of uncommitteds upon the substantive outcomes of the 1957 and 1960 proceedings is that the group consisted primarily of Republicans who, logically, were of a classic conservative ideological bent. Of the senators who remained uncommitted in 1957 and 1960, that is of the twenty-six and thirty-three, respectively, at least 39 percent in 1957 and 64 percent in 1960 were Republican. And, in line with their party's traditional mode of thinking, the mostly Republican group was less than enthusiastic about the sizeable government role encapsulated in many of the proposed civil rights bills. Their ideological preference was for the reverse, namely, smaller government and less government intervention, as would be expected. This predisposition clearly went against the grain of the policy reforms envisioned by civil rights advocates. Advocates' reform goals almost of necessity required an active antidiscrimination role on the part of the federal government in order to protect the rights of blacks in the South.

The specific provisions that advocates and moderates disagreed about most in 1957 were those structuring the attorney general's enforcement powers and those detailing the rights of defendants charged under the bill. What Senate civil rights advocates wanted in 1957 was relatively minimal in comparison to later aims. In 1957, the objective was to simply enforce the constitutional guarantee of equal voting rights and, importantly, to enforce the Supreme Court's 1954 *Brown* decision, especially in the face of the South's outright defiance of the decision. So, Part Three of the four-part original proposal entitled "To Strengthen the Civil Rights Statutes, and for Other Purposes," in Section 121, authorized the attorney general to seek an injunction, restraining order, or other court order to protect the civil rights granted by an 1861 federal law that made it a crime to (1) interfere with an officer performing his duties; (2) obstruct justice; and (3) deprive persons of "the equal protection of the laws, or of equal privileges and immunities under the laws."[34] Part Four made it a crime to interfere with the right to vote in federal elections and authorized the attorney general to institute civil action to redress interference(s) with federal voting rights. The same section also granted federal district courts jurisdiction over cases brought under the act. The first two parts established the U.S. Commission on Civil Rights for a period of two years and provided for an additional assistant attorney general in the U.S. Department of Justice.

Moderates objected to Part Three, saying it gave excessive powers to the attorney general because it did not specify which rights came under the bill nor, as a result, in which areas the injunctive process might operate. They also argued that the bill did not grant the right of a jury trial to defendants prosecuted under the bill and, therefore, sacrificed a fundamental American right. They rejected advocates' contention that Part Three did nothing more than enable the federal government to protect constitutionally guaranteed rights, that there was no constitutional right to a jury trial in all cases, and that the inclusion of a blanket guarantee would mark a significant departure from legal tradition.

Certain of the 1960 bill's provisions divided advocates and uncommitteds on grounds having primarily to do with the extent and nature of the federal government's role in enforcing the bill. Supporters sought to strengthen the weak federal voting rights protections enacted in 1957 by creating a more straightforward enforcement structure, namely, one that would authorize the use of appointed federal registrars to enlist voters. They also wanted to proscribe the use of violence against civil rights activists and demonstrators in the South. Also included in the 1960 original proposal was authorization for federal funding of state school desegregation efforts. Finally, Title VII of the original version of the 1960 bill created a Commission on Equal Job Opportunity under Government Contracts to help ensure nondiscrimination in companies awarded federal contracts.

It was moderates' contention, however, that advocates' proposal to provide for administrative enforcement of the voting rights provisions lodged too much power in bureaucratic agencies. They believed, instead, that federal courts should be entrusted with the power to correct voting discrimination. The version they preferred provided that the attorney general could seek an injunction against one or more persons denied the right to vote because of race and, once granted the injunction, ask the Court to also make a finding of a "pattern or practice" of voter discrimination. If the court found a pattern of discrimination, a black person could then petition the court for voter registration and the court, in turn, could itself register the petitioner or appoint a referee to register him or her. The schisms generated by advocates' remaining policy objectives in 1960, such as desegregation funding and the jobs provisions, were so far beyond repair that they received scant attention.

Critical to fully grasping why the early civil rights policy outcomes emerged as they did is knowing that, given the political forces tied to race, these differences could not be taken lightly and negotiated with the same degree of political detachment as in the case of pork barrel or even regulatory policymaking. Republicanism supplied moderates with their ideological predisposition toward race-related proposals and led them to embrace their particular views regarding the proposed civil rights provisions. However, it was because of the growing political significance of race within the party system that they came to insist upon policy concessions during the early civil rights policy negotiations. The controversial nature of racial politics during the late fifties effectively precluded many of the usual means for resolving policy differences. Just as opponents' cost calculus relative to racial politics prompted them to depart from the restraint norm, so too did that of moderates, only in different ways. Uncommitteds were unwilling to abandon their principles relative to individual freedom and limited government control, especially not on such a high profile issue as race. There was too much at stake. Advocates would have to bring the bills in line with moderates' racially conservative Republican ideology.

Early Civil Rights Policy Concessions and Provisions

The specific changes made to address moderates' concerns affected those titles of the bill that most directly shaped its potential real-life impact. Part Three of the 1957 proposal was removed by adoption of the Anderson-Aiken-Case amendment in a 52 to 38 vote. This change effectively limited the power of the attorney general and the bill itself to voting rights alone, rather than civil rights in general. Also, a right to trial by jury was included in Part Four of the Senate bill by way of adoption of the O'Mahoney amendment in a 51 to 42 vote. Part One, which established the U.S. Commission on Civil Rights, and Part Two, which created an additional assistant U.S. attorney general for civil rights, remained largely intact.

Revisions to the 1960 legislation that were tailored to meet moderates' concerns also restricted the bill's scope and enforcement. The choice to pursue the House version of the bill due to procedural considerations had decisive substantive consequences. The House version did not include provisions for school desegregation funds or for the creation of a Jobs Commission. Nor were there any serious attempts to incorporate these titles into the House bill. Lastly, the presidentially appointed registrar approach that supporters advocated was rejected in three separate votes, first in a 53 to 24 vote rejecting a Douglas-Javits amendment, again in a 51 to 43 vote rejecting a Javits-Clark amendment, and finally in a 58 to 26 vote rejecting a Hennings amendment. The House voting rights provision was adopted instead. It authorized federal courts to appoint referees to assist in the registration of black voters in districts where there was a court finding of a "pattern or practice" of discrimination.

In the end, neither the Civil Rights Act of 1957 nor the Civil Rights Act of 1960 proved to be terribly significant pieces of legislation in terms of actually improving the sociopolitical progress of blacks. The 1957 act, as one senator remarked, did not bring the vote to one person.[35] The Commission on Civil Rights' first voting rights report would later substantiate this claim.[36] The addition of a jury trial right proved especially devastating as it virtually ensured that violations of the bill's provisions in the South would go unpunished by predominantly white southern juries. Even opponents labeled the bill a testimony to their success. Russell stated: "the fact that we were able to confine the Federal activities to the field of voting and keep the withering hand of the Federal Government out of our schools and social order is to me . . . the sweetest victory of my 25 years as a Senator from the State of Georgia."[37]

The 1960 act had an equally insignificant impact. Deleting the FEPC provisions left unaddressed employment discrimination in various industries where blacks were systematically denied jobs, restricted to lower-paying salaries, and/or barred from powerful labor unions. Abandoning the school desegregation provisions delayed implementing the *Brown* decision on the part of even willing school districts that were strapped for funds. Finally, the adoption of the court voting rights enforcement approach would eventually prove to be the slower, more intimidating, more cumbersome approach to ensuring black registration, as compared to the administrative approach. It would yield a great many court suits, but no meaningful increase in black political participation.

CHAPTER SUMMARY

In summary, race was a critical issue in American politics during the early years of modern civil rights politics. It was an issue that split the nation in fundamental ways as it lay at the center of the major regional and partisan cleavages existent at the time. The political salience of the divisions engendered by race was evident in the South's preoccupation with maintaining its racial caste system and in the increased amount of attention devoted by the two major parties to the race problem and the black vote. The heightened scrutiny of race handicapped Senate civil rights advocates' ability to secure the enactment of strong civil rights legislation and to do so through the usual procedural channels. Southerners could not be dissuaded to forgo the obstruction of civil rights legislative proposals, which ultimately imposed upon supporters an extraordinarily demanding alternative process. Uncommitteds could not be won over through the usual quid pro quo bargaining tools and this is why the early modern civil rights laws proved to be almost inconsequential. It is, at bottom, the debilitating nature of racial politics that explains why early civil rights policymaking efforts faltered as they did, both procedurally and substantively.

3

The Peak Years of Civil Rights
Legislative Reform

The explosiveness of racial issues during the sixties surpassed that of every other period in modern American history. In fact, the sixties were, in several respects, the most critical years of the modern civil rights era. It is during this period that racial discord and its national visibility peaked. The historic regional divisions attendant to race were in full force at the same time the partisan differences pertaining to race became firmly anchored. The politics of race during the sixties were essentially transformed so that they were more antagonistic and more salient than ever before. What was true of racial politics during the period leading up to the sixties was even more true during the sixties.

The impact of the extremist nature of racial politics upon America's national governing institutions and processes during the sixties was particularly poignant. Race succeeded in altering congressional legislative process virtually beyond recognition. The 1964, 1965, and 1968 civil rights debates are unique not only in comparison to the average contemporary proceedings, but also as against all proceedings in Senate history. The longest debate in Senate history, the largest number of quorum calls for a single measure, and the first successful civil rights cloture vote ever are just some of the records set during the sixties civil rights era.

There is little question that the provisions of the civil rights laws enacted during this period represent a significant departure from what was previously accomplished or even sought; but they also constitute major failures on the part of civil rights advocates. Race reform advocates aimed during the sixties to correct racial inequities in sensitive areas such as education, employment, and housing. School desegregation and equal public accommodations were the most publicized issues of the sixties race reform effort and of the protest movement that unfolded in full force during the decade. But, policy advocates wanted to provide more than just legal victories. They wanted to equalize the life chances of blacks and whites, to extend the right of "life, liberty, and the pursuit of happiness" to black as well as white Americans. In the end, however, the civil rights laws of the sixties, like their predecessors, fell far short of what race reform advocates had hoped to enact; and, despite their frontiersmanship, they did not redress the race problem in ways that truly mattered.

This chapter shows that race's incompatibility with governance was never before, or has ever since been, more evident than it was during the 1964, 1965, and 1968 civil rights proceedings. What was true of the impact of race upon governance during the period leading up to the sixties was even more true during the sixties. It explores the dynamic interplay between racial politics and institutional processes during the time when the relationship between the two was most intense. Understandably, this is the period most civil rights scholars focus on in formulating an interpretation of civil rights politics because this period lends itself relatively easily to scholarly examination. The analysis presented here seeks to synthesize a comprehensive analysis of racial politics during the sixties with an in-depth analysis of the congressional procedural and policy outcomes of the sixties. In doing so, it places the critical years of civil rights within a broader spectrum. It examines the sixties period not as a rare aberration that is unique unto itself, but as one that is distinctive in terms of depth, but similar in nature to other periods of the modern civil rights era. In other words, it explores the sixties civil rights era as but one facet of a long-term historic trend that started before the sixties and continues to the present.

The discussion is divided into three sections, each focusing on one major aspect of the relationship between race and governance. The first section explains the intrinsic characteristics of racial politics during the critical years of the modern civil rights era. In the second section, a portrait of the institutional consequences yielded by racial politics during the sixties is presented. The third section illuminates how the politics of race led to a major dilution of the racial policy reforms that were advanced by civil rights advocates in the sixties civil rights debates.

THE POLITICS OF RACE DURING THE SIXTIES

Whereas in the past the South had been on the offensive in its efforts to ward off even modest attempts to redress the race problem, during the sixties things changed significantly. Now southerners were very much on the defensive as the pressure to improve the lot of blacks had mounted and gained considerable ground. The balance of competing forces relative to race had shifted in a way that greatly intensified the North versus South struggle over racial equality. At the same time the regional "tug of war" relative to race had advanced to a critical point, so too did the partisan tussle over race. The sixties witnessed what is, in many respects, the birth of modern Republican racial conservatism. Fundamentally, at the same time that racial divisions across geographical and party lines had deepened in notable ways, race, as a political issue, had trumped virtually all other issues in terms of political significance. Few issues could compete with the attention race commanded during this period as the nation and even the international community became fixated on the issues and events of the sixties civil rights movement.

What follows is an overview of the regional and partisan politics of race during these critical years. In particular, the discussion examines the South's position on race as reflected in its actions toward blacks; the extent to which the racial status quo in the South made it the most likely region for reform; and the degree to which the South had in fact become the target of the sixties racial progressive movement. Also examined is the deepening partisan racial division and, lastly, racial saliency in each of these spheres.

Racial Divisions of the Sixties

Regional Division

The South's position on the race reform proposals of the sixties was succinctly characterized in the following statement of Senator Russell Long of Louisiana: "These forced integration bills are generally and overwhelming[ly] opposed by the people of my State and the people of the other States of the South. . . . Many of us believe that racial preference, racial separation, and racial segregation are part of the law of nature that has come down throughout the law of centuries."[1] These sentiments were evident in the South's actions relative to voting, education, and the National Association for the Advancement of Colored People (NAACP), a central organizational component of the sixties reform movement.

Great effort was invested in maintenance of the region's legally segregated school system and its tradition of voter discrimination. Despite the Supreme Court's invalidation of many of the South's disenfranchisement tools, including the Grandfather Clause and the white primary, among others, the Commission on Civil Rights noted in its 1961 report that it had received 382 sworn complaints of voter discrimination and that "all such complaints originated from Southern States."[2] The report proceeded to detail a wide variety of schemes contrived by southern states to prevent blacks from voting. Also, the U.S. Supreme Court's 1954 *Brown v. Bd. of Education* decision declaring public school segregation unconstitutional[3] was denounced and defied by southern officials. The "Southern Manifesto," which characterized *Brown* as an unconstitutional abuse of judicial power, was signed by nineteen southerners in the U.S. Senate and seventy-seven in the House of Representatives shortly after *Brown*'s announcement. It stated: "We pledge ourselves to use all lawful means to bring about a reversal of this decision which is contrary to the constitution and to prevent the use of force in its implementation."[4] Some states enacted measures declaring *Brown* null and void within their boundaries. In others, laws were enacted to evade *Brown*. In 1956 alone, according to C. Van Woodward, some 106 anti-*Brown* measures were adopted, and by 1964, as many as 450 laws and resolutions were on the books.[5]

The South's defiant resistance to integration during the sixties emerged in other areas besides voting and education. One development symbolizing the region's stance was its campaign to immobilize the NAACP, a pivotal player in the civil rights movement. Actively and, often, successfully challenging racial segregation in courts since its inception in 1910, the NAACP became a prime target of numerous attacks by southern state officials. Several states, including South Carolina, Mississippi, Texas, Arkansas, Georgia, and Alabama, conducted intense anti-NAACP campaigns.

Further exacerbating the South's distinctiveness on the race question was the fact that racial disparity remained notably problematic there. This made it the likely focus of whatever federal reforms would be adopted. Blacks and whites were more sharply unequal in the South than anywhere else in the country. The region's racial gap in voting, education, employment, and housing opportunities in particular was substantial. Shown in Table 3.1 are voter registration data for both groups in the eleven-state South in 1962 and 1964. As indicated, southern whites had a significant advantage over blacks. On average, white registration in 1962 was more than twice that of blacks'. And, in 1964, white voter registration exceeded blacks' by an average of 27.3 percent.

In addition to voter inequality, the South was plagued by severe educational inequalities to a much greater extent than other regions. Specifically, there was more racial disparity in the South relative to years of schooling completed. Table 3.2 compares the level of education completed by blacks and whites, by region. It reveals that southern whites received almost three years more education than their black counterparts. The 1960 southern black-white ratio with respect to years of schooling completed was 0.68. This compared to a slightly more equitable 0.83 black-white ratio outside the South.

Differences in employment also fell more sharply along racial lines in the South than elsewhere during the sixties. The general unemployment rate of black and white males (age 14 and older) compared more favorably in the South than in the North.[6] However, one source[7] suggests that this fact could be misinterpreted so as to mask the more serious underlying problems experienced by southern black workers. A closer look at employment data reveals that, more so in the South than in the North, black employment

Table 3.1
Estimated Voter Registration Rate by Race for Eleven Southern States, 1962 and 1964 (in percentages)

	1962			1964		
	Black	**White**	**Diff**	**Black**	**White**	**Diff**
Alabama	13.4	62.4	49.0	22.8	68.4	45.6
Arkansas	34.0	57.1	23.1	41.5	65.1	23.6
Florida	36.8	67.0	30.2	63.8	74.8	11.0
Georgia	26.7	60.8	34.1	44.8	65.8	21.0
Louisiana	27.8	69.3	41.5	31.7	79.7	48.0
Mississippi	5.3	49.6	44.3	6.7	70.2	63.5
N. Carolina	35.8	88.0	52.2	46.8	92.5	45.7
S. Carolina	22.9	50.7	27.8	38.8	78.5	39.7
Tennessee	49.8	49.8	0	69.4	72.9	3.5
Texas	26.7	41.2	14.5	57.7	35.2	-22.5
Virginia	24.0	47.5	23.5	29.1	50.1	21.0
SOUTH AVG.	27.6	58.5	30.9	41.2	68.5	27.3

Source: Compiled by author. See Appendix D on voting for source(s) and details.

opportunities consisted of low-skilled, low-paying jobs. Shown in Table 3.3 is a racial and regional breakdown of occupational status. While both regions experienced racial inequality in employment, as of 1960, blacks in the South were far less likely to obtain employment in white collar, skilled higher-paying jobs than were blacks outside the South. A total of 17.75 percent of blacks worked in skilled jobs in the North compared to less than half that, only 8.30 percent, in the South. Conversely, southern blacks were far more likely than northern blacks to work in low-skilled, low-paying jobs, with 41.56 percent of southern blacks employed in low-skilled jobs compared to 18.6 percent of blacks in the North.

Racial inequality in housing was also more problematic in the South than elsewhere during the sixties. Curiously, residential segregation was less of a problem in the South than in the North. With an index of 100 representing total racial separation and an index of 0 representing random distribution, a study of twenty-nine metropolitan areas, including eleven in the South, shows that black-white residential segregation in the South registered an average 75.3 index, while that in the North registered a slightly higher index of 82.4.[8] However, on at least one direct measure of housing quality, blacks and whites diverged to a greater degree in the South than elsewhere. Data measuring housing conditions are shown in Table 3.4. While the data show

Table 3.2
Level of Education: Mean Years of School of Male Wage Earners Ages 25–64 by Race and Region, 1940, 1950, and 1960

	Southern* Whites	Southern Blacks**	B-W Ratio	Northern Whites	Northern Blacks	B-W Ratio
1940	8.71	5.13	.59	9.15	7.31	.80
1950	9.37	5.88	.62	10.6	7.98	.75
1960	10.13	6.91	.68	10.83	8.94	.83

*Here the South includes the eleven former Confederate states as well as Delaware, Washington, D.C., Kentucky, Maryland, Oklahoma, and West Virginia; the North includes all other states.
**"Black" refers to non-white.

Source: Horton and Smith (1991)

a greater proportion of blacks in the South (19.6%) lived in "newer" housing than those residing in the Northeast (9.5%) or the North Central (9.1%) regions, far fewer southern blacks lived in "sound" housing than did non-southern blacks. More specifically, fewer than one-third of southern blacks lived in "sound" housing, while more than half of blacks in the Northeast and North Central regions and two-thirds in the West did.

In addition to the fact that the South essentially reinforced its traditional stance against racial progressivism and was in more need of reform than any other region, also agitating the regional divide over race was the fact that civil rights advocates continued to single out the South for public censure. Most of the major, large-scale movement-related events and demonstrations of the sixties either occurred in the South and/or concerned chiefly segregation in the South. In many respects, the sixties civil rights movement, especially at its peak, was tailor-made for the South. The "sit-in" campaign that began in 1960 continued throughout southern states in a variety of forms. A bus-riding campaign designed to desegregate bus facilities was initiated in 1961 in Washington, D.C., and set out to make stops throughout the South. The headlining campaign launched in Alabama in 1963 was staged in Birmingham because, according to civil rights leader Dr. Martin L. King, Jr., the city epitomized the South's resistance to racial change and was considered the economic center of the South.

Several other mass demonstrations in 1963 targeted the South, including the record-setting march involving some 250,000 participants, known as the "March on Washington." Though some of the speeches made at its conclusion noted the worrisome trends emerging in the North, the keynote speakers primarily criticized the South and its system of racial segregation. In his historic "I Have a Dream" speech, Dr. King spoke about blacks being "crip-

Table 3.3
Occupation of Employed Males 14+ Years by Race and Region, 1960

	SOUTH*		NORTH*	
	% Brkdown	**% Brkdown**	**% Brkdown**	**% Brkdown**
	of Blacks	**of Whites**	**of Blacks**	**of Whites**
Professional & Technical	2.94	9.96	4.97	11.31
Management Workers	1.48	12.63	3.19	11.11
Clerical Workers	2.90	6.60	7.47	7.32
Sales Workers	.98	7.71	2.12	7.28
TOTAL SKILLED	**8.30**	**36.90**	**17.75**	**37.02**
Craftsmen	8.59	20.49	11.99	20.48
Operative Workers	22.20	19.16	24.92	19.65
Private Household Workers	.81	.06	.66	.09
Service Workers	12.63	4.01	14.94	5.61
TOTAL SEMISKILLED	**44.23**	**43.72**	**52.51**	**45.83**
Farmers	7.18	7.18	1.16	5.05
Farm Laborers and Foremen	11.44	2.96	2.17	2.10
Laborers (excl: farm & mine)	22.94	5.23	15.27	5.77
TOTAL LOW SKILLED	**41.56**	**15.37**	**18.60**	**12.92**
Occupation Not Reported	5.94	4.01	11.17	4.25

*Here the South includes the eleven former Confederate states as well as Delaware, Washington, D.C., Kentucky, Maryland, Oklahoma, and West Virginia; the North includes all other states.
**"Black" refers to non-white.

Source: Derived from *Census of Population 1960,* Table 103, at p. 1–243.

pled by the manacles of segregation" and the need for America to "rise from the dark and desolate valley of segregation."[9] He admonished gatherers to "go back to Mississippi, go back to Alabama, go back to South Carolina," confident the racial situation would improve. A more militant Student Non-violent Coordinating Committee (SNCC) spokesperson, John Lewis, offered the following: "The next time we march, we won't march on Washington, but will march through the South, through the Heart of Dixie, the way Sherman did."[10] Besides these, there were other 1963 demonstrations staged in the South, including a series of marches in Savannah, Georgia, involving between 2,000 and 3,000 blacks in June, July, and August 1963 as well as demonstrations in Jackson, Mississippi, led by Medgar Edgars and Roy Wilkins, involving some 700 participants. In addition, a 1964 project known as "Freedom

Table 3.4
Housing Conditions: Percentage Occupying "Newer" and "Sound" Housing Units by Race and Region, 1960

	BLACK**		ALL	
	Newer***	Sound****	Newer	Sound
South*	19.6	30.6	32.2	63.4
Northeast	9.5	57.9	20.5	80.6
North Central	9.1	57.0	23.4	74.5
West	23.7	66.6	37.2	81.8

*Here the South includes the eleven former Confederate states as well as Delaware, Washington, D.C., Kentucky, Maryland, Oklahoma, and West Virginia; the North includes all other states.
**"Black" refers to all non-white persons.
***Structures built between 1950–1960.
****Source notes: "Sound, with all plumbing facilities."

Source: Derived from *Census of Housing 1960*, Table 1 at p. 1–1, and Table 22 at p. 1–120.

Summer," organized by the Council of Federated Organizations (COFO) representing SNCC, Congress of Racial Equality (CORE), and Southern Christian Leadership Conference (SCLC), was launched; its primary purpose was to register black voters in Mississippi. Two more historic demonstrations later took place in the South, including the 1965 Selma to Montgomery march, involving some 25,000 participants, and the 1966 "Meredith March against Fear," which involved almost 15,000.[11]

On the whole, the South had become increasingly at odds with the rest of the country on the race issue during the sixties. This development, in effect, exacerbated the long-standing regional division that existed for much of the post-Reconstruction period. Now the tensions were even more heated and even more problematic. The events leading up to, the underlying socioeconomic trends, and reactions to civil rights demonstrations and policy initiatives during the sixties served to buttress the South's opposition to race reform.

Partisan Division

Like the regional differences concerning race, the parties' racial differences also intensified during the sixties. What we see happening at this point is the solidification of the bipolarity of the party system relative to race. Whereas previous years witnessed the gradual emergence of decidedly different party views, the sixties signal the firm establishment of an ideological base from which the two parties would develop their respective racial policy agenda during the years to come. More specifically, during the sixties, the Republican party articulates a conservative belief system to complement and undergird the conservative stance on racial policies it had come to assume in previous decades. At the other end of the spectrum, the Democratic party carves out not only a set of beliefs opposite to those espoused by the Republican party, but also embraces a policy agenda that unmistakably, unapologetically, and very directly advocates active government reform on the issue—in very clear contrast to that of the Republican party.

To gauge the partisan division over race during the sixties, we can again look to the actions and rhetoric of their respective presidential candidates and administrations. The presidential politics of the sixties help to demonstrate the relatively firm establishment of the Republican party as the conservative party on civil rights and the Democratic party as the Republican alternative. This is clear in both the 1960 and 1964 presidential election contests and administrations.

The 1960 John F. Kennedy versus Richard Nixon campaign was key in laying the groundwork for the fundamental shift around race that occurred within the party system and came to fore during the sixties. Republican presidential candidate Nixon, who, earlier as vice president, had at least publicly placed himself on the side of civil rights, offered in 1960 a candidacy devoid of any concrete pledges to move forward on civil rights and, instead, one with negative racial overtones as far as civil rights reformers were concerned. Although instrumental in liberalizing his party's 1960 civil rights platform,[12] Nixon the presidential candidate adopted a conciliatory stance toward the South in an effort to win the electoral votes in the region that now appeared up for grabs due to the Democratic nominee's racial liberalism. On the campaign trail, Nixon characterized Democrats' pro–civil rights platform as radical. He, in classic southern tradition, argued in defense of local government rule relative to civil rights and supported voluntary rather than government-enforced desegregation. Generally, Nixon's campaign was considered weak and unspecific in the area of civil rights.[13]

Democratic nominee Kennedy, on the other hand, offered a candidacy strongly supportive of civil rights. Like Nixon, Kennedy also attempted to court the southern vote, as was evident in his selection of Lyndon B. Johnson for a running mate.[14] Author Carl Brauer notes, however, that when campaigning in the South "Kennedy did not hide his views on desegregation, nor did he call attention to them."[15] Kennedy made clear he would not betray the cause of civil rights for political expediency. Also during his campaign, he stated that federally assisted housing could be desegregated by the stroke of a presidential pen. Finally, he appointed a committee to prepare a comprehensive civil rights bill embodying the Democratic platform that he said would be introduced "at the beginning of the next session of Congress" and enacted "early" in 1961.[16] As president, Kennedy was less forthcoming with regard to specific executive and legislative action than his campaign promises predicted, but compared to previous Democratic presidential administrations, there can be no question that he represented a move forward. Two years would pass before he issued an executive order on housing and before he actually submitted a civil rights package to Congress. Still, Kennedy appointed a large number of blacks to high-level positions. And, he issued Executive Order 10925 in 1961, the first federal government order ever to explicitly require that contractors take "affirmative action" to ensure nondiscrimination in employment.

The broader significance of Kennedy's initiatives is that they exemplified a major change in the Democratic party's stance on race, especially in comparison to the Republican party's. No other president since Lincoln had so publicly endorsed racial reform. As Brauer explains, the Kennedy administration had extended a new degree of rhetorical support at the national level to the civil rights cause and changed the tone of governmental behavior toward racial discrimination. In the same stroke, Kennedy changed also the perceived tone of the party for which he spoke.

The 1964 Johnson versus Goldwater presidential contest signaled the culmination of the trend toward complete divergence, at least in ideological tone, where the two parties were concerned. Republican Arizona senator Barry Goldwater ran one of the most racially charged, racially conservative presidential campaigns of the modern civil rights period. Although careful to note that he was "in agreement with the objectives of the Supreme Court as stated in the *Brown* decision,"[17] he believed: "the federal Constitution does not require the States to maintain racially mixed schools."[18] He was critical of Nixon's efforts to strengthen the civil rights plank of the Republican party's 1960 platform[19] and led the states' rights wing of the party that year to challenge a number of liberal positions. Goldwater was one of only six Republican senators who voted against the landmark Civil Rights Act of 1964. Also, his presidential candidacy won overwhelming support from southern segregationists at his party's 1964 national convention. Of the 279 votes controlled by southern delegates from the eleven-state South, 271, or 97 percent, were cast for Goldwater.[20] Lastly, despite his unpopularity among many northern liberal Republicans, five million of whom Sundquist says abandoned the party as a result of his candidacy,[21] Goldwater was the choice of the Republican party. In a seven-name context, he received 883, or nearly three-quarters, of the 1,308 votes cast in the first ballot.[22]

In sharp contrast to the Goldwater candidacy, Lyndon B. Johnson's administration continued the tradition of Democratic racial liberalism propelled by the Kennedy administration; and he backed it with aggressive policy action. Johnson listed passage of a comprehensive civil rights package as one of the "immediate tasks" in his first address to Congress in November 1963. In his first State of the Union message in 1964, he urged the "elimination of barriers to the right to vote" and led the way to passage of the Voting Rights Act of 1965. Again in 1966 and 1967, he requested more legislation to address problems in juries, civil rights protection, and housing. On his own initiative, too, he issued a series of civil rights executive orders that added to the nondiscrimination requirement of previous orders, including Executive Order 11246 in 1965, requiring federal contractors to develop written affirmative action plans, and the inclusion of nondiscrimination clauses in all government contracts.

In essence, the Goldwater versus Johnson campaign, much like that of the Kennedy versus Nixon contest, reveals the extent to which the party split concerning race had evolved to a point of no return. The parting of ways that had begun very gradually around the turn of the century became a permanent gulf during the sixties, one that, in later years, would become even wider, more well defined, and more combative.

Salience of Race during the Sixties

A major contention of this book is that race did more than just stimulate a great deal of disagreement, and that the disagreement engendered by race was itself politically significant. Racial dissension was of pivotal importance within the overall context of American politics during the sixties, and much more so than most other types of political dissension. That racial division is a high stakes game has never been more vividly clear than it was during the sixties. Race was at the top of the nation's priority list and also commanded a great deal of attention abroad as America sought to democratize the rest of the world, thereby adding greater exposure to the denial of equal opportunity to blacks within its own borders. As in previous decades, the political significance of race manifest itself in terms of the priority attention it was accorded in the South and also the national party system, conceptualized here as an embodiment of the larger world of national politics beyond the South.

First, let us consider the South's preoccupation with race during the sixties. There can be no question but that race eclipsed virtually every other problem confronting the region during the sixties. Many southern senators likened the sixties racial politics to the Civil War and a Second Reconstruction. Still, driving the potency of race in the South during the sixties was the fact that it was the region where most blacks lived. As noted in chapter 2, as of 1960, of the roughly 18.9 million blacks living in the United States, at least 9.9 million lived in the eleven-state South. This meant that the impact of whatever reforms were enacted would not only be concentrated primarily in and perhaps throughout the South, but also that race reform, read "black justice," was foremost a southern thing. For this reason, it was a preeminent concern of the region. Survey data also give us some sense of how substantial a role race played in the region. They tell us that the South's prioritization of race exceeded that of other regions. Specifically, according to National Election Studies data, southern whites were more likely than non-southern whites to place great importance on racial issues during the sixties.[23]

Race's significance in party politics also comes into full view during the sixties, so much so that it, in effect, graduates to being one of the handful of issues into which parties invest a substantial portion of their energy and pitch their superiority over one another. The sixties national party conventions were dominated by racial concerns. Each party's southern delegates sought to utilize the platforms as a way of stemming the tide of racial progressivism, while civil rights proponents in each camp attempted to use the platforms to further the cause. And, whereas race's reappearance as a major agenda item on party platforms, starting in 1940, most clearly captures the attention devoted to it by both national parties prior to the sixties, the party platforms' continued emphasis on race post-1940 reflects the degree to which it had advanced to the select class of concerns forming the main battleground of party politics. National platforms indicate the degree to which Democrats' and Republicans' racial differences were of central importance to each party. In particular, the amount of space devoted to the discussion of race in each party's 1960 and 1964 platforms and also the variety of subjects for which both parties believed race was relevant, speak to race's national importance.

In the 1960 Democratic platform, of the total thirty-eight sections comprised by it, two entire sections, "Discrimination in Employment" and "Civil Rights," were devoted primarily to civil rights matters. And, outside of these two sections, an additional subsection entitled "Intergroup Relations" dealt primarily with race relations. Race was mentioned also in at least two other subsections, including one entitled "Clean Elections" and another called "Civil Liberties." The Republican 1960 platform too placed race in the spotlight, as one of its fourteen sections, entitled "Civil Rights," was centered on race relations. And, although no other subsections besides those in the civil rights section focused entirely on race, it was mentioned in at least three other subsections, including the "Education," "Economic Growth and Business," and "Government Administration" sections.

The 1964 campaign platforms continued the trend, tying race to a number of key issues and alluding to it throughout. At least three of the 1964 Democratic platform's forty-eight relatively short sections were devoted to civil rights, including a lengthy section entitled "Civil Rights" and two other relatively shorter sections entitled "One Nation, One People" and "Discrimination in Employment." Although, beyond these, no other subsections were entirely devoted to civil rights, race was mentioned in a subsection entitled "Welfare." Similarly, the 1964 Republican platform, although it did not devote any of its four lengthy sections exclusively to race (or any other single issue), a substantial portion of one of its major subsections, entitled "Faith in the Individual," concerned civil rights issues. Additionally, race was mentioned in a separate subsection entitled "Discord and Discontent."

In addition to regional and partisan politics, the significance of race during the sixties is evident in public opinion survey data. The findings from survey questionnaires asking respondents to rank the importance of racial issues in relation to other issues reveal that the amount of public attention race commanded peaked during the sixties. Specifically, the National Election Studies' (NES) direct measure of the public's prioritization of race shows that a substantial portion of Americans considered race to be among the nation's most important problems. Gallup poll data suggest that almost 50 percent of the national public named civil rights as the most important problem in 1964. NES data suggest a much smaller percentage, but they also indicate that it was during the sixties that racial saliency peaked for the public as a whole.[24]

In should be noted as an aside that the sixties is unique in this regard because it is the only time period during which we observe a substantial number of Americans explicitly noting race as a priority agenda item. In the years to follow, the potency of race for the American public is much more evasive to survey tools designed to measure direct assessments of race's priority. Nonetheless, its significance to the public in later years is ascertainable through other, indirect measures. The point here is that, for the sixties, the evidence indicates unequivocally that race is a national, salient issue.

In sum, between 1961 and 1968, the South became even more adamantly at odds with the national push for racial progressivism as evident by its response to *Brown* and to NAACP activities. Deepening still further the division between the South and non-South was the fact that the "race problem" was more readily apparent in the South than in other areas of the country. Added to this was civil rights advocates' strategy to "reform" the South of its ills. The partisan divisions over race deepened as reflected in the 1960 Kennedy versus Nixon contest and the 1964 Johnson versus Goldwater contest. These contests show, in essence, an ideological parting of ways between the two parties. Importantly, the nation's differences concerning race occupied the epicenter of American politics during the sixties. It continued to dominate the South's politics. It consumed substantial portions of both parties' policy agendas. And, survey research showed that even the American public had come to openly and directly express its concern over race. In essence, the politics of race during the sixties epitomized the politics of division in the spotlight.

CIVIL RIGHTS PROCESS AND PROCEDURES DURING THE SIXTIES

One of the two major consequences of the heated nature of racial politics during the sixties was the emergence of procedural processes never before observed in the Senate. Because race reform was diametrically opposed to the South's way of life, advocates stood no chance whatsoever of convincing its Senate representatives to confine their legislative strategy to the use of traditional parliamentary tools. Southerners were obligated to utilize every conceivable procedural prerogative to defend their home states from what was perceived as a frontal attack. Thus was borne obstruction of the sixties civil rights proceedings, obstruction that brought the Senate to a standstill in each of the sixties debates. In short, the regional contention relative to race led to a breakdown in normal legislative process, prompting advocates of civil rights to turn to alternative routes of passage. These routes proved to be so much more demanding than the normal process that, arguably, what emerged was an entirely separate form of congressional process.

This section describes the makeup of the civil rights opposition coalition in the Senate. Then, it briefly outlines how opponents went about the task of obstructing civil rights legislative proposals. Next it demonstrates the end result of opponents' obstruction, namely, the onset of formal legislative proceedings that departed substantially from the Senate's normal process.

Civil Rights Opposition in the Sixties

More so than at any other time during the modern civil rights era, southerners had compelling reasons during the sixties to resist race reform, and, for this reason, obstruction of civil rights was a largely southern enterprise. Likewise, the vast majority of southerners in the Senate partook in the obstruction. The group engaged in the 1964 filibuster numbered twenty-seven senators, at least twenty-one (or 78%) of whom were from the eleven-state South. Helping to block the 1964 civil rights proposals through the use of procedural tactics were both senators representing Alabama, Arkansas, Florida, Georgia, Louisiana, Mississippi, North Carolina, South Carolina, Tennessee, and Virginia. Also joining the group in 1964 were John Tower of Texas, Robert Byrd of West Virginia, and five Republican senators representing non-southern states. The 1965 opposition coalition claimed twenty senators, nineteen (or 95%) of whom were from the South. This group comprised both senators representing nine former Confederate states and also Robert C. Byrd of West Virginia and John Tower of Texas. The 1968 group involved the efforts of twenty-three senators, with nineteen (or 83%) of them representing southern states. In addition to the representatives of nine former Confederate states were John Tower of Texas and the following four Republican senators from non-southern states: Senators John Williams of Delaware, Paul Fannin of Arizona, Bourke Hickenlooper of Iowa, and Jack Miller of Iowa.

Not only was obstruction of civil rights a southern enterprise during the sixties, but the overwhelming proportion of the "South wing" of the Senate was devoted to the obstructionist strategy. A total of 95 percent of the southern coalition actively supported blockage of civil rights legislation in 1964 and a total of 86 percent did so in both 1965 and 1968.

Obstruction of Civil Rights Legislative Proposals in the Sixties

The sixties civil rights debates witnessed what is arguably the fiercest active opposition ever pitted against a set of legislative proposals. Every major stage of the 1964 proceeding was blocked by southern filibustering, and all but the consideration stage proved an impediment in the 1965 and 1968 proceedings. The obstacles created were formidable enough to defeat and/or delay one or more versions of the various civil rights proposals introduced. Again at the committee stage, Eastland was crucial to the opposition strategy. Buttressing Eastland's efforts during the sixties were those of civil rights opponent Sam Ervin, who chaired the Subcommittee on Constitutional Rights. Together they successfully prevented the committee from voluntarily reporting any of the Senate versions of the sixties bills. Committee defeat of the 1965 Senate bill did not actually come to fruition because supporters managed to employ a preemptive strategy; however, it was evident that the committee represented a likely obstacle to the bill. Eastland said of the bill: "I am opposed to every word and every line in the bill." Beyond the committee stage, various other prerogatives were marshaled by opponents, most of which were derived from the rules. Specifically, lengthy speechmaking and debate of even routine items, extensive parliamentary maneuvering, untimely quorum calls, and refusal to agree to a time limitation were used to maintain the blockade. Opponents even divided into teams with rotating responsibilities at the floor. Fully 216 quorum calls were made in 1964, 186 of which were live. During the 1964 debate, Senator Robert Byrd spoke for over fourteen hours in opposition to the bill. And, right up until the end, even minutes before passage, Senator Albert Gore, Sr., of Tennessee submitted a motion to refer the 1965 bill back to the Judiciary Committee. In 1965 as many as seventy quorum calls were made, and in 1968 a total of 116 quorum calls were made.

Routes of Passage during the Sixties

Taken as a whole, the impact of southerners' obstruction during the 1964, 1965, and 1968 civil rights proceedings dramatically changed the nature of Senate process. Making civil rights policy during the sixties was not at all similar to making other types of policies. Confronted with numerous obstacles preventing movement of civil rights proposals through the usual channels, proponents had to turn to other means of passage. Rather than a process characterized by a degree of predictability, stability, and minimal procedural demands, civil rights policymaking during the sixties resembled a process that was the exact opposite. The alternate routes exacted a great deal more from supporters not only in terms of support, energy, time, skill, and so forth, but also in terms of the need to be innovative and quick witted.

Committee Stage

Traditionally, the committee stage of the process involves a select group of senators and requires, at most, their participation in committee hearings and markup. To get the 1964 bill beyond committee obstruction, direct placement of a House version was eventually chosen, but only after a host of other routes were considered, including committee cloture, discharge, multiple referral, rider amendment, and referral with instructions. Senator Jacob Javits, a supporter, raised the question of invoking cloture within the Judiciary Committee. Eastland's response was that he would recognize a cloture motion if sixteen or more members of the committee signed a petition for cloture, which was impossible since there were only fifteen members. Discharge was dismissed because it was considered "extremely cumbersome and impossible to accomplish."[25]

Multiple committee referral was utilized, but primarily as a backup. In addition to Judiciary, the bill was referred to the Committee on Commerce, headed by supporter Warren Magnuson, and the Committee on Labor and Public Welfare, headed by opponent Lister Hill. The Commerce bill was to be the first choice, if the House bill could not get past the committee stage.[26] Both the Commerce and Labor bills were reported and placed on the calendar, but never taken up at the floor. The leadership's view was that these bills dealt only with certain portions of the overall civil rights package and, as such, restricted the kind of amendments that could be incorporated at the floor, particularly under cloture. The rider amendment approach was rejected for similar reasons. The committee instructions procedure was also considered, but rejected, because, supporters argued, a substantial information record was already available from the printed hearings of the Commerce and Labor committees and because referral of the 1960 bill with instructions had yielded only a one-page report listing the committee's meeting dates and witnesses. A motion by Senator Wayne Morse to refer the House bill to Judiciary with instructions to report it back by April 8, 1964, was rejected on March 26 in a 50 to 34 tabling vote.[27]

Eventually advocates dealt with the 1964 committee obstruction by altogether bypassing Judiciary via direct placement of the House passed version of the bill. The House passed its version on February 10, 1964, and sent it to the Senate. The first reading occurred on February 17. Mansfield, following a second reading of the bill on February 26, 1964, objected under Rule 14 to further proceedings on the bill. Russell raised a point of order against use of the direct placement procedure, but was overruled by Acting President Pro Tempore Lee Metcalf. Russell's subsequent appeal to the floor was rejected in a 54 to 37 vote. The bill was placed directly on the calendar.

In 1965, anticipating the committee would not act on civil rights, a decision was made by supporters in advance to refer the bill with instructions. None of the other alternatives for bypassing Judiciary was seriously considered. Immediately after introducing the bill (S. 1564) on March 18, 1965, on behalf of the Johnson administration, himself, and Republican leader Dirksen, Mansfield moved that the bill be referred to Judiciary with instructions to report it back to the floor by April 9, 1965. The Mansfield-Dirksen motion to refer the bill was agreed to in a roll call vote of 67 to 13. Later, on April 9, 1965, following nine days of hearings, several amendments, and crafting of a substitute, the bill was reported to the floor, without any recommendations.

Referral with instructions was also the method chosen to steer the 1968 bill beyond the committee stall. The House passed its version of the 1968 legislation (H.R. 2516) and sent it to the Senate. Mansfield moved on August 25, 1967, that the bill be referred to Judiciary with instructions to report it back to the floor within sixty days, by October 24, 1967. The question was put and the motion agreed to immediately in a voice vote. The committee later reported the bill to the floor on November 2, 1967, the original deadline having been extended by unanimous consent.

Consideration Stage

It is common for a bill to be taken up at the floor of the Senate with almost no active involvement on the part of supporters or even the leadership. In 1964, a motion to take up the House version of the comprehensive civil rights bill was presented by Mansfield on March 9, 1964. The motion was adopted on March 26, 1964, in a 67 to 17 vote. During the interim, a great deal was required in the way of active support and advocacy. Various adjustments were made to the Senate's schedule. Daily sessions were extended into the evening and a total of eight Saturday sessions were held during debate of the motion. Also, a recess schedule was implemented, whereby the Senate recessed from day to day rather than adjourned. From March 9, when a motion to proceed was first made, until March 26, when it was adopted, the Senate remained in the same legislative day, despite some eighteen calendar days having passed. Under the rules, supporters would have had to resubmit a motion to proceed at the start of each new legislative day following adjournment, which meant debate and proceedings would have to start anew. Recessing also placed some restrictions on the number of speeches southerners could make, since the rules prohibit senators from speaking twice on one subject in the same legislative day. At the floor, the sergeant-at-arms dealt with failed quorum calls. This move was geared to prevent a forced adjournment and to spare supporters from having to bear the brunt of the calls while opponents rested. A strict application of the rules was followed. And, a one-track system was imposed that prevented other measures from being considered.

Lastly, the threat of cloture on the motion to take up the 1964 bill played a key role in convincing southerners to abandon their filibuster at this stage because of three considerations. First, the possibility that a cloture petition would be filed was a very real one. In a key strategy meeting of supporters it was considered important that "it be made known that there was no question but that it would be attempted if necessary."[28] Second, the possibility that a civil rights cloture vote would very likely succeed was quite real. Negotiations between supporters and uncommitteds were well underway for the purpose of building the support needed. As early as March 11, Humphrey noted that the two groups were "not too far apart" on the more controversial sections of the bill.[29] Lastly, opposition senators took the possibility of a successful cloture vote on a motion to proceed seriously and, moreover, wanted to avoid cloture. In a radio address, opponent Senator Allen Ellender explained: "Under the rules of the Senate, the motion to take up a bill is debatable, it is possible, however, that should southerners talk at length on a motion to take up the bill, a cloture move could be successful."[30] In a meeting between Mansfield and Russell, Russell indicated there would be much delay on the motion to take up the bill, but that he would not force the issue of cloture on the motion because, he said, "if cloture was imposed on a procedural matter of this kind it would very likely be successful and the momentum would react against the opponents of the legislation."[31]

At the consideration stage of the 1965 proceedings, because there was no obstruction on the part of opponents, there were no unusual costs to be absorbed in supporting the bill at this juncture. Mansfield formally moved on April 13, 1965, that the Senate proceed to consider Calendar No. 149, the Voting Rights Act of 1965 (S. 1564). Even though no agreement had been officially arranged, once Mansfield assured Ellender that no action would be taken before April 21, 1965, the Senate agreed in a voice vote to formally proceed to the bill.

At the consideration stage of the 1968 proceedings, advocates had to expend little effort. This was because Mansfield acted singlehandedly to prevent the bill from being blocked by opponents at this stage. On December 15, 1967, the day the Senate adjourned the first session of the 90th Congress, Mansfield made a motion to proceed to consideration of the House-passed civil rights protection bill (H.R. 2516). It was presented toward the very end of the day, only thirty minutes before the Senate adjourned for the session. At the time the motion was made, a substantial amount of end-of-the-session work was being transacted, so the motion went largely unnoticed. The motion was submitted, the question put by the presiding officer, and then adopted in a voice vote. Only a handful of senators were present in the chamber when the bill was taken up. No quorum calls had been made to alert absent senators that the vote was about to occur. No prior notifications had been sent to the opposition informing them of the leadership's plans to move to the bill. Mansfield's action essentially eliminated the need for any special counterfilibuster strategy, which meant the 1968 filibuster strategy did not impact much at all at the consideration stage.

Final Vote Stage

Normally, the procedural demands at the floor are relatively straightforward and are provided for, often in detail, by prearranged unanimous consent agreements. However, the consequences of obstruction at the final vote stage of the 1964 proceedings were significant enough that advocates had to launch the most extensive counterfilibuster strategy ever undertaken in the Senate. Since the bill had been completely stymied by opponents, advocates were forced to invest enormous efforts into maintaining its procedural viability and moving it toward a final vote on passage.

The group's extensive plan of coordination was laid out and communicated by way of a daily newsletter published solely for the 1964 debate. Humphrey and Kuchel, bill managers on each side, planned to meet three times a week to discuss "all strategy decisions jointly." Floor leaders were to meet with their floor captains, in addition to joint meetings of all captains.[32] At the beginning of each day, Humphrey was to meet with Democratic captains to lay out the daily agenda. Each evening was to involve a staff meeting with senators to draft the following day's agenda.

Great emphasis in the newsletter was placed on responding to quorum calls. Groups of supporters were assigned quorum duty. Six senators were responsible for producing quorums, each of whom was to know the whereabouts of senators who were on quorum duty.[33] A quota of thirty-six Democrats and fifteen Republicans was followed to ensure quorum coverage. A new buzzer and light signal system was installed to replace the old system that had failed to work on several occasions in certain parts of Senate office buildings. Also, the quorum effort was helped considerably by a newly instituted method of conducting a quorum call. It essentially set aside twenty minutes for each quorum call, during which the clerk would re-call the names of absent senators, rather than announce a failed quorum whenever fewer than fifty-one senators responded to the first call of the roll. This method was intended to reduce the chances of a failed quorum call by enabling supporters to respond in adequate numbers as required.

Scheduling adjustments were made. It was believed that "long and inconvenient" sessions would convince some that cloture might be desirable.[34] There was some discussion of all-night sessions. Mansfield rejected the approach, however, saying: "I have always been opposed to the idea of around-the-clock sessions" because "the ultimate effect would be to wear out proponents rather than the opponents,"[35] since, he argued, supporters would have to produce fifty proponents for a quorum at all times during the night, while the opposition needed to produce only three- or four-man squads, with the remainder of their forces resting.

The Senate continued to recess from day to day and remained in the same legislative day from March 30 to June 19, although some fifty calendar days passed during the interim. Supporters extended little to no lenience in applying the rules governing debate. Rule 7 was insisted upon, which required that debate be germane during the first three hours of debate following the morning hour or after the pending business was laid before the Senate. Senate Rule 19 was pushed because it limited to two the number of speeches a senator can make on a subject in the same legislative day. Also under Senate Rule 19, which provided that speaking senators may yield the floor only for the purpose of obtaining a question, supporters objected to lengthy yields whereby speaking senators allowed their counterparts to interject entire speeches, ostensibly as questions. The one-track system instituted earlier in the proceedings was continued. In fact, there was no morning hour or call of the calendar.

In the end, cloture was the means by which supporters defeated the opponents' 1964 filibuster strategy. Mansfield had pitched cloture as necessary to ensure passage of the pending civil rights bill and also uphold the reputation and integrity of the Senate's legislative process.[36] He submitted a formal motion for cloture on June 8, 1964, that was signed by a bipartisan group of thirty-nine senators. For the first time in Senate history, the floor voted 71 to 29 two days later in favor of limiting debate on a civil rights bill. Debate on the 1964 bill came to a conclusion on June 19, 1964, when the Senate voted 73 to 27 in favor of passage. It was sent to the House where it was passed on July 2, 1964. It was signed into law the same day by President Johnson.

The final phase of the 1965 proceedings was relatively less demanding than that of the 1964 debate. A number of things that had been used by supporters in previous civil rights proceedings were missing from supporters' 1965 strategy. No teams were devised to ensure floor coverage. There were no special warnings from the leadership to anticipate untimely and/or surprise motions and quorum calls. There was no insistence on a strict application of the rules at the floor. Nor was any use made of the sergeant-at-arms to enforce response to quorum calls. No scheduling adjustments were made. Daily sessions were not lengthened. Business proceeded as usual as far as the Senate's business at the floor was concerned. The Senate adjourned from day to day, rather than using the recess option. Whereas 97 percent of the debate days in 1964 ended in recess, only 14 percent of those days in 1965 did. Following adjournments, the usual morning hour was had, lasting the first two hours of the daily session and, on several occasions, longer. The one-track system used in previous debates was not used in 1965. On two occasions, the civil rights bill was temporarily laid aside so the Senate could consider first a supplemental appropriations bill and later a military bill. There was even a call of the calendar during several of the sessions.

Still, two key elements distinguished the 1965 proceeding from most normal Senate proceedings. First was the extended discussion to which the bill was subjected, indicating the lack of a time limitation agreement. And, importantly, cloture was the centerpiece and, in many respects, the most involved element of supporters' 1965 counterstrategy. Cloture had been seriously considered from the outset. Mansfield remarked the day of his first attempt to obtain a limitation agreement: "In view of the fact that it seems impossible to arrive at a unanimous-consent agreement on the amendments and the bill . . . we shall have to give very serious consideration to filing a motion for cloture at an appropriate time."[37] Bill manager Phillip Hart submitted a motion for cloture on May 21, 1965, sponsored by Senators Mansfield and Dirksen and 36 other senators. The Senate adopted the cloture motion on May 25 in a roll call vote of 70 to 30, three votes more than required under the rule. One day after invoking cloture, the Senate adopted the 1965 bill in a 77 to 19 roll call vote. The bill was sent to the House where it was adopted in a 333 to 85 vote on June 9. It was signed into law by President Johnson on August 6, 1965.

At the final vote stage of the 1968 housing proceedings, advocates again relied primarily on cloture, but little else beyond cloture was involved in the counterfilibuster at this juncture. Missing from advocates' floor strategy in 1968, as in 1965, were several components that were critical in earlier debates. There were no substantial schedule adjustments. Morning hours were not shortened. Daily sessions were not lengthened. And, the Senate routinely adjourned rather than recessed. A one-track system was not insisted upon as in previous debates. However, while committee meetings were permitted regularly by unanimous consent until the last week of debate, when Dirksen registered a standing objection to the meetings, he said, to ensure quorums during the final days of the debate. Also, a loose coordination plan was implemented as a safety precaution.

Eventually, supporters chose to invoke cloture as it was considered the only effective response to the filibuster. But, even this cloture-centered strategy exacted its costs. A total of four separate cloture motions were submitted, three of which were rejected. The first failed on February 20, 1968, in a 55 to 37 vote of the floor; the second was unsuccessful on February 26, 1968, in a 56 to 36 vote; and a third was rejected on February 28, 1968, in a 59 to 35 roll call vote. Finally, on February 28, a fourth cloture motion was adopted in a 65 to 32 vote. A vote on passage of the bill was held on March 11, 1968, when the Senate adopted it in a 71 to 20 vote. The bill was sent to the House and adopted there on April 10. The next day it was signed into law by President Johnson.

On the whole, in 1964, 1965, and 1968, the intense active opposition stimulated by the politics of race in the South led to the transformation of each of the major stages of the Senate's formal procedural process. Their efforts forced supporters to utilize extreme measures in order to secure passage of the sixties civil rights proposals. And, in the end, the costs exacted by these measures, in the form of votes, time, strategic planning, energy investment, and so forth were enormous and, importantly, far beyond that of the average Senate debate. Among other things, a supermajority was required in each instance, and, until it was obtained, the Senate was brought to a virtual standstill by obstructionists. In the end, the sixties civil rights proceedings remain unparalleled—thanks, once again, to the regional conflict inherent in racial politics and, specifically, the South's racial dissonance.

CIVIL RIGHTS POLICY OUTCOMES IN THE SIXTIES

In addition to the formal policy proceedings on civil rights legislative proposals, also affected by the contentious nature of racial politics during the sixties were the actual policy provisions yielded by these processes. They, too, were outside of the norm. As laudable as the racial policy reforms of the sixties may be, their makeup and accomplishment pale in comparison to that of the policies originally proposed by advocates. There is ample evidence that the sixties laws encompass only portions of the bills originally sponsored. Relative to each of the sixties proposals, advocates sought blanket application of the bills and, in almost all cases, administrative enforcement. And, in each proceeding, they were forced to retreat.

More important to our analysis, however, is that the reason the bills were substantially weakened is that race was an extremely controversial political issue. Once again, the divisiveness and saliency of race placed constraints on Senate advocates in their attempts to recruit additional members to their effort. Given the higher support demands of the alternative procedures forced by southern obstruction, proponents had to turn to uncommitteds for help in saving the bills. And, when they did, they found these members were willing to go only so far to facilitate race reform.

The discussion to follow demonstrates the factors driving the policy outcomes of the sixties, specifically the "moderating" influence of uncommitteds. First, it details the vote deficit resulting from active southern opposition. Second, it outlines potential supporters' differences with advocates. Third, it explains these uncommitteds' unwillingness to bargain those differences away, due to the heated nature of race's partisan politics.

Negotiating Race in the Sixties

The most basic factor contributing to uncommitteds' decisive role in the sixties civil rights proceedings was the civil rights coalition's need for additional votes to defeat obstructionists. Cloture was the most effective approach to dealing with the filibusters, especially since there was every indication opponents would never voluntarily permit a vote on final passage of the sixties proposals. Advocates lacked the two-thirds support required for cloture. They numbered fifty-seven, sixty-one, and fifty-nine members at the outset of the 1964, 1965, and 1968 proceedings, respectively.[38] Of the remaining senators, at least twenty-seven, twenty, and twenty-three, correspondingly, were actively involved in the opposition effort. This left roughly sixteen, nineteen, and eighteen senators in each of these debates, respectively, who were not wholly committed to the original versions of the bills. So, assuming 100 percent attendance at the floor during a vote on cloture, in order to defeat opponents and secure a vote on passage, supporters needed to convince at least ten senators in 1964, another six in 1965, and an additional eight in 1968 to vote on behalf of the bill. This need laid the basic groundwork for the decisive policy role played by uncommitted moderates.

In addition to the fact that their votes were indispensable, uncommitteds' policy role was shaped also by the fact that they were mostly Republican. Of the senators in the uncommitted camp in the 1964, 1965, and 1968 proceedings, a corresponding 69 percent, 90 percent, and 67 percent belonged to the Republican party. Importantly, these Republican uncommitteds followed foremost their party cues relative to racial policy proposals. And, once again, the partisan-based ideological divide between uncommitted moderates and advocates concerned the role of government. Specifically, Republicanism dictated government restraint, especially at the federal level.

The overriding concern in 1964 was that of who would be affected by the bill and how the bill would be enforced. Advocates wanted the bill to reach virtually all employers, virtually all educational institutions, virtually all public facilities, and so forth. The intent was to ensure each of the major areas of life in American society would provide equal opportunities for blacks. Moderates agreed with advocates relative to the general goal of greater racial equality, but differed on the question of how best to achieve that goal. They were wary of some aspects of advocates' original plan for achieving those goals.

Dirksen outlined moderates' reaction to each of the titles in the original 1964 proposal in a manuscript, entitled "The Civil Rights Bill: Some Observations by Senator Everett McKinley Dirksen."[39] Dirksen, whom bill manager Humphrey referred to as a "very key person" who "exerted influence and provided leadership for members of his party in the Senate,"[40] voiced many of the moderates' concerns relative to the 1964 proposal. In the manuscript, Dirksen noted he was "concerned about the impact of the already heavy case load on our federal courts" that Title I would have since it permitted the attorney general or any defendant to request a special three-judge court to hear voting rights discrimination cases brought under the title. The language in Title II, he thought, could force small operations to confront the enforcement machinery of the federal government. He questioned the original "full and complete utilization of any public facility" language in the public accommodations provisions of Title III, saying it would be more appropriate to substitute it with "equal utilization of any public facility."

In regard to Title IV, Dirksen asked: "Isn't the school board or other agency entitled to some opportunity to correct the situation complained of before the Attorney General institutes suit?" He suggested also that the bill left unclear whether the attorney general could seek to achieve desegregation "through the assignment of students to public schools in order to overcome racial imbalance." And, he argued that the Commission on Civil Rights' authority outlined in Title V should be "subject to the same rules of procedures" applied to other government agencies and outlined in the Administrative Procedure Act because the commission was achieving a somewhat permanent temporary status. The federal funding provisions of Title VI, according to Dirksen, could deny defendants plausible defenses provided for under existing law.

More concerns were expressed by Dirksen about the equal employment provisions of Title VII than any others. He believed the House bill was not clear regarding which records employers were required by Title VII to keep and for how long. He questioned the Commission on Civil Rights' "carte blanche authority" to examine and copy evidence obtained from employers. And, he believed each state should be given a voice in employment suits, so as to determine the effectiveness of their agencies. Also, the term "employer" was used too broadly so that seasonal workers could bring small-scale employers under coverage of the act. He questioned whether seniority systems would remain intact. And, in his view, action under the title should be restricted to the individual affected and it should not be initiated on his or her behalf by others, such as civil rights organizations. The remaining titles raised fewer objections, but nonetheless evoked similar concerns relative to careful structuring of government power under the bill.

As in 1964, in 1965, substantive differences divided civil rights advocates and uncommitteds; and, once again, it was the federal government's power under the bill that was in dispute. Advocates wanted to concentrate the federal government voting-rights enforcement apparatus specifically in those states identified as having the longest, most egregious record of voter discrimination. They also wanted to, in essence, prevent such states from being able to exercise such discrimination in the first place.

Moderates opposed advocates' attempt to ban the use of poll taxes in state elections by way of congressional statute, arguing that Congress did not have the power to do so, except by way of a constitutional amendment. Their stance on the poll tax issue first surfaced in committee. Of the twelve out of fifteen committee members who endorsed a statement supporting the bill, Dirksen was one of two who voted in favor of reporting the bill, but against including a poll tax amendment. In speaking against a statutory ban on the use of poll taxes in state elections, he noted he had cast votes in favor of measures banning the state poll tax while serving in the House, but that the Supreme Court in a 1937 case, *Breedlove v. Suttle*, and a 1951 case, *Butler v. Thompson*, had upheld the validity of poll taxes as a condition for voting in state elections. Dirksen also referenced a letter from the attorney general advocating adoption of a poll tax ban, but recommending a constitutional amendment rather than a statutory provision.

Relative to the 1968 bill, moreover, moderates' concerns were also anti–big government. Advocates wanted to provide greater protections for civil rights demonstrators. Some also sought to revive a failed 1966 initiative to establish and provide federal protections for housing rights. The bill was formally framed as a civil rights protection bill. Housing first became an issue when, following through on a January 24, 1968, presidential message to Congress, Senator Walter Mondale proposed on February 6, 1968, a fair housing amendment.

Moderates were again at odds with supporters over the substance of the policy proposal. Dirksen initially opposed any form of federal fair housing legislation, but eventually began to work toward a compromise. He took credit for the failure of a 1966 cloture vote on open housing and had argued then that "if the Federal Government is given the power sought here to regulate the sale and occupancy of living quarters, there is practically nothing left in this country that will not eventually come under the supervision of and required to be performed to the satisfaction of some bureaucrat here in Washington."[41] By 1968, the idea of a fair housing law had become more acceptable to moderates; but they wanted to ensure it was carefully tailored. One of their chief concerns was that the bill provide appropriate exemptions in those instances wherein the machinery of the federal government was potentially harmful, such as in the case of single-family, owner-occupied housing sold without the assistance of an agent. Here, according to Dirksen, the federal government's intrusion was unwarranted and the burdens of complying with federal government regulations would be too great. The most important concern was whether to provide enforcement through the Department of Housing and Urban Development or through federal courts.

Aside from the fact that uncommitteds parted ways with advocates on the merits of the bill, of fundamental importance to understanding uncommitted Republicans' decisive role in shaping civil rights laws is the fact that the politics surrounding the bills effectively precluded certain means of resolving their differences with supporters. The racial politics of the sixties foreclosed use of the standard bargaining tools for building support. The extremely high visibility of race along with the deepening of racial divisions led Republicans to regard it as too risky to barter their principles for political expediency.

As a result, despite moderates' general support of the sixties efforts, there was little doubt they would not supply the votes needed to invoke cloture in each of the proceedings without the improvements they believed necessary. Dirksen hinted as much in 1964 in the following remark made the day the final compromise agreement was offered at the floor: "As a result of the various conferences, and by the process of give and take, we have at long last fashioned what we think is a workable measure. I trust it will . . . command sufficient votes ultimately to bring debate to an end."[42] In 1965, Dirksen's refusal to endorse the committee report recommending adoption of a poll tax ban amendment was a clear indication he would not vote to invoke cloture if a poll tax ban were added to the bill, nor would he deliver the votes of other moderates that were needed in order for a cloture motion to succeed.

And, in 1968 too, moderates refused to endorse the bill in its original form without the changes they proposed being included in the bill. This is most evident in the failure of the first three cloture petitions filed. They all failed as a result of limited moderate support. The first two cloture motions filed were opposed by Dirksen. Just before the first vote, Dirksen explained the bill was still at that point unsatisfactory to him. Just before the second cloture vote as well, Dirksen noted that even though substantial progress was being made in the negotiations, an acceptable agreement had not yet been reached. Even after Dirksen would have worked out a compromise agreement with supporters, some moderates continued to withhold their support. Senator Miller, a Republican moderate who had voted against the third motion stated: "We can still make a great step forward in the cause of civil rights . . . but it is going to require a greater willingness to compromise than has been demonstrated so far."[43] Even the 65 to 32 victory vote of February 28, 1968, indicated a substantial number of moderates were still unwilling to bend.

Civil Rights Policy Concessions and Provisions of the Sixties

The revisions made to the sixties civil rights proposals were designed chiefly to meet the objections of Republican moderates. The changes made either limited the scope of the bills and/or limited the enforcement authority and activities of the federal government, particularly that of the U.S. attorney general. Several of the 1964 act's major provisions were changed by an agreement adopted at the floor of the Senate on June 17, 1964. The provisions were brought in line with virtually all of the concerns outlined by Dirksen in his initial memorandum and in a series of meetings. I will mention here the most significant changes.

Amendments to Title I of the comprehensive 1964 bill limited the use of three-judge courts to cases in which the attorney general alleged a "pattern" of discrimination. Changes to Title II required the attorney general to give officials in states with public accommodations laws thirty days to act before filing suit and exempted from coverage of the public accommodations provisions small operations, such as boarding houses. Title IV was changed so that the attorney general was required to notify local authorities of school segregation complaints he had received and specified that the bill did not authorize the attorney general or courts to order school busing to redress segregation in schools. Title V stipulated that standard procedural requirements be established to govern investigations by the Commission on Civil Rights. The Title VI federal funds cut-off provision was amended to include a requirement that there be a hearing and a finding of discrimination before funds were cut off.

Changes to Title VII included the addition of an exemption of employers of seasonal workers; deletion of authority for outside groups such as the

NAACP to file a suit on behalf of an individual; restriction of official authority to bring suit to the attorney general and not the Commission on Civil Rights; a requirement that the individual bringing the suit give local officials in states with equal employment laws sixty days to act first; and a requirement that the Court find "intentional discrimination" on the part of defendants charged under the act.

The final provisions of the seven main titles of the Civil Rights Act of 1964 as enacted into law are as follows. Title I provides additional voting rights protections. Title II bars discrimination in public accommodations, such as restaurants, hotels, lodging houses, and so forth. Title III empowers the attorney general to bring federal suits to enforce desegregation of state and local public facilities, and Title IV empowers U.S. education officials and the attorney general to enforce public school desegregation. Title V extends the U.S. Commission on Civil Rights and broadens its duties to include serving as a national clearing house on civil rights information. Title VI requires nondiscrimination in federally assisted programs and provides for the cut-off of federal funds. The landmark title, Title VII, outlaws discrimination in a number of employment areas, including hiring, classification, and union membership. It also establishes the five-member Equal Employment Opportunity Commission to investigate and report to Congress job discrimination and to assist in the settlement of employment discrimination suits.

Moreover, the 1965 voting rights act was also revised to meet the objections of Republican moderates, although the changes were less drastic, in comparison to those made to the other sixties proposals. Much of the 1965 bill's original coverage and enforcement mechanisms were left intact. In fact, what the Senate balked from doing in 1960 was accomplished by way of the 1965 bill, namely, the authorizing of administrative registrars to enforce voting rights. Nonetheless, rather than adopt the flat ban on the use of poll taxes in state and local elections, as advocates wanted, the choice was made to implement a much weaker poll tax provision. The flat ban was first rejected in committee, even though a clear majority of the committee (10 out of 15) supported an amendment providing for the "elimination of the use of a poll tax or any other tax or payment as a precondition of registering or voting."[44] A second version of the flat ban offered by Senator Edward Kennedy at the floor was defeated in a 45 to 49 vote on May 11. Then, in its place, a compromise poll tax amendment was agreed to in a 69 to 20 vote on May 19, 1965, and later included in a Mansfield-Dirksen substitute bill adopted in a 78 to 18 vote on May 26, 1965. The compromise amendment, which was enacted, stated that Congress was against the use of poll taxes as a condition for voting, but it did not actually ban the use of the taxes.

The Voting Rights Act of 1965, as originally passed, contains ten main sections, the first of which is relatively minor. Section 2 contains a prohibition on racial discrimination in voting. Section 3 empowers courts to authorize the appointment of federal examiners to ensure voting rights in states proven in court to have discriminated. One of the two most critical provisions of the bill, Section 4, automatically suspends the use of voter qualification tests or devices in states where less than 50 percent of voting age residents were registered to vote in the 1964 presidential election. It also makes completion of the sixth grade evidence of voter literacy. The second critical provision, Section 5, requires states below the 50 percent threshold to obtain approval from the U.S. District Court for the District of Columbia in order to change their voting laws and practices.

The remaining sections address mostly procedural matters. Section 6 authorizes the federal district courts or the attorney general to appoint federal examiners in states covered by the 50 percent–1964 trigger formula in Section 4. Section 7 empowers federal examiners to "promptly" list qualified applicants as eligible voters who, in turn, are to be placed on the official voting list by state officials. Section 8 empowers the Civil Service Commission to assign observers at the request of the attorney general. Section 9 lays out the procedures for challenging the lists compiled by examiners. Finally, Section 10 contains a statement saying Congress disapproved of the use of poll taxes as a condition for voting and that it found the poll tax requirement to have been used in a discriminatory fashion. It also includes a declaration that the constitutional right to vote was denied by the poll tax requirement.

Like the 1964 and 1965 bills' provisions, the provisions of the 1968 housing bill were the product of strained negotiations between advocates and supporters. Hammered out in a series of conferences held in Dirksen's office, the agreement effectively limited the bill's scope of coverage. More specifically, it reduced coverage from 91 percent to 80 percent of the housing market. This was accomplished by the inclusion of various exemptions. A key exemption eliminated from coverage single-family, owner-occupied housing sold or rented by the owner rather than a real estate agent. Most importantly, the agreement with moderates provided for court, rather than administrative, enforcement of the 1968 bill's provisions. Whereas advocates' original version of the bill provided for the Department of Housing and Urban Development (HUD) to enforce the bill, the compromise entrusted federal courts with enforcement responsibilities. A motion to table the advocates' version was adopted at the floor on February 18, 1968, in an 83 to 5 roll call vote. The final compromise bill was adopted on March 8, 1968, in a 61 to 19 vote.

As enacted into law, Title I of the Civil Rights Protection Act of 1968 prohibits interference with any person attempting to vote, attend a public school, or enjoy facilities or services provided by the state or any hotel, cafeteria, lunch counter, and so forth. It also prohibits the incitement of or participation in riots. Titles II through VII expand certain Native American rights. And Title VIII prohibits discrimination in the sale or rental of housing; the financing of housing; and the provision of brokerage services.

The Impact of the Sixties Civil Rights Laws

Because all of the sixties civil rights legislative proposals were, in effect, stripped of their most critical enforcement provisions, they have failed to bring about the kind of widespread racial change advocates had hoped they would. From the outset, the sixties laws met very limited success in altering or even arresting certain racial inequality trends. Evidence of this is the continuance of overt discrimination against blacks in the South well beyond the sixties and seventies, accompanied by the "spread" of the race problem to areas outside the South. More specifically, the 1964 policy concessions placed significant constraints upon enforcement of the bill and left blacks vulnerable to the same extent and forms of discrimination to which they had been previously subjected. Restricting the right to sue under Title VII to the individual; excluding from Title VII's coverage employers of seasonal workers, many of whom in the South were black; restricting the use of three-judge courts to the attorney general only, thus slowing down litigation under the act; and limiting the enforcement authority of the attorney general and the Commission on Civil Rights, key agencies in the bill's overall enforcement, placed severe limitations on the bill's potential to restructure the racial status quo in the South and elsewhere. The rights accorded by the bills were largely litigable rights, but the bills limited even litigation strategies.

The 1965 policy compromises were also debilitating. But, in comparison to earlier civil rights compromises, the 1965 changes were less devastating. Still, failure to enact a poll tax ban left the five southern states with the largest black residential populations free to continue using the poll tax as a means of denying the vote to a substantial proportion of black voters. These states were Alabama, Arkansas, Mississippi, Texas, and Virginia. The Twenty-Fourth Amendment to the U.S. Constitution, adopted in 1964, had banned the use of poll tax requirements in federal elections, but not state elections. In 1966, the Supreme Court declared their use in state elections unconstitutional. Congress missed its opportunity to do so in 1965.

Despite the weakening changes made to the 1965 bill, it still had a very noticeable, positive impact on black registration rates and is, arguably, the most effective federal civil rights legislation ever enacted. This is largely due to the fact that the bill's coverage formula brought half of the South under the watchful eye of the federal government. And, it suspended in at least six southern states the use of tests and devices proven to have a racially discriminatory impact. States brought under coverage of the bill included Alabama, Georgia, Louisiana, Mississippi, South Carolina, and Virginia. Additionally, Alaska and counties in North Carolina, Arizona, and Idaho were also brought under coverage.

Lastly, the effect of the 1968 concessions was to virtually ensure that the elimination of housing discrimination would take place at a slow pace. The decision to invest enforcement authority wholly in the courts would yield time-consuming and costly consequences. In addition, the exemptions added to the bill would leave fully 20 percent of the housing market (namely, the 20% that was relatively more affordable to blacks) free to discriminate on the grounds of race in the sale of housing. The choice of a court-enforcement approach and the inclusion of exemptions cut into the heart of the 1968 housing bill.

CHAPTER SUMMARY

Overall, because race was such a highly contentious political item, Republican moderates, whose votes were needed to satisfy the supermajority requirements of the altered process, were unwilling to give up their racial ideology for political expediency. Rather than concede to advocates, they insisted instead that many of the key provisions in the sixties civil rights proposals be reformulated to fit their racially conservative ideology. This resulted in the enactment of weak laws. Though more progressive with respect to the shift in concern toward the social and economic aspects of the race problem, the sixties civil rights laws, like their predecessors, depended upon the slower judicial approach for enforcement. These policy outcomes were facilitated in large part by the extraordinarily demanding procedural process to which the sixties proposals were subjected, a process that, in effect, made the votes of Republican moderates indispensable. Both this process and its policy output were borne of racial conflict and controversy. Racial discord stimulated the opposition's obstruction of the normal process. And, the heightened scrutiny of racial policymaking limited advocates' ability to win over moderates without sacrificing policy achievement in the process.

4

Race and Civil Rights
Policymaking in Transition

The political meaning of race changed during the seventies so that the regional division attendant to race throughout much of American history began to dissipate. The race problem spread more noticeably beyond the South. Also, the partisan racial divide that began to emerge in the late fifties and crystallized during the sixties began during the seventies to take the form of contradistinctive policies—that is, Republicans and Democrats began to counter each other with concrete administrative and legislative proposals to complement their opposing ideological principles. There was yet another critical development in racial politics during the seventies: race came to assume an even more important role in party politics than it had in earlier years.

Still, even as the broad political meaning of race changed in critical ways during the seventies, the end result within America's governing institutions continued to be that of broken processes and, even more, broken promises. In particular, the procedures used to enact the civil rights laws of the seventies were less deviant from the norm than were the procedures of the late fifties and sixties; however, the parliamentary dimensions of civil rights policymaking were still abnormal—only less so. Also, the provisions of the seventies legislation were inadequate to the task of altering persistent racial inequalities, much like their precursors. In fact, the seventies legislative initiatives were in many respects even more of a failure because they were further from their intended mark than the sixties legislation.

Advocates had hoped during the seventies to shore up many of the civil rights laws originally passed during the sixties. Specifically, they sought enactment of the stronger enforcement provisions that had been sacrificed in order to secure passage of the sixties legislation. Chief among the seventies goals was to authorize administrative implementation of the fair employment provisions of the 1964 bill, that is, to give the Equal Employment Opportunity Commission (EEOC) cease-and-desist authority. This was not accomplished. Advocates also missed the mark relative to voting. Here the objective was to preserve the forceful effect of the landmark 1965 bill by restricting application of the law and, thus, concentrating the implementation resources to those areas where they were most needed. This was also not accomplished. On the whole, even where the "follow-up" bills of the seventies are concerned, both in form and substance, Congress' civil rights policymaking mode prevailed.

This chapter highlights the interplay between race and formal structure during the seventies, specifically, major changes in the politics of race and the corresponding changes in federal civil rights lawmaking that occurred. The first section describes the reformulation of racial division and saliency during this period. The next section assesses the procedural consequences of the seventies brand of racial politics in the 1970, 1972, and 1975 Senate civil rights proceedings. Finally, the last section details the impact of the "transitional" politics of race upon substantive policy outcomes.

THE POLITICS OF RACE DURING THE TRANSITION YEARS

That race was no longer simply a matter of the South versus the North was perhaps the most vivid aspect of the transition in racial politics that occurred in the years following the sixties. An equally significant change during the same time period was the exacerbation of partisan racial differences. In the first instance, we observe less opposition to race reform in the South. We also find a decline in racial inequality in the region, juxtaposed to an increase of the same in other areas of the country. Also, advocates of racial change shifted their focus to areas beyond the South and characteristically "southern" issues. With respect to the partisan politics of race, moreover, starting in 1968, the Republican party not only embraced a more conservative racial ideology than its counterpart, but also began to formulate and advocate specific policy proposals designed to actualize its particular brand of race reform. In essence, we see the concretizing of racially conservative principles. Alongside the occurrence of major shifts in racial divisions, also evident during the seventies was the enduring political saliency of race. So that, the antagonisms spurred by race remained among the nation's more important political conflicts. I will now offer a more detailed explication of each of these claims.

Racial Divisions of the Transition Years

Regional Division

The regional cleavage attendant to race continued into the seventies, but in a diminished capacity. The South continued to embrace an oppositional stance relative to race reform; but simultaneous with this was a softening of its anti–civil rights stance as revealed by a number of developments. In the first instance, the persistence of racial discrimination in the South assumed a variety of forms. Voter discrimination there shifted to the aggregate level, away from the individual level where much of the historical disenfranchisement had occurred. Included among the contemporary disenfranchisement tools were those in which the black vote was diluted or split through gerrymandering schemes, such as those utilizing at-large elections, county consolidations, multimember districts, and so forth.[1] The U.S. Commission on Civil Rights' (USCCR) 1968 report detailed the region's increased reliance on racial gerrymandering. It also cataloged various other incidents that it said "characterize the typical difficulties experienced by Negro candidates and voters in the South because of their race since the passage of the Voting Rights Act."[2] These other post-1965 devices included many that effectively prevented blacks from becoming candidates or obtaining office.[3] And, although many of these schemes were subsequently challenged in court, often successfully, a later report of the commission, entitled "The Voting Rights Act: Ten Years After," concluded that some of the barriers put into place in the South immediately after passage of the 1965 act remained intact as late as 1975.[4]

Despite the persistence of voter discrimination in newer forms, certain other signs reflected progress. The same USCCR report that detailed persistent voter discrimination actually began by explaining that, in the South, "substantial progress has been made toward full enjoyment of political rights."[5] Many of the more blatant forms of political exclusion were conspicuously absent. The use of violence to control black sociopolitical behavior was a thing of the past. Thousands of blacks were added to the rolls. Thousands voted. According to the 1968 USCCR voting rights report, the black vote was a major factor in elections across the South, supplying the winning margin in 1966 for a U.S. senator in South Carolina and at least one governor in Arkansas.[6]

Most notably, blacks were beginning to gain a foothold in the South's political structure as evidenced by the hundreds of blacks elected to public office in the region. In 1972, Yvonne Jordan of Houston and Andrew Young of Atlanta became the first blacks from the region to be elected to Congress since Reconstruction.[7] Overall, black representation increased substantially at all levels. Following the 1966 elections, black elected officials (BEOs) in the eleven-state South numbered 159, and by 1967 exceeded

Table 4.1
Black Elected Officials in the South, 1968–1974, Selected Years

STATE	1968	1970	1974
Alabama	24	86	149
Arkansas	33	55	150
Florida	16	36	73
Georgia	21	40	137
Louisiana	37	64	149
Mississippi	29	81	191
N. Carolina	10	62	159
S. Carolina	11	38	116
Tennessee	26	38	87
Texas	15	29	124
Virginia	24	36	63

Source: 1968 data: USCCR (1968); 1970 and 1974 data: Joint Center for Political Studies (1974)

200, which, according to the 1968 voting rights report, was more than twice the number serving in 1965 when the original voting rights act was passed. By 1974, this number had increased sixfold as shown in Table 4.1. Most black elected officials had acquired minor posts; however, some held more powerful positions, including eleven elected to state legislatures in the South.

Most analyses of the increased political participation of southern blacks emphasize the role of the 1965 voting rights act in facilitating the increase. The act was indeed enormously helpful in this respect. Nonetheless, the trend is also a reflection of how the politics of race in the region had changed. Whatever the impetus, southern racial politics had been transformed so that blacks could run their own candidates, vote for their own candidates, and witness their own candidates actually assuming public office. Significantly, much of this occurred without the violent response on the part of southern officials that had typified earlier years. Thus, inasmuch as a black political presence was now a factor in the region's politics, the South had become more receptive (or at least permeable) to black progress.

More generally, the region's anti–civil rights stance had begun to wane. Incidents of overt racial discrimination in the region were far less common in the seventies than in previous years. State laws containing disadvantaging racial classifications were now part of a seemingly distant past, in part because many were nullified by federal courts, removed by state legislatures from the law books, or simply made moot as a result of nonenforcement on

Table 4.2
Estimated Black Voter Registration Rate in the South, 1960–1976, Selected Years (in percentages)

	1960	1970	1976
Alabama	13.7	62.0	58.4
Arkansas	38.0	62.0	94.0
Florida	39.4	63.3	61.1
Georgia	29.3	59.5	74.8
Louisiana	31.1	53.1	63.0
Mississippi	5.2	66.3	60.7
N. Carolina	39.1	47.3	54.8
S. Carolina	13.7	51.4	56.5
Tennessee	59.1	74.5	66.4
Texas	35.5	64.0	65.0
Virginia	23.1	52.8	54.7

Source: Compiled by the author. See Appendix D for sources and detailed figures.

the part of state and local officials. Gone too were the "white only" and "colored only" signs that were a prime target of the explosive sixties protest movement. Finally, acts of violence and intimidation against blacks previously employed to control their social and political behavior were also uncommon. In short, by the seventies, many of the social and political patterns that were central components of the South's post-Reconstruction history were no more.

In addition to being less resistant to racial change, the South was also less likely to be impacted by the seventies reform proposals as it had begun to make great strides toward racial parity—this occurred as the need for reform beyond the South became more evident. Trend data on voter registration, employment, and family income show that the South's racial status quo began to change for the better and at a faster pace than that outside the South. As indicated in Table 4.2, every state in the South witnessed dramatic increases in black voter registration between 1960 and 1970. Mississippi's 1970 rate was almost thirteen times the 1960 rate. Virtually every other southern state's rates had nearly doubled between 1960 and 1970. While a few experienced some minimal decline between 1970 and 1976, most experienced improvement. For example, Arkansas' 38.0 rate was topped in 1970 with a rate of 62.0, which, in turn, was topped in 1976 with a 94.0 registration rate, the highest for the region. Table 4.3 shows that, as of

Table 4.3
Estimated Voter Registration Rate by Race for South and Non-South, 1966–1976, Selected Years (in percentages)

	1966			1970			1976		
	Black	White	Diff	Black	White	Diff	Black	White	Diff
South	51.8	71.2	19.4	58.9	63.9	5.0	63.1	67.8	4.7
Non-South	68.4	71.8	3.4	62.6	70.8	8.2	54.8	68.5	13.7

Source: Compiled by the author. See Appendix D for sources and detailed figures.

1966, the South remained behind the non-South with respect to black registration, but by 1970 and 1976, it had surpassed the non-South on this measure. Where the South had witnessed improvement in black electoral participation, areas outside of the South began to experience a downturn. Between the mid-sixties and seventies, the difference in registration rates between southern blacks and whites decreased from 19.4 percent to 4.7 percent, while the difference for non-southerners actually increased from 3.4 percent to 13.7 percent.

In addition to improvements in voting, the South also witnessed improvements in socioeconomic equality during the seventies. The overall socioeconomic status of southern blacks was still worse than that of blacks in other areas; however, southern blacks had begun to make notable strides in comparison to southern whites. This is reflected in a comparison of the two groups' occupational status and income. Again during the seventies, as before, unemployment was worse among non-southern blacks than among those in the South; however, the practical importance of this with respect to the overall economic vitality of southern blacks at the time is diminished by the fact that a large number of "employed" southern blacks were in seasonal positions that were necessarily temporary in nature. This is why I have chosen to focus on what is a more meaningful measure of employment opportunity, namely, occupation.

What we find in looking at occupational breakdown is that, generally, blacks in both the South and the non-South were less likely to be employed in skilled jobs and more likely to be employed in low-skilled jobs than their white counterparts (see Table 4.4). As for comparisons among blacks across both regions, in 1970, 20.2 percent of southern blacks were employed in skilled jobs, while slightly more, 33.4 percent of northern blacks were. Conversely, southern blacks were more likely than northern blacks to be employed in semiskilled jobs and were two times more likely to be employed in low-skilled jobs. But, whereas the 1960 occupation data provided in chapter 3 show that less than 10 percent of southern black males were employed in skilled jobs, these 1970 data clearly reveal progress.[8] Similarly, where the

Table 4.4
Occupation: Employed Persons 16+ Years by Race and Region, 1970

	SOUTH*		NORTH	
	% Brkdown of Blacks	% Brkdown of Whites	% Brkdown of Blacks	% Brkdown of Whites
Professional & Technical	7.6	14.8	9.1	15.7
Management Workers	2.0	9.7	2.7	8.7
Clerical Workers	9.0	17.9	18.8	18.6
Sales Workers	1.7	8.0	2.9	7.5
TOTAL SKILLED	**20.2**	**50.5**	**33.4**	**50.6**
Craftsmen	8.8	15.4	9.3	14.0
Operative Workers	22.9	17.4	24.5	16.8
Private Household Workers	11.5	0.7	4.9	0.8
Service Workers	20.0	8.7	20.1	10.9
TOTAL SEMISKILLED	**63.2**	**42.3**	**58.8**	**42.4**
Farmers	1.0	2.1	0.2	2.0
Farm Laborers and Foremen	4.2	1.3	0.5	1.0
Laborers (excl: Farm & Mine)	11.4	3.9	7.2	4.0
TOTAL LOW SKILLED	**16.6**	**7.3**	**7.8**	**7.0**

*"South" includes the eleven former Confederate states and also Delaware, Washington, D.C.,
    Kentucky, Maryland, Oklahoma, and West Virginia.
**"Black" refers to non-white.

Source: Derived from *Census of the Population 1970,* Table 133 at p. 1–454

data in chapter 3 show that 42 percent of southern blacks were confined to
low-skilled jobs as of 1960, the data shown here indicate that only 17 percent of blacks in the South were so employed as of 1970. A second measure
of socioeconomic status, income, also indicates that the South continued to
lag behind the North, but had made notable improvement following the
sixties. Consider the median family income for both races between 1953
and 1974. The gap between black and white families in the South closed
between 1953 and 1974, while the gap outside the South actually widened.
The black to white income ratio in the South was 0.56 in 1953 and improved to 0.61 in 1969, but dropped slightly to 0.58 in 1974. On the other
hand, the black to white ratio outside the South was 0.75 in 1953, but by
1974 had dropped to 0.67, which, again, suggests the North was falling
behind as the South was making nominal gains.[9]

On the whole, what the change in the political and socioeconomic racial status quo in the South did was essentially close the regional gap between the North and South in ways that necessarily meant less division.

A third way in which the regional conflict relative to race had begun to subside during the seventies is that fewer civil rights demonstrations occurred within the South's borders, concerned the South, or addressed what had been traditionally "southern" issues. Increasingly, many of the large-scale movement activities previously reserved primarily for the South were being conducted in northern cities. Of course, the sixties movement was never entirely restricted to the South; however, those activities that did occur outside the South during the sixties did not approach the scope or frequency of those that took place within the South.[10] By the late sixties and early seventies, the handful of large-scale demonstrations capturing national attention that did occur took place, not in the South, but beyond its borders.[11]

Because legally sanctioned racial classifications were largely nonexistent in the North, much of the protest conducted there was aimed at dismantling de facto segregation in various areas, especially education and housing. In 1967, nine prominent civil rights leaders, including Dr. King, announced plans to initiate demonstrations in Cleveland. A 1968 march known as "The Poor People's March to Washington," involving some 50,000 participants, began in Memphis, Tennessee, and officially opened later in Washington, D.C., in what was termed the "Solidarity Day March." Another 1968 march took place in Chicago that involved roughly 300 demonstrators. And, in 1972, what was in many respects the last massive organized protest activity specifically aimed at dismantling racial barriers was a school boycott in New York in which the overwhelming majority of blacks and Puerto Rican students in a Harlem school district participated.

Beyond the traditional forms of protest activity, perhaps the series of events that best reflect a gradual shift of concerns to areas outside the South is the race riots of the late sixties and seventies. Several small-scale riots had taken place in the early sixties. The watershed year was 1967, when as many as 164 riots occurred in urban cities throughout the United States. A review of the 1967 rioting reveals that more disorders erupted outside the South than within. Table 4.5 shows that fully 84 percent of the 1967 riots occurred in states outside the South and its border states and that nearly two-thirds, 61 percent, occurred specifically in the eastern and midwest regions. The disorders, and especially their regional distribution, were symptomatic of the growing racial problem in northern urban areas. The Kerner Commission study of the 1967 riots, "The Report of the National Advisory Commission on Civil Disorders," identified several conditions as the basic causes. Foremost among these were pervasive discrimination and segregation in employment, education, and housing, which, according to the report, resulted in the continued exclusion of large numbers of blacks from the benefits of

Table 4.5
Race Riots, 1967

Region	Number of Riots	% Distribution
East	57	35
Midwest	59	36
West	27	16
South and Border States	21	13
TOTAL	164	100

Source: U.S. National Advisory Commission on Civil Disorders, *Report of the National Advisory Commission on Civil Disorders* (1968)

economic progress. Second was the growing white exodus from, and concentration of blacks in, major cities, seeding a crisis of deteriorating inner cities. Third was the solidification of black ghettos wherein segregation and poverty produced excessive crime, drug addiction, welfare dependency, and other social disorders.

Most importantly, the report made it clear that these problems were especially endemic to the North and the concerns of that region. A post-riot survey of neighborhoods in Detroit and Newark revealed that fully 74 percent of the rioters were reared in the North. And, the specific grievances of the rioters listed by the report were as follows: (1) police practices; (2) unemployment and underemployment; (3) inadequate housing; (4) inadequate education; (5) poor recreation facilities and programs; and (6) ineffectiveness of the political structure and grievance mechanisms. These were all newly emerging issues outside the South. More generally, the Kerner Commission brought into clearer focus the race problem's contemporary dimensions by squarely identifying the racial problem as a national one. The report concluded: "Our Nation is moving toward two societies, one black, one white—separate and unequal."[12] This statement very clearly symbolized the general locus of racial discrimination, revealing that its historical roots had begun to produce problems far beyond the South's borders. Southern-style discrimination was no longer the preeminent concern in regards to race. As of the seventies, the "race problem" was no longer a regional matter.

Partisan Division

As the regional differences pertaining to race began to wane, the partisan divisions intensified. The stances of presidential candidates and administrations are used here to illustrate the extent to which the two parties diverged to an even greater extent during the seventies than previously. In particular, presidential politics suggest that the Republican party's previously conservative tone was translated during the seventies into concrete conservative policies. This occurred as the Democratic party's liberalism became virtually commonplace. The 1968 and 1976 presidential campaigns and administrations are especially telling in this regard.

The 1968 Nixon versus Humphrey presedential election contest made it unmistakably clear that Republican racial conservatism was well on its way to becoming etched in a permanent party racial agenda, in much the same way that Democratic racial liberalism was. Democratic candidate Hubert Humphrey advocated reform. Humphrey's background was a resume of civil rights advocacy. Nelson Polsby suggests Humphrey was largely responsible for the re-introduction of race into mainstream politics in 1940 when he spearheaded the inclusion of a civil rights plank on the Democratic party's national platform for the first time in decades.[13] As mayor of Minneapolis, he was largely responsible for the first local fair employment law in the country. And, while serving in the U.S. Senate, he proposed as many as thirteen major civil rights laws between 1949 and 1963. During the 1968 presidential campaign, he endorsed aggressive governmental action in the field of civil rights, stating: "it is grievous error to assume that governmental action can do nothing to cause a change of heart. . . . If we succeed in eliminating discrimination by law, we have reason to expect that the lessening of prejudice will be a byproduct of our success."[14]

Nixon, on the other hand, both as party candidate and as president served to reinforce his party's ever-increasing racial conservatism. Nixon as vice president and as 1960 presidential candidate offered at least moderately supportive overtones; however, by the late sixties and seventies, he was decidedly less apt to forthrightly side in favor of progressive racial policies. It was his 1968 campaign that first put into place what became known as the "Republican southern strategy" wherein the party's leadership actively courted southern whites who were dissatisfied with the Democratic party. During the 1968 Republican national party convention, Nixon assured southern delegates he would not run an administration that would "ram anything down your throats," that he opposed school busing, that he would appoint "strict constitutionalists" to the Supreme Court, and that he disapproved of federal intervention in local school board affairs.[15] Later, as president, Nixon wrote: "This country is not ready at this time for either forcibly integrated housing or forcibly integrated education. . . . We simply have to face the hard fact that the law cannot go beyond what the people are willing to support."[16]

The Republican party implicitly endorsed Nixon's viewpoints. During the 1968 convention, Nixon's southern strategy won the votes of 228,[17] or 78 percent, of the 292-member southern delegation in the very first ballot and, in the second ballot, the entire delegation voted for Nixon. Later, during the 1972 convention Nixon won 100 percent of the southern delegation. Also in the 1968 general presidential election, Nixon won a large percentage of the southern white vote.

Significantly, Nixon's conservative perspective on race was carved into the executive and legislative policies during his tenure in office. His administration not only failed to advocate on behalf of integration in various areas, but actually fought certain pro-integration efforts pushed by those within as well as outside his administration.[18] A case in point is his administration's actions relative to education and voting. Within a week of his inauguration, Nixon postponed for sixty days a federal funds cut-off deadline for five southern school districts that had failed to abolish segregated schools. He did so, ostensibly, to allow more time to study the cases. A year later the Justice Department petitioned the Supreme Court to postpone desegregation deadlines in six southern states. The administration also voiced strong opposition to busing.[19] Nixon went so far as to support a constitutional amendment banning mandatory busing, although he later backed away from the idea. He endorsed instead a moratorium on court-ordered busing and an equal educational opportunity bill that would strictly limit busing, while providing federal funding for schools serving poor children.[20] Six weeks after taking office, Nixon withdrew federal voting registrars from Mississippi and proceeded to, in effect, underenforce the Voting Rights Act of 1965.[21] A measure introduced in 1969 in the House on behalf of the administration sought to eliminate the 1965 bill's preclearance requirement and to remove the exclusive authority of the federal district court of Washington, D.C., to hear cases brought under the bill, an authority civil rights advocates believed was critical to ensuring effective voting rights enforcement.

The Nixon administration was not wholly devoid of favorable civil rights action; nonetheless, what was put in place by the administration fell far short of the objectives underlying not only the policies advanced by most civil rights groups, but even those of the administration itself. Two programs geared to implement Nixon's black capitalism program, the Minority Business Enterprise program and the Philadelphia Plan, were themselves weakly enforced under Nixon's leadership. The Commission on Civil Rights found that the Office of Federal Contract Compliance, which oversaw the Philadelphia Plan, seldom applied sanctions against those in noncompliance.[22] Michael Genovese reports that by 1971, Nixon had all but forgotten about the minority business enterprise and had no other real plan for promoting minority economic development.

Like the 1968 presidential politics, the 1976 presidential contest between Jimmy Carter and Gerald Ford revealed a hardening of partisan racial fault lines. Ford had adopted Nixon's positions on busing and government intervention. At the 1964 Republican National Convention he denounced busing. And, during his first press conference as president, he criticized a federal court decision that ordered busing. His remarks, noting his belief that busing should be used to correct the effects of intentional segregation and not to remedy unintentional segregation,[23] prompted harsh criticism from the Commission on Civil Rights in September 1975.[24]

Whereas the Nixon and Ford administrations hinted at the Republican party continuously moving toward the right, Jimmy Carter's administration showed just the opposite as far as the Democratic party was concerned. Even on difficult subjects, he advocated aggressive action. In his statement to the Platform Committee of the 1976 Democratic Party National Convention, he said: "I believe that our platform should reflect a strong commitment to enforcement of the Open Housing Act of 1968 and the Community Development Act of 1974."[25] He continued: "we should enable the Equal Employment Opportunity Commission to function more effectively and expeditiously in employment discrimination complaints."[26] With regard to reversing the high unemployment rate among black youth, Carter stated: "it doesn't take just a quiet or minimum enforcement of the law. It requires an aggressive searching out and reaching out to help people who especially need it."[27]

As president, Carter undertook efforts to redress racial inequality across the board, utilizing mostly administrative approaches, but legislative and judicial remedies as well. He proposed an amendment to the 1968 Fair Housing Act that would have enabled the Department of Housing and Urban Development to issue cease-and-desist orders.[28] Minority government contracts more than doubled as did federal deposits in minority-owned banks. His Justice Department argued in a major Supreme Court case, *Hazelwood v. U.S.* (1977), that Title VII of the 1964 Civil Rights Act did not bar only those actions with a discriminatory intent, but those with a discriminatory effect as well. And in *University of California v. Bakke* (1978), it supported the view that race may be taken into account as a positive factor in employment and education decisions, provided doing so did not result in quotas. Finally, Carter appointed a record number of blacks to executive and judicial posts.[29] He appointed more blacks to federal judgeships (37) than did the Johnson, Nixon, Ford, Reagan, and Bush administrations combined (32).[30]

In essence, during the seventies, national party differences concerning race widened as Republicans began to more actively champion policy restraint and even retreat. This occurred even as the Democratic party essentially expanded and diversified its racial liberalism to include not only legislative, but also administrative and judicial civil rights activism.

Salience of Race during the Transition Years

Importantly, the broader political significance of these divisions remained intact, even as the nature of these differences began to change. Racial discord's importance specifically in the South was waning; but, in the party system, which I have argued best exemplifies the national importance of race, it remained very much a top priority. Party platform attention is used here again to demonstrate the salience of race within the party system. Analysis of the platforms show that both the Republican and Democratic parties devoted one or more sections of their 1968, 1972, and 1976 national party platforms to expound what they considered the best approach to racial problems and/or address issues such as discrimination, equal opportunity, black civil rights, and so forth. In doing so, they each implicitly recognized race as relevant to a variety of policy areas. This is clear from their discussion of race in connection with various other types of issues. What the level and nature of attention in the party platforms essentially reveal is that race was a major ticket item.

First, the Republican and Democratic 1968 platforms gave significant attention to racial issues. Democrats included a subsection devoted to racial issues entitled "Toward a Single Society" and discussed race-related issues in at least six other parts, including those entitled "The People," "The Nation," "Housing," "Opportunity for All," "Education," and "Justice for All." Republicans did not devote an independent section to race in their 1968 platform, but the topic was addressed in as many as five different parts of their platform, including the preamble and four subsections entitled "Domestic Policy," "Crisis of the Cities," "Human Development," and "The Poor."

Again in 1972, civil rights was a major concern of both parties. In fact, the Democrats' platform contained two civil rights subsections, one entitled "The Right to Be Different" and the other called "Equal Access to Quality Education"; and the issue was discussed in at least thirteen other parts of the platform, all addressing a range of topics from jobs to social justice to government partnerships to crime to administrative agencies to education and housing. The Republican 1972 platform included a subsection entitled "Ending Discrimination" and articulated a civil rights position in connection with at least six other areas, including the platform's preamble and other subsections under the following headings: "Small Business," "Health Care," "Education," "Law Enforcement," and "Arts and Humanities."

Finally, in 1976 both parties again devoted much attention to race. Democrats included two sections on race, one entitled "Equal Employment Opportunity" and the other called "Civil and Political Rights." It also touched on racial subsections in eight other portions of the platform, namely, the preamble and the following sections: "Full Employment Opportunities," "Small Businesses," "Health Care," "Education," "States, Counties, and Cities," "Housing and Community Development," and "Law Enforcement and Law Observance." And, the 1976 Republican platform gave significant space to civil rights, devoting an entire section to the subject, entitled "Equal Rights and Ending Discrimination." In addition, the platform described its civil rights position in discussions of at least four other policy issues, "Small Business," "Education," "Working Americans," and "Arts and Humanities."

In sum, the racial divisions of the seventies had changed, but their overall importance within American national politics remained the same.

CIVIL RIGHTS PROCESS AND PROCEDURES DURING THE TRANSITION YEARS

The reformulation of racial conflict during the seventies directly affected how formal institutional processes accommodated race reform initiatives. Although the South's distinction on the race question would become a thing of the past by the close of the seventies, as explained above, remnants of it remained during much of the seventies. Consequently, the active opposition to congressional civil rights legislative proposals was still supplied primarily by the South. Though smaller in number, southern opponents of the seventies, like their predecessors, could not be persuaded by advocates to forgo the use of filibuster tactics as a means of blocking the proposals' adoption. They continued the tradition of obstructing civil rights process. As such, they stimulated a breakdown in the standard legislative process. And, thereby, they imposed upon civil rights advocates an unconventional process.

The discussion to follow analyzes the makeup of civil rights opposition in the Senate during the seventies; the extent of obstruction pitted against the seventies proposals; and the resulting nature of the demands of the formal procedural process through which the seventies proposals were enacted.

Civil Rights Opposition in the Transition Years

Given the continued, albeit diminished, controversiality of race in the South, the majority of senators obstructing the bills continued to be drawn from the South; however, unlike in the past, most senators representing the South did not participate in the seventies obstructionist effort. At least 89 percent (16) of senators obstructing the 1970 bill were from states in the deep South. The coalition was comprised of both senators from Alabama, Georgia, Louisiana, Mississippi, North Carolina, and South Carolina. Also part of the 1970 opposition group were Arkansas senator, John McClellan; Florida senator, Spessard Holland; Nebraska senator, Roman Hruska; Texas senator, John Tower; Virginia senator, Harry Byrd, Jr.; and West Virginia senator, Robert C. Byrd.

In 1972, the coalition again was composed of mostly southern senators, with at least 77 percent (13) of the group's members representing the eleven-state South. Included were both senators from Alabama, Arizona, Louisiana, Mississippi, and North Carolina. Also joining the group were Herman Talmadge of Georgia; James Buckley of New York; Milton Young of North Dakota; Strom Thurmond of South Carolina; Brock Hill of Tennessee; John Tower of Texas; and Harry Byrd of Virginia. Lastly, the 1975 obstructionist effort was also a largely southern undertaking, with at least 85 percent (11) of its members representing the South, including both senators from Alabama, Mississippi, and Virginia. Also included were Arkansas senator, John McClellan; Georgia senator, Herman Talmadge; Nevada senator, Paul Laxalt; North Carolina senator, Jesse Helms; South Carolina senator, Strom Thurmond; Texas senator, John Tower; and Wyoming senator, Clifford Hansen.

As alluded to above, even though civil rights obstruction continued to be a mostly southern enterprise during the seventies, the proportion of southern senators committed to the obstructionist effort declined substantially during the seventies as fewer of the South's twenty-member representation in the Senate took part in the obstruction. The overall average (61%) of southern Senate representation in the obstructionist camp during the seventies debates compares to a higher overall average of 90 percent participating in the sixties debates. What is more, a gradual decline began to take place across the seventies debates. At least 73 percent of the southern bloc, helped to obstruct civil rights in 1970, while 59 percent did in 1972, and only 50 percent did in 1975.

Obstruction of Civil Rights Legislative Proposals in the Transition Years

Southerners' procedural impediments of the seventies continued to cause breakdowns in the normal process. They were less imposing obstacles than before, but obstacles nonetheless. Opponents' use of the rules was somewhat scaled down in comparison to their earlier use. And, as before, the obstacles proved formidable; however, the range and intensity of tactics involved was much smaller in scope. Starting in the seventies, lengthy speechmaking and refusing to vote were mostly used to maintain the blockages and only in limited instances was there excessive use of quorum calls and amendment motions. We begin to see a diminution in the civil rights obstruction strategy. But, what we get is still blockage in every proceeding.

Four versions of the 1970 bill referred to Judiciary never emerged out of committee. The 1972 bill was spared obstruction at the committee stage as it was referred to the Labor Committee, chaired by civil rights supporter Senator Edward Kennedy. The 1975 bill was eventually voluntarily reported out of Judiciary, but only because of Eastland's absence due to illness and, even so, the committee's action came too late, after the Senate had already abandoned its own version of the bill to pursue the House's version. During the seventies, only the 1975 proposal was blocked at the consideration stage. However, all of the seventies bills were subjected to filibusters at the final vote stage.

Routes of Passage during the Transition Years

The breakdowns caused by opponents' obstruction in the seventies again necessitated use of alternative procedural routes, in particular more costly routes. Advocates relied on a smaller range of formal and informal "non-traditional" motions during the seventies than in previous debates. Procedures such as direct placement, committee instructions, and cloture were used; however, only minimal use was made of other formal procedures and even less use was made of informal tactics, such as scheduling adjustments, a one-track system, strict application of the rules, and so forth. However, even though somewhat less involved as of the seventies, as compared to normal process, civil rights lawmaking was still quite distinctive.

Committee Stage

The seventies civil rights committee procedures were abnormal, with the exception of the 1972 committee route. Ordinarily, little is involved at this point in the policy process. But, this was not the case in regard to the seventies civil rights legislation, namely the 1970 and 1975 bills. The 1972 bill was sent to the Labor Committee, which was favorable to civil rights. It was referred to the committee on September 14, 1971, and by October 28, 1971, the subcommittee and full committee had completed hearings, markup, and reporting of the bill. In 1970, however, advocates were forced to pursue a House-passed version of the bill, rather than the Senate version in committee. Pursuit of the House bill was complicated as it was channeled first through the direct placement route and then later through the instructions procedure. The House had passed its version of the bill on December 11, 1969, and sent it to the Senate where it received a first and second reading on December 12 and 15, 1969, respectively. Immediately following the second reading of the bill, Senator Hart objected to further proceedings under Senate Rule IV. Opponents complained that "no bill has ever been held on the calendar by the invocation of this procedure except so-called civil rights bills."[31] The House bill was later removed from the calendar and referred to Judiciary with instructions to report it back. This was done in exchange for opponents agreeing to permit the bill to be taken up without debate. On December 16, 1969, Mansfield requested unanimous consent to refer the bill to Judiciary with instructions to report it back by March 1, 1970. On Saturday, February 28, 1970, the bill was reported to the floor by Eastland, with no committee recommendations.

The 1975 committee strategy also involved pursuit of an unconventional procedure. Direct placement of the House-passed version of the voting rights act was again the chosen route. The House version of the bill received a first and second reading in the Senate on June 5, 1975. Following the second reading, Minority Leader Scott objected to further proceedings under Rule 14. Allen tried to block the procedure, but registered his objection too late, after the presiding officer had already ruled the bill would go directly to the calendar. Interestingly, the Judiciary Committee did subsequently report the Senate version of the 1975 bill. Senator Eastland, who had thus far succeeded in stalling committee action on the 1975 proposals had taken a leave of absence due to illness. During his absence, civil rights supporter Senator Hart acted as chair and successfully chartered the bill through hearings and markup and finally to a 10 to 4 vote in favor of reporting it to the floor on July 18, 1975. The action, however, came too late. The bill was set to expire on August 6, 1975, and the Senate's scheduled date of adjournment for the session was August 1, 1975. As a result, the House bill was utilized instead.

Consideration Stage

Proceedings at the consideration stage of each of the seventies civil rights proceedings were closer to normal, with the exception of the 1975 debate. By convention, the consideration stage is the least demanding of the remaining stages. And, during the seventies, this was mostly true of civil rights proceedings as well. The unanimous consent agreement that had provided for the 1970 voting rights bill to be referred with instructions also provided for it to be made the pending business "at the conclusion of morning business on March 1, or the first legislative day thereafter."[32] As a result, at the conclusion of morning business on March 2, 1970, the House version of the bill was officially made the pending business of the Senate. The 1972 proceedings at the consideration stage were uncomplicated due to the growing pressure on the leadership to invoke cloture. On the last day of the first session of the 92nd Congress, December 17, 1971, Mansfield asked for unanimous consent that the fair employment bill be made unfinished business so that, when members reconvened in January, it would be the pending business.

In 1975, advocates' input at the consideration stage was considerable. First, it took two separate roll call votes (one on a point of order and another motion to instruct the sergeant-at-arms), two live quorum calls, and a vote on a motion to recess simply to enable Majority Leader Mansfield to obtain the floor in order to submit a motion to proceed to the House-passed civil rights bill. Securing a vote on the motion itself involved even more effort. There were a number of things absent from the advocates 1975 floor strategy that were part of earlier debate strategies, such as strict application of the rules, a one-track system, scheduling adjustments, and so forth. In fact, a number of "debate-containing" items specifically suggested in a memorandum to the majority leader were not utilized, including "[i]importuning all supporting Senators to minimize usage of their time and the introduction of amendments"; "conserving leadership's available time for disposing of procedural questions"; and "preparing various parliamentary procedural alternatives for dealing with procedural dilatory tactics."[33] However, several of the remaining "civil rights" procedures were utilized. Amendments were subjected to tabling motions. There were also the usual warnings from the leadership regarding quorum calls and other items. Byrd stated: "Quorum calls can come at any time. . . . Motions to recess, motions to adjourn, motions to send the Sergeant at Arms to request the attendance of absent Senators—all these motions can result in roll call votes."[34]

Cloture was the focal point of the 1975 strategy at the consideration stage; but even it was complicated. This time, a motion for cloture on debate of the motion to proceed was coupled with the motion to proceed. Within moments after Mansfield had submitted the motion to proceed, Byrd sent a cloture motion to the desk. Both were submitted on a Friday. Under Rule 22, the Senate was to vote on the cloture motion the following Sunday. However, because supporters were not expected to be in ample supply until Monday, the leadership pushed for a vote on the following Monday, instead of Sunday. The plan to accomplish this entailed holding a Saturday session, but adjourning early Saturday afternoon. Doing so would ensure the cloture vote did not take place until Monday. But, when the opposition attempted to gain the floor Saturday morning in an attempt to continue discussion of the bill throughout Saturday, thus forcing a vote on Sunday, Byrd counteracted. He first moved for a recess immediately after the session was convened on Saturday and then retained the floor for the entire Saturday session, refusing to yield except for limited purposes. And, as a safety precaution, a second cloture motion was submitted by Mansfield on Saturday in the event opponents tied up the floor, forcing a Sunday vote.[35] The motion to shut off debate on the motion to proceed was adopted the following Monday in a 72 to 19 vote, twelve votes more than were required under the newly revised three-fifths requirements of Rule 22.

Final Vote Stage

Demands at the final vote stage of the seventies civil rights proceedings were also excessive in comparison to what is normally required, with the exception of the 1970 proceedings. In most cases, procedurally, the final vote stage is relatively straightforward as much of what occurs here is ordinarily structured by pre-floor agreements. And, during the seventies, much was missing. In the past supporters usually had to undertake a taxing civil rights floor strategy. Now, there were no special warnings from the leadership to be on guard for surprise motions and quorum calls. The one-track system was abandoned as supporters agreed on several occasions to temporarily lay aside the voting rights bill to consider other measures. There were no major adjustments to the daily session schedule, nor were Saturday sessions held. And, rather than recess from day to day, the Senate adjourned at the end of each day virtually throughout the debate, so that, of the fourteen daily sessions that encompassed the debate, at least twelve, or eight-six percent, were adjourned. The only rule for which advocates demanded strict application was the germaneness rule, which requires that debate be germane to the pending business during the first three hours of discussion following the close of morning business. This strict application of the rules was the only significant departure from the Senate's normal proceedings. The debate reached a "natural" conclusion after Allen was dissuaded from continuing his filibuster due to Senator Long's argument that continuing to block a final vote could cost the opposition needed alliances. On March 13, 1970, the Senate adopted the House bill in a 64 to 12 vote. The House, on June 17, 1970, agreed to the Senate amendments in a 272 to 132 vote. President Nixon signed the bill into law on June 22, 1970.

Advocates' 1972 civil rights strategy at the floor was more involved. Acting majority leader Byrd warned throughout the debate that surprise votes could occur at any time and that supporters should be prepared to deliver them as necessary. Adherence to certain debate rules was insisted upon. For example, supporters objected on several occasions when filibustering senators yielded to other senators for purposes other than to ask a question. Objection was made also to speaking senators being able to maintain the floor once they had yielded. Additionally, the Pastore rule requiring that debate be germane the first three hours following the close of morning business was strictly enforced. Scheduling adjustments were made. The morning hour was shortened, on average, to between fifteen and thirty minutes rather than the usual two hours. Daily sessions were also lengthened, primarily to strain southerners' physical endurance. A memorandum to bill manager Senator Williams contained the following: "The general consensus (your Leadership Conference friends) is that it is time to start putting Senators Allen and Ervin's feet to the fire by keeping the Senate in session until at least 7:00 or 8:00 P.M." It went on: "Senator Ervin is reported to have said he has enough amendments to keep going until July. This sounds like bravado but he should be put to the test."[36]

Cloture was the main vehicle for action at the floor in 1972, and it took three separate tries before it was successfully invoked. The first cloture motion was submitted on January 28, 1972, by Williams and Javits and rejected, on February 1, 1972, by a vote of 48 to 37. A second cloture motion was filed the same day, over many advocates' objections. It too was rejected, on February 3, 1972, by a vote of 53 to 35. A third cloture motion was submitted on February 18, 1972, after a major compromise amendment had been adopted on February 15, 1972. The petition for the motion was endorsed by fifty-three signatures and adopted at the floor in a 73 to 21 vote on February 22, 1972. The bill was passed in the Senate the same day in a 73 to 16 vote. The Senate later approved on March 6 a conference report, which was subsequently adopted by the House on March 8 in a 303 to 110 vote. The bill was signed by President Nixon and became law on March 24, 1972.

The 1975 floor strategy was also relatively involved, but not as much as the 1972 strategy. For the most part, the Senate carried on its business at a relatively normal pace, on a two-track basis. However, daily sessions were lengthened by roughly two hours, on average. And, a recess schedule was put in place, which caused the Senate to remain in the same legislative day until the bill was passed (the Senate recessed from July 21 through July 24). Again in 1975 at the floor, for the second time during this debate alone, supporters turned to cloture. Mansfield submitted a cloture petition signed by twenty-six senators to close debate on the bill on July 21, 1975, only minutes after the motion to consider was agreed to and the bill had become unfinished business of the Senate. The motion to close debate on the bill was agreed to in a 76 to 20 roll call vote of the floor as scheduled, on July 23, 1975. The bill was adopted on July 24 in a 77 to 12 roll call vote. It was adopted in the House on June 4, 1975, in a 341 to 70 vote. President Ford signed the bill into law on August 6, 1975.

In summary, the strategy advocates used to enact the seventies civil rights legislation was relatively scaled down in comparison to the sixties legislative efforts. However, as compared to most bills enacted in the Senate, the seventies civil rights procedures were still far more taxing. Much less attention has been paid by scholars to the Senate debates of the seventies than has been devoted to the sixties debates, in part because the seventies proceedings were less overtly abnormal. Nonetheless, as the preceding discussion has shown, they represented a departure from the norm in much the same way that the infamous sixties proceedings did, only to a lesser extent.

CIVIL RIGHTS POLICY OUTCOMES IN THE TRANSITION YEARS

Abnormal civil rights policymaking continued into the seventies as did the weakening of race-related legislative proposals. As a consequence of the limited consensus surrounding the race problem and its controversiality, those seeking to make real the promise of the sixties legislation later encountered the same bargaining challenges as those who had initially obtained those promises. More specifically, given the higher procedural demands of the seventies policy process, sponsors of the seventies bills were dependent upon the votes of uncommitteds in order to secure passage of any form of legislation. The problem they faced once again was that their hands were, in effect, tied in negotiations with uncommitteds, as the range of bargaining options available to them was severely limited. Once again, the only means of winning over the additional votes was by altering the substance of the proposals. For the mostly Republican group of uncommitteds, race remained too divisive, too salient, and, thus, too much of a high stakes issue on which to play politics as usual.

The end result of the diminished bargaining leverage relative to race was the enactment of weak legislation. Advocates had hoped to shore up the

enforcement structures established in the original voting rights and fair employment laws of the sixties, but were unable to do so. In particular, the
aim was to extend the original voting rights act with a few changes, especially the trigger formulas in Sections 4 and 5. A simple extension of these
provisions, they believed, would constrict southern states' ability to exclude
black voters from participation in elections, particularly in those states with
well-known histories of black disenfranchisement. As far as employment discrimination was concerned, advocates pushed for wider coverage, but importantly, they wanted to put more teeth into Title VII of the 1964 bill.
Under the original Title VII, EEOC was authorized only to litigate on
behalf of complainants. The goal in 1972 was to enable EEOC to do something about the complaints.

   This section demonstrates the mediums through which the impact of racial politics upon the seventies civil rights laws was mediated. First, it shows
that uncommitteds' votes were indispensable to the passage of any form of
civil rights legislation. Then, it highlights the conditions advocates faced in
their attempts to win over uncommitteds' votes, conditions shaped largely
by the nature of racial politics. Lastly, it outlines the actual policy losses
suffered in return for victory on passage of the seventies civil rights bills.

Negotiating Race in the Transition Years

   Moderates' pivotal role in diluting the seventies bills arose foremost from
the fact that none of the bills could have succeeded without their votes.
Advocates lacked the supermajority support needed to bypass southern obstruction. Supporters initially claimed the votes of only sixty-three members
in 1970 and fifty-five in both the 1972 and 1975 debates, while opponents
claimed eighteen members in 1970, seventeen in 1972, and thirteen in
1975.[37] This left roughly nineteen members uncommitted in 1970 and
twenty-eight in 1972. With only ninety-nine members in the Senate during
much of 1975 due to a disputed seat, thirty-one senators remained outside
of the two coalitions during the 1975 proceeding. In order to invoke cloture
in 1970, then, at least four of the nineteen uncommitteds had to be convinced to switch their position, whereas twelve of the seventeen in 1972
had to be won over. And, with the 1975 change in Rule 22, which reduced
from two-thirds to three-fifths the number of senators needed to invoke
cloture, the support of only five more senators was needed to enact the
1975 civil rights legislation.

   In addition to the fact that their votes were absolutely critical to civil
rights success, also important for understanding their impact on the seventies legislation is that, once again, most were members of the Republican
party who held conservative views relative to government activism. Of the
senators on the fence in 1970, 1972, and 1975, at least 79 percent, 64
percent, and 45 percent, respectively, were Republican. For them, the fed-

eral government's power was to be carefully limited to those areas in which it had a clear, legitimate role to play. Following the sixties, their views regarding a minimal role for government became especially poignant relative to race. Many had come to believe that certain of the sixties congressional policies, Supreme Court decisions, and executive orders and actions had overextended their reach by implementing forced busing and various other schemes to achieve racial proportionality. Government had simply gone too far in its attempt to improve the lot of blacks, and it had reached the point where the government's efforts were unfairly intruding into the lives of other American citizens.

During the seventies proceedings, Republican uncommitteds' racial conservatism took the form of objections to the scope and enforcement provisions of the seventies proposals. With respect to the 1970 proposal addressing voting, moderates expressed three main concerns. First, advocates did not want to switch the base year of the trigger formula in the 1965 act because they believed doing so would release from coverage those states with the worst history of voting discrimination. Moderates believed, however, the switch would make the bill fairer and better tailored. Second, supporters believed that nationalizing the 1965 bill's provisions would jeopardize its constitutionality because it would be difficult to justify the federal government's interference in all fifty states. They believed expanding the bill's coverage would stretch enforcement resources and, thereby, limit the bill's effectiveness in areas where it was most needed. But, moderates supported several versions of the 1970 bill that provided for nationalization of the 1965 voting rights act's provisions. Senator Everett Dirksen introduced on behalf of the Nixon administration a bill (S02507) designed to do this. Third, almost all uncommitted senators preferred a constitutional amendment as a means of lowering the voting age, rather than the statutory route advocated by supporters.

In 1972, uncommitteds objected to advocates' attempt to invest "cease-and-desist" authority in the Equal Employment Opportunity Commission, which had been established by the Civil Rights Act of 1964. Supporters believed that channeling employment discrimination suits through the EEOC, rather than the federal court system, was a more expeditious route to eliminating barriers faced by blacks and other minorities in the workplace. Senator Javits for years had complained about the 1964 act's employment provisions, saying: "Title VII pays lip service to the idea of equal employment opportunity but the hard fact is that the compromise worked out in 1964 under which the . . . Commission was emasculated, has destroyed the Act as an effective tool to end discrimination in employment in this country."[38]

Moderates strongly disagreed with advocates, arguing that under the cease-and-desist approach pushed by advocates, "the EEOC . . . writes most of the rules and regulations, acts as an investigator . . . acts as a prosecutor.

. . . (f)inally the commission acts . . . to decide whether or not its own personnel have acted properly."[39] In effect, the EEOC was made prosecutor, judge, and jury. For them, the preferred approach was the judicial approach. Under it, EEOC would have the authority to identify discrimination, but the attorney general would be entrusted with the authority to prosecute, and the federal courts would actually make the final determinations as to whether discrimination had occurred and, if so, what the appropriate remedy would be. Toward this end, Republican Colorado senator, Peter Dominick, the spokesperson for the moderate coalition, sponsored an amendment to provide for court enforcement.

Unlike the first two seventies proceedings, the 1975 proceeding involved fewer major differences between the mostly Republican group of uncommitteds and the advocates. Advocates sought a simple ten-year extension of Sections 4 and 5 of the 1965 act and fought against nationalizing these sections of the bill. Again, their basic contention was that "there was no clear evidence to justify Congress exerting such authority in all 50 states."[40] A handful of Republicans, however, wanted to have these provisions nationalized, saying "the Attorney General can be the same Attorney General in all the 50 states that he is in this little area that is designated in the bill." For these reasons, Republican Senator Richard Stone sponsored an amendment that would have nationalized Sections 4 and 5.

There were substantive differences between advocates and uncommitteds relative to each of the seventies civil rights proposals, and, these differences stood in the way of having the seventies proposals adopted in the Senate. In theory, there were a number of ways advocates and uncommitteds could have met on common ground, such as the commonly used quid pro quo approaches: "you vote with me now and in return I'll vote with you later," or "you vote with me now and in return you will be rewarded later." However, race continued to be a major partisan issue during the seventies. As explained above, given the extensive amount of attention accorded by each party to racial issues during the seventies, Republicans' and Democrats' views on race took on greater political meaning than did their differences on most other issues. The practical result of this was that whatever benefits inhered in the traditional quid pro quo approaches were offset by the costs associated with defecting from one's political principles for political gain. In effect, the politics of race during the seventies had restricted the "barginability" of racial legislative proposals of this time period.

Moderates conditioned their support of final passage of the seventies bills on the inclusion of changes they deemed necessary. It was clear many would not support invoking cloture on the 1970 bill without the revisions they sought. The timing of the cloture announcement is telling. Not until after the major differences between supporters and moderates were resolved and a final agreement was formulated did the leadership actively seek cloture. Immediately after the policy negotiations were concluded, Mansfield indicated on March 12, 1970, he would seek cloture.[41] And, in 1972, Dominick, who spoke for several uncommitteds, remarked: "I must confess in all candor, that if we do not adopt an amendment substantially similar to the one I have here, we will not get a bill out at all.[42] He added, "I remain firm in my resolve not to desert 45 of my colleagues who faithfully supported the court enforcement procedure and not to compromise my principles concerning the superiority of the court enforcement."[43]

The 1975 civil rights debate is the only seventies proceeding in which moderates did not insist upon policy concessions in return for their votes. In a July 21 letter to Mansfield, President Gerald Ford indicated his support for "broadening the Act" so as "to expand the protection of the Act to all citizens,"[44] but stressed he wanted the Senate "to move promptly—first, to assure that the temporary provisions of the Voting Rights Act do not lapse."[45] Later, in a July 24 conversation with Minority Leader Scott, President Ford reportedly advised Scott to drop the nationalization provision because he did not want to jeopardize the bill's passage by insisting on its inclusion."[46] However, as will be explained shortly, moderates' acceptance of the bill in its original proposal form was, arguably, of little meaning as far as its actual impact is concerned.

Civil Rights Policy Concessions and Provisions of the Transition Years

In the end, huge policy concessions were made to accommodate moderates' main concerns and to secure passage of the 1970 bill and also the 1972 bill. Specifically, the 1970 voting rights policy compromises addressed moderates' views regarding national coverage, the base year of the coverage formula, and the method for lowering the voting age. An amendment changing the base year of the trigger formula in Sections 4 and 5 from 1964 to 1968 was adopted in a 50 to 37 vote on March 10, 1970. Also, the lower voting age provision was adopted on March 11, 1970, by a 64 to 17 vote after it was modified in an 84 to 7 vote so that the prohibition would apply "except as required by the Constitution."[47] Finally, a provision partly nationalizing the bill so that it banned the use of literacy tests in all states was included in the final compromise package adopted in a 51 to 22 vote on March 13, 1970.

In its final form, the Voting Rights Act of 1970 comprised three titles. Title I switched the base year of the trigger formula in the 1965 voting rights act from 1964 to 1968, and it also extended for an additional five years the prohibition on the use of tests and devices in certain states caught under the trigger formula. Title II prohibited in all states the use of literacy tests for federal, state, and local elections, until August 6, 1975. Finally, Title III established eighteen as the voting age in all states in all elections "except as required by the Constitution," effective January 1, 1971.

The 1972 civil rights proposal was also revised in line with Republican preferences. The final compromise agreement essentially incorporated the provisions of Dominick's amendment and was finalized in a series of steps. The first two votes on Dominick's amendment failed, the first in a 41 to 31 roll call vote on January 24, and the second in a 46 to 48 vote on January 26. But, on February 15, 1972, the amendment was adopted in a 45 to 39 vote. It provided for the EEOC to bring suit in federal court to enforce equal job opportunity and for the court to, in turn, make a finding of discrimination and implement the appropriate remedies.

As enacted into law, the Equal Employment Opportunity Act of 1972 contained thirteen sections. Seven are key. The first of these, Section 2, amended Section 701 of the 1964 act by extending coverage of the act to business and labor organizations with fifteen or more employees or members, to state and local government employees, and to employees of educational institutions, but it exempted religious institutions. Originally, the 1964 bill applied to employers with twenty-five or more employees and did not cover educational institutions, including religious schools; private clubs; or federal, state, or local government. Section 4 of the act amended Section 706 of the 1964 act by authorizing the EEOC's general counsel to bring civil suit in federal court against an employer found to have discriminated and with whom the EEOC had failed to secure a conciliation agreement, provided sixty days had elapsed after state proceedings would have begun in states that had Fair Employment Practice (FEP) laws. Section 4 also authorized courts to order employers to halt discriminatory practices and to institute corrective action, including affirmative action. Section 5 amended Section 707 of the 1964 act by transferring the authority to sue employers engaged in a pattern or practice of discrimination to the EEOC from the Department of Justice. Section 8, which amended Section 705 of the 1964 act, established an independent counsel to handle EEOC prosecutions. Section 10 established the Equal Employment Opportunity Coordinating Council to coordinate and implement all federal fair employment efforts. Section 11 banned the federal government from discriminating and authorized the Civil Service Commission to carry out this mandate. Finally, Section 13 provided that no government contract could be suspended under the bill without a full hearing, provided the employer had not substantially deviated from an equal opportunity program that had already been approved by the federal government.

Because moderates' support for cloture in 1975 was not conditioned on changes being made to the 1970 voting rights proposal, there were no compromises adopted during the proceedings to appease them. Only one minor change was made to the bill, and its approval came only after supporters in the Senate were assured by House leaders that the amendment would not delay House concurrence with the Senate bill. That amendment was unrelated to moderates' preference for nationalization. Submitted by Senator

Robert Byrd, the amendment reduced the bill's extension from ten years to seven years. It was considered toward the very end of the debate and adopted in a 52 to 42 roll call vote on July 23, 1975. In actuality, nonetheless, the more important policy concessions were already built into the original 1970 proposal. Advocates had essentially capitulated even before the proposal was taken up at the floor. Switching the base year of Sections 4 and 5, a subject of considerable controversy in 1970, was proposed and adopted in 1975 without much ado. In effect, the original proposal was itself a major policy concession.

As enacted, the Voting Rights Act of 1975 comprised three titles. Title I made permanent the national ban on the use of literacy tests (the 1970 bill had established 1975 as the deadline for application of the national ban). Title II switched the base year of the coverage formula in Sections 4 and 5 from 1968 to 1972. Title III prohibited discrimination against language minorities and required bilingual election materials, such as voting notices, instructions, ballots, and assistance, where more than 5 percent of the voting age population was a language minority. It also established completion of the fifth grade as evidence of literacy for language minorities.

The Impact of the Seventies Civil Rights Laws

What were the real-life consequences of the seventies legislation and, in particular, the revisions made to accommodate uncommitteds' conservative policy views? Once again, they were significant in a way that was hurtful to the bills' effectiveness. The impact of the 1970 compromises was, as advocates had feared, to stretch the enforcement resources under the bill. The switch in the base year from 1964 to 1968 brought more states under the bill than were covered under the 1965 bill. Now the states covered under Sections 4 and 5 included several states in the South, namely, Alabama, Georgia, Louisiana, Mississippi, South Carolina, Virginia, and North Carolina as well as districts and/or counties in Alaska, Arizona, California, Idaho, New York, and Oregon. Some of these non-southern states' lower voter turnout in 1968 was not indicative of a history of deliberate disenfranchisement, as was the case for the southern states, but was instead the result of other factors. Thus, the bill's resources were now being expended in areas where they were not especially needful and, therefore were less available in those areas where they were. As for the language regarding the lower voting age, it ultimately proved inconsequential as the Twenty-sixth Amendment to the Constitution, adopted in 1971, lowered the voting age to eighteen in all federal, state, and local elections.[48] Finally, the national ban on literacy tests did have some positive benefits as it promoted the political participation of many racial and language minorities who were previously excluded from electoral participation as a result of the literacy tests.

The real life consequences of the 1972 compromise were especially significant. The choice of court enforcement virtually ensured that complaints of discrimination would not be expeditiously handled, nor for that matter redressed. A series of federal government studies by the U.S. Commission on Civil Rights, published intermittently during the seventies and eighties, revealed a serious backlog in federal employment discrimination cases as well as a host of problems arising from coordination of the federal government's legal activities under the bill across several agencies. Finally, the practical importance of the one policy change adopted during the 1975 proceedings was relatively minor. At most the amendment extending the bill for seven years, rather than ten, simply left advocates three fewer years during which to re-extend the bill if it became necessary. Thus, efforts would have to begin anew in 1982 rather than in 1985.

CHAPTER SUMMARY

On the whole, achievement of even the modest civil rights policy goals of the seventies was inhibited by the enduring conflict surrounding race. Advocates' attempts to improve upon the sixties landmark legislation in ways that would better ensure real-life reform were hampered by the fact that (1) their efforts continued to encounter intense opposition from southern legislators and (2) their success in winning enough votes to defeat the opposition hinged upon abandoning the very goals they sought to achieve. It is true that the politics of race began to change in critical ways, primarily in ways that detracted from the South's political stake in race reform and, therefore, from the regional cleavages underlying racial politics. At the same time, however, vestiges of the region's anti–civil rights stance were still in place, and partisan dissension pertaining to race intensified.

With these critical features of racial politics still in place, the parliamentary aspects of congressional civil rights legislating remained distinctively abnormal. Admittedly, civil rights process departed from the norm to a lesser degree than it had in previous years; nonetheless, it still did not compare to the Senate's standard legislative process. Relatedly, with race remaining a heated political issue, and now even more so in the party system, the price of winning indispensable moderate votes and, thus, of passing civil rights legislation remained that of sacrificing the heart of the legislation.

5

The Contemporary Politics
of Racial Policymaking

The substance of contemporary racial politics is very different from that of years past. The most fundamental change in racial politics that has occurred since the seventies is the disappearance of regional divisions relative to race. At the same time that the regional division concerning race has vanished, something quite different has occurred as far as the party system is concerned. Here the cleavage has deepened. More specifically, in previous decades Republicans had begun to take a more proactive conservative racial stance by actively pushing for alternative policies more in line with their preferences. Recently, they have gone beyond reactionary measures. Instead, they have undertaken initiatives to reduce the federal government's overall civil rights laws and have vigorously pursued dismantling of affirmative action in particular. Republican control of the presidency for much of the eighties, along with control of both houses of Congress as of 1995, brings into clearer view both the increased polarization of parties around race and the continued prominence of race within national American politics.

What remains as an essential characteristic of racial politics, moreover, is its contentiousness. As a consequence, the procedural and policy outcomes engendered by the "new" politics of race mirror in important ways those wrought by the historical politics of race. Specifically, the effect of existing racial dissonance upon the bargainability of the eighties and nineties race-related legislative proposals is largely the same as that of previous decades. All that has really changed in this regard is the openness of civil rights proceedings and negotiations, so that much of it now occurs outside of public view. Behind the scenes, partisan racial conflict continues to significantly inhibit the bargainability of race. Supporters still meet little success in warding off active intense opposition, which continues to drive the now traditional procedural obstruction of civil rights proposals. In addition to congressional obstruction, and new to the post-seventies civil rights efforts, is another factor. The conflict inherent in racial politics has led to a form of presidential obstruction. In addition to intra-congressional obstructions, supporters have encountered vetoes and veto threats, primarily from the Reagan and Bush administrations. The end result is that, well past the sixties and seventies, advocates still have to bow to moderates in order to secure enactment of civil rights legislation. In essence, given advocates' continued limited success in negotiations with opponents and uncommitteds, the procedural and policy outcomes of recent civil rights proceedings are much the same as those of previous decades—only with much less fanfare.

The contemporary policy aims of civil rights proponents are quite distinguishable from those of the sixties and, to a lesser extent, those of the seventies as well. Whereas the proposals pushed during previous decades sought to establish new legislative prohibitions and requirements in the civil rights field, recent proposals are not designed to expand rights, but, instead, to preserve them. They are, primarily, attempts to restore and maintain rights secured during the sixties proceedings. More specifically, the laws enacted during the eighties and nineties constitute either extensions of earlier laws or legislative reversals of Supreme Court decisions that restricted the application of earlier laws. Despite their fairly nominal objectives even at the outset, these bills too are weakened by policy concessions forced by procedural obstructions.

The discussion in this chapter shows how the interplay between contemporary racial politics and institutional structure yields essentially the same processes and policies that are often mistakingly looked upon as sixties phenomena. The first part presents a portrait of how the politics of race have evolved through the nineties. The second part describes the procedural fallout in the Senate engendered by the "new" politics of race. And, the last section discusses the nature of laws that have emerged from recent congressional civil rights proceedings.

THE CONTEMPORARY POLITICS OF RACE

A fundamental change in the conceptualization of the race problem since the seventies has altered the dominant features of racial politics. Until the eighties, the race problem had been viewed and discussed in terms closely tied to racial discrimination; and, while this remains the case, the "race problem" is no longer a purely racial problem. What does this mean in concrete terms? First, the race problem has become partly a class problem. The importance of socioeconomic class variables and conflict are more recently perceived as inextricably linked and relevant to the race problem.[1] Second, the race problem has been reformulated as a problem of diversity, one to which more than just racial and ethnic groups can lay claim. The policy concerns of developmentally disabled persons, the elderly, and gay rights groups as well as women are in recent years consistently included under the rubric of civil rights issues. Third, partly because of the confluence of race and class and also because of the expansion of the ideological and political boundaries of civil rights issues, the contemporary race problem is a problem of national proportions, that is, one that the country as a whole confronts. Together, all of these things mean, at the very least, that the regional division that had previously dominated racial politics no longer pervades.

Yet another outcome of the reformulation of the race problem is the Republican and Democratic parties' departure from what little common ground had existed between them after the sixties. Whereas in the past both parties were at least in agreement concerning the basic goal of civil rights advocacy, more recently they sharply disagree not only on the question of how best to grapple with the race problem, but even on the question of what the goal of civil rights reform ought to be. The manifestation of extreme poverty in black and Hispanic communities, along with striking disparities in employment and education have shifted the bulk of party discourse to these subject areas. Democrats actively support racial preferential policies in these areas, both because they ascribe to the belief that socioeconomic equality along racial lines is a necessary and proper goal of government and because they see racial preferential programs as one means of achieving that goal. Republicans, in contrast, are less supportive of the cause of socioeconomic equality from a governmental perspective and vehemently oppose preferential policies. Though not opposed to the goal of race reform, its achievement is not a more pressing governmental policy priority of Republicans, than is preventing reverse discrimination.

Underlying each of these phenomena, both the disappearance of regional racial demarcations and the intensification of partisan racial division, is the continued salience of race. On the one hand, the "Negro phobia" that had pervaded southern politics in the past has become little more than a keepsake item that is confined largely to displays of the Confederate flag. The more critical features of southern politics are no longer defined in racial terms. Within the party system, on the other hand, Republican opposition to affirmative action has become a rallying ground for its leadership and its rank and file. The modern Republican party has placed a high political premium on its stance on affirmative action, while at the same time decrying Democrats' endorsement of the same as a fundamental point of separation between the two.

The discussion to follow explores in more detail the unfolding of racial politics in the South, beyond the South, and within the party system during the eighties and nineties.

Table 5.1
Black Elected Officials in the South and Non-South, 1997

	Number	Percentage
South*	5456	63
Non-South	3200	37
Total	8656	100

*"South" includes the eleven former Confederate states.

Source: Calculated from Table 2 at p. 9 in Bositis (1997)

Regional Division

As alluded to above, most notably absent from present-day manifestations of racial division in American politics is the regional separation that, until the close of the seventies, had distinguished the South from the rest of the country on the race matter. Indeed the passing of the Old South's intransigence to race reform marks a critical juncture in the evolution of civil rights politics in America. The South has shed its historic reputation of repression and mistreatment of blacks. Though not entirely purged of high-publicity incidents of discrimination, most of the egregious acts of discrimination against minorities in the South are isolated and are not part of the larger pattern that was reflective of a more general regional stance on the issue in the past. Evidence of this is the fact that contemporary black political clout in the United States is arguably greater in the South than in any other region of the country (and certainly greater than at any other point in the region's post-Reconstruction history). Even Alabama Governor George Wallace, who in 1963 declared "segregation now, segregation tomorrow, segregation forever," appointed in January 1993 two blacks to key cabinet posts in his administration. In addition four black legislators were appointed committee chairmen in the state's legislature. National civil rights advocate, Jesse Jackson, by invitation, became the first black since Reconstruction to address a joint session of the Alabama state legislature.

The majority of black elected officials (BEOs) in the United States currently hold office in southern jurisdictions. Of the country's 5,160 BEOs in office during 1982, fully 50 percent were elected to posts in the eleven-state South; and, again in 1990, an even larger percentage held office in the South, with 59 percent of the country's 7,335 BEOs occupying offices in the region.[2] The current breakdown of BEOs is shown in Table 5.1. The South is, in many respects, the primary locus of black "power" in electoral politics, even though it is no longer the primary locus of the U.S. black population.

Table 5.2
Estimated Black Voter Registration Rate in Eleven Southern States, 1980–1990,
Selected Years (in percentages)

	1980	1982	1986	1988	1990
Alabama	62.2	57.7	75.4	68.4	65.3
Arkansas	62.6	63.3	62.5	68.0	50.8
Florida	58.2	50.3	61.3	57.7	53.3
Georgia	59.8	51.9	55.3	56.8	57.0
Louisiana	69.0	68.5	71.9	77.1	72.0
Mississippi	72.2	75.8	75.9	74.2	71.4
N. Carolina	49.2	43.6	57.1	58.2	60.1
S. Carolina	61.4	53.3	58.8	56.7	61.9
Tennessee	69.4	67.1	73.0	74.0	68.5
Texas	56.4	43.2	66.0	64.2	60.0
Virginia	49.7	53.6	66.5	63.8	58.1

Source: Compiled by author. See Appendix D for details on sources and figures.

Another bit of empirical evidence demonstrating the blurring of regional lines relative to race is that existing racial disparities are most prevalent in non-southern states—that is, it is in areas outside the South where blacks and whites are most unequal. Specifically, current trends in voter registration, education, income, and housing all suggest a shift in the locus of the race problem. As indicated in Table 5.2, since 1980, black voter participation has witnessed almost continuous improvement in every state in the deep South. Between 1980 and 1990, southern black rates have climbed from 55.8 to 61.1, on average.

In fact, while gains in southern black rates have been substantial, those of every other group have fallen (see Table 5.3). Between 1980 and 1990, southern white rates fell from 72.4 percent to 62.6 percent. Those of blacks outside the South have fallen by 6.9 percentage points and those of whites outside the South by 2.8 percentage points. Currently, the gap between white and black registration is smallest in the South.

Besides voting, disparities in other policy areas are also greatest outside the South. For example, blacks have reached a level of educational attainment that closely resembles that of southern whites. Whereas in 1970, southern whites had completed 11.2 years of school compared to southern blacks' 8.53 years, by 1980, as indicated in Table 5.4, the education gap between the two groups had shrunk from 2.69 to 1.59 years. As of 1980,

Table 5.3
Estimated Voter Registration Rate by Race for South and Non-South, 1980 and 1990 (in percentages)

	1980			1990		
	Black	White	Gap	Black	White	Gap
South	55.8	72.4	16.6	61.1	62.6	1.5
Non-South	63.6	67.0	3.4	56.7	64.2	7.5

Source: Compiled by author. See Appendix D on voting data for details on source and figures.

the gap between the two groups in the South, moreover, was not far from that in the non-South, as whites outside the South exceeded blacks by 1.01 years of school. This means that, with respect to equal educational opportunity as of 1980, the South and the non-South differed by just one-half of a school year.

The problem of segregation that had plagued southern politics for years has also shifted. But, where the South had legally mandated segregated schools, in schools outside the South, segregation formed without the aid of law. By 1995, as shown in Table 5.5, de facto school desegregation is primarily a phenomenon of the non-South. On the list of the top ten most segregated city school systems there are only two in southern states. The most segregated schools exist outside the South.

Another measure of socioeconomic status, income, also indicates that the South had made notable improvement by the seventies, even though it continued to lag behind the North. Shown in Table 5.6 are data on the median family income for both races. It shows the gap between black and white families in the South closed between 1953 and 1980, while that outside the South actually widened. This suggests the South has moved increasingly toward racial parity as areas outside the South have regressed. Further and, most importantly, by 1980, with regard to income, regional distinctions have become relatively insignificant as the black-white income ratio in the South is quite similar to that outside the South.

The contemporary housing opportunities available to southern blacks are comparable to that of other groups, as shown in Table 5.7. Blacks in the South are still more likely than other groups to live in houses without complete plumbing, but the overall proportion has dwindled substantially since 1960. Also, southern blacks are still more likely to live in "newer" homes than their northern counterparts. Another measure, the monetary value of housing, indicates that the South has, at the very least, approached a level of equality comparable to that of other regions. In the South, the value of black homes was roughly 59 percent of white homes, which was nearly equal to the 0.58 black-white ratio in the North Central region and not very far behind the 0.63 ratio of the Northeast.

Table 5.4
Level of Education: Mean Years of School of Male Wage Earners Ages 25–64 by Race and Region, 1970 and 1980

Year	Southern* Whites	Southern Blacks**	Difference	Northern Whites	Northern Blacks	Difference
1970	11.22	8.53	2.69	11.80	10.20	1.60
1980	12.48	10.89	1.59	12.92	11.91	1.01

*Here the South includes the eleven former Confederate states as well as Delaware, Washington, D.C., Kentucky, Maryland, Oklahoma, and West Virginia; the North includes all other states. The source used here does not indicate this, however. Its primary source is the 1940–1980 Census of the Population, which in previous years configured the South to include these fifteen states.
**"Black" refers to non-white.

Source: Horton and Smith (1991)

Beyond statistical trends, yet another indication of the explicitly nonregional dimensions of race is the manner in which civil rights issues have been advocated. In essence, they are advocated in a "regionally neutral fashion," very much unlike years past. In fact, advocacy of race reform has changed in several respects. First, protest politics is much less common and what little "movement" activity has occurred since the seventies is no longer southern-bound. The "movement" activity during the eighties consisted of scattered, reactionary demonstrations that occurred on a much smaller scale than those of the sixties. There were only a dozen or so demonstrations that involved a sizeable number of participants and commanded some national attention, and only a few of these were guided by a grand vision or purpose. Most importantly, almost none were designed to draw attention specifically to the South or the plight of blacks living there. Rather than discrimination in the South, the bulk of the few eighties demonstrations that did take place had a transregional focus.

Significantly, the bulk of modern-day civil rights advocacy closely resembles traditional forms of political activism. Much of it revolves around voting and campaigning. These contemporary forms of black political participation, too, are devoid of a specifically southern focus. Katherine Tate's *From Protest to Politics*[3] examines the extent to which various elements of the sixties black protest movement have been subsumed into the new electoral-centered black politics. We can glean from her detailed analysis that the new black politics have emerged, in essence, with a broader, national focus. Jesse Jackson's presidential campaigns is one case in point. Tate describes Jackson the presidential candidate as a "Black American championing minority causes" and intimates that the majority of the main policy issues addressed by Jackson's campaigns were unrelated to any "regional" concerns. Instead, they

Table 5.5
School Segregation: Percentage of Black Students Attending White-Majority Schools in "Most Segregated" States, 1995

State	% Blacks in White Schools
New York	15
California	20
Illinois	20
Michigan	20
Mississippi	26
New Jersey	27
Maryland	28
Wisconsin	30
Pennsylvania	31
Louisiana	32

Source: Smith and Horton (1997)

had to do with the Democratic party's nominating procedures, anti-apartheidism, D.C. statehood, and increased set-asides for minority contractors. Tate notes further that the one issue that did have regional implications, namely, ten southern states' use of the run-off primary, had little political meaning for most blacks, and, by 1988, it had lost so much of its usefulness to the Jackson campaign as well that it was abandoned.

Wholly aside from the contemporary evolution of racial politics, the fact is that black politics now face a much more formidable enemy than the southern enemy of the past. Indeed, the new challenge confronting "mainstream" black politics is that of identifying a discriminatory target of any kind, be it the South or otherwise. The source(s) of the inequities civil rights advocates had sought for decades to eliminate have proven to be more elusive than ever before. In the past, it was believed, first, that full black political participation would, in turn, facilitate a more equal footing in other areas, such as education, housing, employment, and so forth. Consequently, securing the franchise for blacks in the South, where they were represented in large numbers, was regarded as a key step in that direction. In addition to voting rights laws, the passage of laws making it illegal to discriminate on the basis of race in education, housing, and employment was also considered necessary for ensuring full inclusion. But, by the eighties, blacks had made notable strides relative to electoral participation in the South and beyond. Yet, the racial socioeconomic status quo wherein blacks continue to

Table 5.6
Income: Median Family Income by Race for South and Non-South, 1953–1980, Selected Years

	South*	Non-South
	Black-White Ratio**	Black-White Ratio
1953	.49	.75
1959	.39	.71
1964	.49	.70
1969	.57	.73
1974	.56	.67
1980	.60	.66

*"South" includes the eleven former Confederate states and also Delaware, Washington, D.C., Kentucky, Maryland, Oklahoma, and West Virginia.
**"Black" refers to non-whites for years 1953–1974.

Source: Derived from U.S. Bureau of the Census, *Social and Economic Status* (1979), and the *Census of the Population 1980*.

be at a disadvantage remains very much intact not only in the South but more evidently in the rest of the country as well. This circumstance has left advocates in the position of having to discern the more deeply entrenched, underlying causes of racial inequality that do not manifest themselves as vividly as the "colored only" and "white only" segregation signs of the past.

Another development with which contemporary civil rights advocates must contend is the diffusion of race reform advocacy into the fray of marginalized issues. The racial component of contemporary civil rights legislative efforts competes even more so with other social, politically marginalized, nonracial interests. The political importance of the policy demands of other previously excluded groups, such as women, the handicapped, and gays, following the sixties, has grown. Racial disadvantage has come to be perceived as one among many types of sociopolitical disadvantages. As a result, although in many respects the legislative reaction to civil rights policies is tied to racial predispositions, within the larger political arena, civil rights is no longer a matter of black and white, but one of disadvantage. The modern civil rights discourse addresses the concerns of racial and ethnic minorities as well as those of other marginalized groups.

Complicating still further contemporary civil rights advocacy efforts is the fact that by 1976 the majority of Americans had come to believe that blacks had made substantial progress and were growing impatient with demands for still further governmental intervention on their behalf. The results of a National Election Studies survey series, shown in Table 5.8, asking respon-

Table 5.7
Housing: Newer, Not "Sound," and Value (Owner-Occupied Units) by Race and Region, 1980

	South		Northeast		Midwest		West	
	Black	**White**	**Black**	**White**	**Black**	**White**	**Black**	**White**
Newer*	26%	35%	7%	16%	7%	22%	16%	34%
Not Sound**	6%	1%	1%	1%	1%	1%	.3%	.5%
Median Value	$25,100	$42,400	$30,300	$47,900	$26,100	$44,800	$57,000	$72,000
Ratio	.59		.63		.58		.79	

*"Newer" refers to those homes built between 1970 and 1980.
**"Not Sound" refers to homes without complete plumbing.

Source: Derived from Table J-31 at p. 1–633 of U.S. Bureau of the Census, *Census of Housing 1980.*

dents whether they believe "a lot of real change had taken place in the position of black people in the past few years," reveals that by the seventies, a majority of whites and southern blacks were satisfied that a *lot* had been done on behalf of blacks and an overwhelming proportion believed that *enough* had been done. Furthermore, and finally, to the extent that there is some consensus that a problem does exist, it is not necessarily regarded as a race problem. The discourse concerning race is increasingly attentive to the class dimensions of the race problem. Rather than their race, blacks and other minorities are now considered to suffer primarily from their class standing. The limited education and training background and also the limited employment skills of inner-city blacks in particular are regarded as critical determinants of the existing racial disparities that civil rights advocacy seeks to redress. The *Kerner Commission Report* of 1968 had labeled the race problem as a matter of black and white. The twenty-year follow-up to this report, *Quiet Riots* (1988), however, emphasized the significance of poverty. And, the 1998 Advisory Board report, stemming from President Clinton's Race Initiative launched in 1997, noted the continuation of large racial disparities due partly to active racial discrimination, but emphasized also the critical "role of education in helping to overcome racial disparities."

Partisan Division

Just as the passing of the Old South marks a critical juncture in the historical and contemporary evolution of civil rights politics, so too does the

Table 5.8
Perceptions of Black Progress: Percentage Believing a Lot of Change Has Taken Place in the Position of Blacks, 1970–1976, Selected Years

	1970	1972	1976
Non-Southern Whites	54	55	61
Southern Whites	58	64	73
Non-Southern Blacks	30	33	23
Southern Blacks	53	53	41

Source: Compiled by the author. See Appendix C on survey data for details.

party system's realignment around race at the start of the eighties. But, here we see not only a deepening, but also the emergence, of diametrically opposed civil rights strategies. The redefinition of race reform so that it more explicitly encompasses socioeconomic reform has significantly altered the partisan politics relative to race, so that affirmative action has become much more important to both parties. It is especially where this item is concerned that the two parties are very sharply divided. Evidence of this is again found in the civil rights stances of Republican and Democratic presidential candidates and administrations. In examining specifically the racial ideologies and policy stances of the Reagan, Bush, and Clinton administrations, as well as the candidacies of Dukakis and Mondale, we find even greater incongruity between the Republican and Democratic parties on the race issue.

Starting in the eighties, Republicans signaled an aggressive retreat that was pitched generally as a push for de-regulation and evolution, but one that had special ramifications for racial policies. Republicans essentially combined a traditional conservatism relative to government intervention with a strong opposition to civil rights governmental activism in particular. The Reagan administration best exemplified the party's shift to the far right on race. Reagan's civil rights rhetoric and policies came out of a long, entrenched history of anti–civil rights politics. He opposed the federal civil rights acts of 1964, 1965, and 1968.[4] As governor of California, he signed legislation prohibiting busing. In a debate with Jimmy Carter during the 1980 presidential campaign, he expressed his belief that the role of the president in the area of race relations should be primarily that of a "bully pulpit," and that the federal government should defer to local governments, rather than actively involve itself in many civil rights issues.[5]

The philosophy embraced during his presidency by Reagan and his appointees, as one writer notes, represented "a clean ideological break with the recent party, not only from the Democratic appointments of Jimmy Carter and Lyndon Johnson, but in some cases from the Republicans installed by Ford and Richard Nixon."[6] Especially on affirmative action, the Reagan administration reflected a willingness to depart from the approach of previous Republican and Democratic administrations. Reagan's assistant attorney general for civil rights, William Bradford Reynolds, remarked: "We [in the Civil Rights Division (CRD)] will no longer insist upon or in any respect support the use of quotas or any statistical formula designed to protect non-victims of discrimination or give them preferential treatment based on race."[7] Reagan's Secretary of Education, Terrence Bell, believed that "in exercising [its equal education] role, the federal government should assume a cooperative rather than a coercive posture"[8] and actively sought congressional endorsement of what he termed his "efforts to decrease the undue harassment of schools."[9] In addressing criticism against the administration "for not enforcing civil rights laws and regulations," he explained: "[It] seems that we have some laws that we should not have, and my obligation to enforce them is against my own philosophy."[10]

The administration's activity in the overall field of civil rights too reveals a shift.[11] A sharp drop occurred in the number of cases litigated by the CRD, so that whereas under Carter, a total of twenty-nine prison inmate cases were litigated in 1980, during 1981, under Reagan, none were. The number of school desegregation cases litigated also dropped under Reagan to ten in 1981, down from twenty-two in 1980. Housing litigation by the CRD as well was slowed.[12] Prior to Reagan an average of thirty fair housing suits a year were filed, whereas in 1981 none were filed and in 1983 only two were filed. Out of a total of twenty-five cases recommended to the Justice Department by HUD for court action, only two were actually filed. In numerous other cases that had been initiated by the Justice Department under Carter, the Reagan administration actually switched sides, aligning itself with the defendants against whom charges of discrimination had been originally made. Also, in January 1982, the Reagan administration announced it was reversing a twelve-year IRS policy that denied tax exemptions to schools that discriminated on the basis of race. Lastly, over a 123-year history, he was the first president ever to veto a civil rights bill adopted by Congress.

Although data on voting rights enforcement under the Reagan administration, according to authors Charles Bullock and Katherine Butler, "do not consistently put the Reagan administration in a poor light," on balance, Reagan was widely perceived as anti–civil rights.[13] In a 1983 report the Commission on Civil Rights stated: "There is a widespread perception that the Federal Government is relaxing its enforcement posture in the area of civil rights."[14] Jack Greenberg of the NAACP Legal Defense and Educational Fund, also a critical player in civil rights advocacy, was much more direct: "The political appointees in the Reagan Justice Department are engaged in a concerted effort to sabotage the gains made since 1954 by minorities and women pursuant to congressional mandate, Supreme Court decisions and established legal principles."[15]

The Bush administration continued with much the same conservative retreat as that initiated by the Reagan administration, although with less antagonistic rhetoric. The basic goal of scaling back administrative enforcement of racial policies was embraced by Bush, just as it had been by Reagan. And, like Reagan, Bush's pre-presidential political career was punctuated with racially conservative overtones. His opposition to the Civil Rights Act of 1964 was a centerpiece of his campaign strategy to win a Texas Senate seat in 1964. He argued minorities' rights should not be guaranteed by law, but should be gradually won through moral persuasion.[16] He said also that the 1964 act was passed to protect 14 percent of the people, but that he was also worried about the other 86 percent, promising to "develop attractive job opportunities both for our growing population and for those displaced from . . . jobs by the new Civil Rights Act."[17]

The Bush presidency was solidly behind the Reagan-initiated policy of regression. Bush's Department of Education announced in early 1990 new policy guidelines that would prevent schools receiving federal funds from earmarking those funds for minority scholarships,[18] and although later withdrawn, their introduction served as a clear indication of where the administration stood. In October 1990, Bush vetoed the Civil Rights Restoration Act of 1990, which he characterized as a "quota bill," although many civil rights advocates deemed it critical for reversing a series of Supreme Court decisions restricting minority rights. During the same year Bush supported long-time civil rights opponent Jesse Helms in his bid for re-election to the Senate, despite evidence out of the U.S. Justice Department that Helms' campaign was engaged in intimidation of black voters.[19] Authors Lucius Barker and Mack Jones conclude that "by its actions the Bush administration had shown little concern or sensitivity toward blacks and minorities."[20]

Juxtaposed to the sharp turn to the right within the Republican party during the eighties and nineties was a move toward the center within the Democratic party where race is concerned. Each of the Democratic nominees during the 1984 and 1988 presidential campaigns espoused a fairly liberal ideological stance relative to race. However, much of their rhetoric suggests racial issues were a political issue for the Democratic party, but not necessarily a policy issue. Both Walter Mondale in 1984 and Michael Dukakis in 1988 discussed the relevance of race in presidential politics, but stopped short of advocating civil rights policies or any concrete action(s) in the field. In fact, neither of these candidates addressed the race issue squarely, but instead conveyed hints of its importance. In his acceptance speech, Mondale described the Democratic party as a "mirror of America," including persons from various socioeconomic and racial and ethnic backgrounds and stated that Americans who voted for Reagan did not "vote to trash the civil rights laws." Beyond this, however, there was little in the way of a policy statement—even as he promised support of the Equal Rights Amendment.

The same is true of the Dukakis candidacy. Much of Dukakis's civil rights campaign strategy centered not around the substance of the issue, but rather its politics. Jesse Jackson, who had achieved a measure of clout in the party in the wake of his 1984 and 1988 presidential bids, was mentioned repeatedly throughout Dukakis's acceptance speech. This suggests an attempt to appeal to the black vote, but not by way of specific policy pledges. A similar approach was used relative to the Hispanic vote. Dukakis was the first major party presidential nominee to invoke the Spanish language during an acceptance speech. Still, his remarks on this score as well did not translate into a call for reform. Together, both Mondale and Dukakis embraced an ideology of inclusion, but not progressivism.

The Clinton administration too signaled development of a more moderate racial liberalism on the Democratic side, but went beyond Mondale and Dukakis's pro–civil rights rhetoric. Clinton's emphasis on the use of universal, urban policies rather than explicitly race-conscious policies as a means of redressing racial inequality are a indication of this. In his 1992 acceptance speech at the Democratic National Convention, Clinton invoked the following platform statement: "The most important . . . minority policy . . . America can have is an expanding entrepreneurial economy of high-wage, high-skill jobs."[21] Also, his failure during two terms in office to request comprehensive civil rights legislation from Congress, as had his Democratic predecessors, is yet another indication of the party's growing moderation. Still, the appointment of blacks and other minorities to high-level cabinet and policy posts, including the appointment of longtime civil rights advocate and Democratic presidential candidate, Jesse Jackson, to an advisory post, reveals the continued importance of race as a political cause of the Democratic party. Finally, Clinton offered a very highly publicized apology to blacks for the system of slavery. Thus, on the whole, it can be argued that Clinton's civil rights stance is at least true in form, if not in substance, to that of earlier Democratic administrations and candidates.

In essence, the increasingly moderate stance of the Democratic party on race bespeaks the party's reorientation on the issue, but it does not connote a convergence within the overall party system. Despite the Democratic move toward center, given the Republican party's significant redirection of civil rights rhetoric and policy, the chasm within the party system has effectively deepened. Race remains a significant point of separation between the two parties.

The most telling indication of at least the perceived dissimilarity between the Democratic and the Republican party on the race issue is the trend in black voting. That blacks vote overwhelming Democratic and have done so fairly consistently since 1968[22] serves as further evidence of the partisan divergence. In 1980, Carter received 85 percent of the black vote, compared to Reagan's 11 percent. In 1984, Mondale received 89 percent of the black vote, compared to Reagan's 9 percent. In 1988, Dukakis won 86 percent of the vote, compared to Bush's 12 percent share. Finally, in both the 1992 and 1996 presidential elections, Clinton lay claim to more than 80 percent of the black vote.

Salience of Race in Contemporary Politics

Precisely how importantly the partisan racial division just described has figured into the larger scheme of contemporary American politics is best seen in the premium each party has placed on its racial ideology. Keeping in mind that party politics are a key indicator of the national salience of race in American politics, party platforms are a useful mechanism through which to gauge racial salience. And, in both parties' national platforms adopted since 1980, race remains a key issue. Specifically, analysis of the 1980 to 1996 platforms demonstrates that race continues to be one of the handful of issues critical in distinguishing the two parties from one another.

Evidence of this is the fact that (1), it was discussed often, and, in some cases throughout the platform(s); and (2), it was discussed in connection with a range of different topics. As far as both parties were concerned, race had a bearing on a wide range of domestic policy issues. References to "race," "blacks," "civil rights," "discrimination," and other like terms are found in a number of sections dealing with a wide range of subjects, from education to housing to business to agriculture. The 1980 platform of the Democratic party either briefly mentioned race or discussed it at length in as many as twenty-two different subsections. Five subsections were either totally or substantially devoted to civil rights, including those entitled "Minority Business," "Economic Inequities Facing Minorities," "Education," "Civil Rights," and "Dr. Martin Luther King, Jr." The Republican 1980 platform referenced or discussed racial issues in only ten different subsections and only one, entitled "Black Americans," was substantially or totally devoted to race. Still, the variety of issues that Republicans connected race to were as wide ranging as those to which Democrats had tied race, namely, education, welfare, neighborhood revitalization, the workplace and workers, training, government reform, and even energy.

In 1984 and also 1988 race was of central importance to both parties as each of their national platforms accorded some spotlight to the subject. The 1984 Democratic platform made reference to civil rights in twenty different subsections. At least four were entirely or substantially concerned specifically with race, including the "Investing in Education," "Small and Minority Business," "The Future if Reagan Is Re-Elected," and "Equal Justice under Law" subsections. Again, the Republican platform offered direct references to race in relatively fewer subsections, specifically nine; but, again, the range of subjects that Republicans believed race had some bearing upon was as extensive as that to which Democrats considered it relevant, including business, housing, health, transportation, education, crime, immigration, individual rights, and family protection. It should be noted that the 1988

Democratic platform was all of seven-and-a-half pages long, compared to a much lengthier, 104-page, Republican party platform. Both 1988 platforms accorded relatively less attention to race as compared to the 1980 and 1984 platforms, and even those of the sixties and seventies as well. Still, in the 1988 Republican platform, racial issues were mentioned or discussed in as many as six subsections. And, of the roughly twenty-six subsections or paragraphs in the 1988 Democratic platform, at least four included some discussion of race.

Finally, the decision of the 1992 and 1996 national Republican and Democratic party conventions, too, was to include race among its priority issues. In each year, both parties' platforms specifically referenced and/or alluded to race throughout the platform and connected it to a wide variety of policy issue areas. The 1992 Democratic platform discussed one or more aspects of the race problem in as many as six different subsections, aside from the "Civil and Equal Rights" subsection, which was devoted entirely to race issues. More specifically, race was mentioned in all three sections dealing with domestic policy issues and problems. In 1996, Democrats noted the importance of observing and/or preserving minority rights in regards to economic growth, the reinvention of government, and what the platform termed the "American community." Just as Democrats placed great importance on race in 1992 and in 1996, so too did the lengthier Republican platforms of these two years. Both platforms, which are similarly worded and organized, alluded to race in as many as six separate subsections, including those focused on homewnership, congressional reform, individual rights, and personal safety.

Beyond party platforms, other developments further demonstrate the contemporary political weight of race. Foremost is the fact that the Republican party has used affirmative action as a virtual litmus test of partisan loyalty and fitness. Republican presidential and congressional candidates and also Republican nominees for federal judge and administrative posts have been gauged for "fitness" by their party's leadership partly on the basis of their views concerning affirmative action. For Republicans, affirmative action is the ultimate betrayal of their party's most basic principles and ideology. It goes against the grain of traditional Republican conservatism relative to administrative government, laissez-faire economics, and individualism. For this reason, it has been at the center of several high profile bouts between, first, a Democratic Congress and Republican presidents and, recently, between a Republican Congress and a Democratic president. Senate confirmation proceedings on the Supreme Court nominations of the Reagan, Bush, and Clinton administrations have hinged partly around the affirmative action controversy. Senators on both sides of the aisle, but especially Republicans, have questioned nominees about their stance on affirmative action. In particular, rejection of Reagan's nomination of Robert Bork, the intense battle over Bush's nomination of Clarence Thomas, and even the strong opposition that was merely foreshadowed in connection with Clinton's nomination of Lani Guinier all demonstrate the pivotal role of affirmative action and, ultimately, of race in contemporary party competition.

CONTEMPORARY CIVIL RIGHTS PROCESS AND PROCEDURES

The new politics of race just described produce the same kinds of abnormal procedural outcomes that were prevalent during the seventies, sixties, and before. This is foremost because of the opposition racial divisiveness creates, which leaves virtually no room in which to bargain. The result is obstruction. On the surface, the formal process of contemporary civil rights lawmaking has begun to approximate the norm, in that there is more frequent use of the normal channels of legislative decisionmaking. However, cloture, the most striking indicator of unconventional lawmaking, remains a strategy of choice for Senate civil rights advocates. And, even though supporters have abandoned the use of certain elements of the sixties and seventies civil rights parliamentary strategy, changes that have occurred within the overall congressional context have yielded particularly problematic procedural and political consequences for civil rights legislative efforts.

What follows is an in-depth discussion of the procedures used to enact current civil rights laws. It begins with an overview of the more recent opposition coalition's makeup and strategy that have prompted use of nonconventional routes.

Contemporary Civil Rights Opposition

Several things are revealed by an analysis of recent civil rights opposition in the Senate. First, it consists of a much smaller coalition than in previous years. Second, it has lost much of its southern base. Many in the small band of senators who have resorted to using the rules in more recent decades are not the typical southerner motivated by a long history of anti–civil rights sentiment. Instead, it is a mostly Republican group of senators who have fought the bills. The group of eight senators actively opposing the 1982 civil rights proposal included Harry Byrd, Jesse Helms, John East, Jeremiah Denton, S. I. "Sam" Hayakawa, Gordon Humphrey, James McClure, and Steven Symms. Neither of the two 1988 housing proceedings confronted obstruction within the Senate. But, the 1991 bill did and this opposition was carried out primarily by the following five senators: Jesse Helms, Daniel Coats, Robert Smith, Steven Symms, and Malcolm Wallop. The 1992 bill was obstructed by the following six senators: Jake Garn, Orrin Hatch, Jesse Helms, Alan Simpson, Steven Symms, and Strom Thurmond.

A total of seven out of eight (or 88%) of the 1982 filibusterers were Republican and all of the 1991 and 1992 filibusterers were. On the one hand, because these numbers represent only 12–15 percent of Senate Republicans, it could be said they do not provide a sufficient basis for conclusively arguing that Republican party ideology alone was the driving force behind the post-seventies obstructionism. On the other hand, however, more than one out of every ten does at least suggest some connection.

One thing that is unmistakably clear about contemporary civil rights obstruction is that it is no longer driven by regional politics. Southerners' contribution has dropped significantly from what it was in earlier decades, so that they represented only 50 percent of the eight-member group obstructing the 1982 bill. The 1991 and 1992 obstructionist coalitions were only 20 percent and 17 percent southern, respectively. These post-seventies numbers are a far cry from the sixties and seventies numbers, wherein southerners had represented the overwhelming majority of obstructionists, with an average of 85 percent of the group drawn from southern states.

The South's twenty-two-member bloc in the Senate has essentially pulled out of the opposing side of civil rights battles. Only 18 percent of the southern contingent contributed to the 1982 opposition effort, while a mere 5 percent did during the 1991 and 1992 debate. In fact, the majority of southern senators have become active supporters, including most of those who had earlier vigorously fought civil rights. Four out of six of the "original" filibusterers still in the Senate in 1982 voted for the voting rights bill. Two out of four voted for the Grove City bill in 1988. Three out of four voted for both the 1988 housing bill and the 1991 Civil Rights Restoration Act. And, Senator Ernest Hollings of South Carolina, the only remaining member of the original filibusterers, also voted for the 1992 bill. Moreover, of the total number of senators representing the eleven-state South, eighteen (82 percent) voted in favor of the 1982 bill and four against. In 1988, of those voting, seventeen (85%) voted for the Grove City bill, and three were against it, while two did not vote. Finally, passage of both the 1988 housing bill and the 1991 bill was endorsed by twenty southerners voting at the floor (95%), opposed by one, and one did not vote. A total of fifteen of the twenty-two (or 68%) southerners voted for the 1992 bill.

Obstruction of Civil Rights Legislative Proposals during the Eighties and Nineties

Procedural obstruction of civil rights proposals during the eighties and nineties debates was considerably scaled down in comparison to that pitted against earlier proposals. Much of opponents' blocking strategy was confined to the consideration stage and centered primarily around refusal to vote, with few other dilatory tactics employed. Republicans' control of the Senate from 1980 to 1986 essentially helped to defray the need to resort to procedural tactics, so that the mostly Republican group of opponents could rely partly on their leadership to stall action. None of the eighties and nineties legislation was blocked in committee, although they were subjected to significant delays due to various other causes. At the consideration stage, all but the 1988 measures were actively blocked by opponents. And, at the final vote stage, only the 1982 bill was subjected to a mild filibuster. Besides refusal to vote, there were no digressions, no grandstands, and no lengthy speeches. Still, there was obstruction.

Routes of Passage during the Eighties and Nineties

Given the continued obstruction of civil rights process, the overall logistics of civil rights policymaking in the Senate have remained relatively more complicated than is the case for most policymaking that occurs in the Senate. The procedures involved in enactment of recent civil rights legislation more closely approximate the norm than did those of earlier decades. Nonetheless, more effort and energy is still poured into securing civil rights bills' passage than is normally the case. Much of the extra effort is invested at the consideration stage. And, cloture, the clearest indication of abnormal policymaking, continues to be an important tool of civil rights strategists. Thus, opponents' rules-based strategy, even if scaled down, continues to yield enormous consequences for civil rights strategists. Moreover, the altered congressional context within which civil rights decisionmaking has unfolded essentially adds to the impact of recent procedural obstruction. Further, presidential vetoes and veto threats are now an added feature of contemporary civil rights obstruction. Let us look in more detail at the nature of the contemporary civil rights legislative process.

Committee Stage

Reliance on unconventional procedures has not been needed to facilitate movement of recent civil rights proposals beyond the committee stage, due to the fact that none of the bills have actually encountered obstruction at this juncture. The 1982 bill and the 1988 Grove City bill proceeded to the floor through normal channels, namely, a voluntary committee vote. However, the direct placement procedure was used to move the 1988 housing bill and also the 1991 and 1992 bills beyond the committee juncture. In these instances, time constraints primarily prompted the use of the procedure, rather than obstruction. The 1988 housing bill manager, Senator Kennedy, was careful to note that the "unusual procedures that were allowed" in bringing the bill to the floor were forced by the tight time frame within which the bill would have to be debated and passed.

The House version of the 1988 bill was placed directly on the calendar on July 7, 1988, when, following a second reading of the bill, Senator Byrd objected to further proceedings. An amended version of the 1991 bill that had originally been considered in Labor and Human Resources was introduced anew at the floor as S. 1745 in September 1991, at which time Senator Wendell Ford obtained unanimous consent to have the bill placed directly on the calendar. In order to meet the August 6, 1992, expiration deadline that loomed over the 1992 proceedings, advocates decided to abandon the Senate version, which would have necessitated House concurrence. The House bill, if adopted by the Senate in its original form, would not. Thus, moving it to the floor "as is" held the promise of timely enactment. Officially received in the Senate on July 28, 1992, the House version of the 1992 voting rights bill (H.R. 4312) was read twice and placed on the calendar.

Consideration Stage

Advocates of the most recent civil rights proposals have been forced to turn to cloture at the consideration stage in at least three of the last five proceedings. Ordinarily, the consideration stage is little more than a brief stopping point; however, this was not so during the 1982, 1991, and 1992 proceedings. Both of the 1988 bills were taken up at the floor by way of unanimous consent. With respect to the 1988 Grove City bill, the leadership's plan to adopt a motion to proceed to the bill, without any debate of the motion itself, was announced in early January 1988 by Majority Leader Robert Byrd. On January 26, 1988, after indicating that an agreement with opponents had been reached, Byrd requested and obtained unanimous consent to take up the bill. On the 1988 housing bill, too, a unanimous consent agreement with opponents was reached on August 1, 1988. It was taken up by unanimous consent on August 2, 1988, also at Byrd's request.

The strategy for taking up the 1982 bill at the floor involved the use of unconventional procedures, many of which were reminiscent of those used in earlier debates. Daily sessions were extended toward the end of the debate, just after Baker warned senators they should "hold onto their hats" because the Senate would remain in session "as late as necessary to make progress on this measure."[23] A limited recess schedule was followed. A strict application of the rules was adhered to by advocates. Kennedy stated he and his group would use the full array of procedures available to them to move the bill along. Something closely resembling a one-track system was imposed as supporter Senator Riegle threatened to "block action on virtually any other items that may come before the Senate." Finally, Stevens and Baker requested that the Senate remain on the act until it was disposed of,[24] upon noting opponent Helms's interest in the balanced budget amendment, which was third in line after the voting rights act.

Cloture was the centerpiece at the outset of advocates' strategy to initiate formal action on the 1982 bill. The same day the motion to proceed was submitted, Minority Leader Robert Byrd inquired how soon a cloture motion would be filed, to which Acting Majority Leader Stevens answered, the following week. Supporters pushed for an early cloture vote. Dole indicated the leadership's time line was too long: "to wait until next Tuesday to file a cloture motion to proceed does not seem to be moving very quickly."[25]

Byrd went further, suggesting that if the leadership did not file a motion for cloture by Monday of the following week, then he would do so himself. A motion for cloture was subsequently submitted by Baker the following Monday morning. The Senate voted overwhelming the next day, 86 to 8, in favor of invoking cloture.

The 1991 strategy of civil rights advocates at the consideration stage also departed from the norm in that it centered almost wholly around cloture. Beyond this, the Senate carried on as usual. Committees met on schedule. Other items on the calendar were disposed of. In fact, all that really occurred during the filibuster was the passage of time. As early as October 7, 1991, a full week before the leadership had planned to take up the civil rights bill, Mitchell coupled a cloture motion with his formal motion to proceed to the bill, but withdrew the motion the next day to accommodate several senators. Again on October 17, 1991, after Mitchell had failed for a third time to get opponents to agree to go to the bill, he submitted a second motion for cloture on a second motion to proceed to the bill. He subsequently withdrew the second motion to proceed, after he had obtained unanimous consent to vote on cloture. The Senate adopted the cloture motion in a 93 to 4 vote on October 22, 1991. Additionally, Majority Leader Mitchell had threatened to force all-night sessions while the Senate was operating under cloture, but later obtained an agreement from opponents that eliminated the need for additional action.

Lastly, a motion to invoke cloture to proceed to the 1992 voting rights bill was submitted by Majority Leader George Mitchell on August 4, 1992. Although the motion was vitiated the next day, after an agreement to vote was reached, its initial pursuit clearly indicates advocates' continued reliance on cloture as a means of facilitating action on civil rights legislation.

Final Vote Stage

The final vote stage of contemporary civil rights proceedings has proven to be relatively less formidable to advocates than that of earlier proceedings. This is primarily because opponents have concentrated their efforts and energies at the consideration stage, trying in essence to preempt a fight at the floor. As a result, much of what normally occurs in Senate legislative decisionmaking once a bill is formally before the floor has applied to recent civil rights proceedings. Advocates have been able to utilize traditional routes once the bills have entered the final vote stage. For example, in 1982, although Majority Leader Stevens threatened to pursue cloture,[26] supporters' actual strategy closely mirrored the norm. Unanimous consent agreements on amendments and a time limitation agreement on debate were arranged by Baker. After the rejection of fifteen opposition-sponsored amendments and relatively little debate, the Senate adopted the bill in an 85 to 8 vote on June 18, 1982, after which it amended the House version of the bill (H.R. 3112) to conform to its own version (S. 1992). On June 23, 1982, the House unanimously passed H.R. 3112, without debate, and President Reagan signed the bill into law on June 29, 1982.

Normalcy prevailed at the floor for each of the remaining post-seventies debates as well. In each of the 1988 debates, consent agreements were arranged to govern amendment activity, debate, and final voting. Debate on the Grove City bill came to a close on January 28, 1988, when the Senate adopted it in a 75 to 14 vote. The House later adopted the bill in a 315 to 98 vote. It was subsequently vetoed by President Reagan on March 16, 1988; and, in less than a week, Congress overrode the veto—in the Senate by a 73 to 24 vote and in the House by a 292 to 133 vote. The amended House version of the 1988 housing bill was adopted in the Senate in a landslide 93 to 4 vote on August 2, 1988. The House adopted the bill as amended by the Senate on August 8, 1988, by a voice vote. The bill was signed into law by President Reagan on September 13, 1988.

Floor proceedings on the Civil Rights Restoration Act of 1991 and the 1992 bill also resembled the norm. In each of these debates, a series of ad hoc consent agreements carried the day. Advocates flatly rejected what they referred to as "deal-breaker" amendments, accepting only two major changes that were the subject of extended negotiations involving congressional leaders and administration officials. All four rejected amendments were killed immediately with tabling votes. The Senate adopted the bill on October 30, 1991, in a 93 to 5 vote. It passed the House on November 7, 1991, in a 381 to 38 vote and was signed into law by President Bush on November 21, 1991. Similarly, the regular order prevailed during floor proceedings on the 1992 bill, with some minor adjustments. A unanimous consent agreement to govern floor action was entered by Mitchell on August 5, 1992. It provided that the voting rights bill would be taken up immediately following Senate action on a separate measure, that only four amendments proposed by Senator Alan Simpson would be allowed, and that a vote on passage would immediately follow debate and votes on the amendments. Mitchell also imposed a one-track system while the bill was pending and extended the daily session late into the evening. Beyond these adjustments, little else in the way of extra input was required of supporters.

Overall, there is little question that opponents' abandonment of lengthy speeches, excessive amendment activity, numerous quorum calls, and other maneuvers has helped reduce the procedural demands confronted by advocates of recent civil rights proposals. However, this advantage has been offset by certain other developments. In the wake of various reforms adopted during the seventies, both the Senate and the House have undergone a transformation.[27] Some of the key changes that have occurred include, foremost, an increased legislative workload. Although the number of bills introduced and enacted in both chambers has declined, the number of pages consumed by the bills suggests the complexity of laws considered and adopted by Congress has increased. This, combined with an increase in the number of roll call votes held at the floor, the number of hours expended in floor sessions, and also the number of committee meetings, suggests that Congress' workload is heavier now than it has been in the past.

Also, stimulated initially by critical membership changes in 1958 and then enabled by the expanded rank-and-file member power and resources provided by the seventies reforms, both the House and the Senate have experienced greater individualism. This is partly evidenced by the increase in floor amendment activity and cloture votes. What this greater individualism means in practice is that congressional norms are far less effective in constraining members' use of the rules to create obstructions. Thus, use of procedural blockages is no longer confined to the southern wing, but has been used more recently on a wider scale. What all of these changes mean is that Congress operates under much greater time constraints than it had previously and it must grapple with a much wider set of policy demands than before.

Against this backdrop of a transformed legislative context, even the scaled-down version of recent obstruction of civil rights legislation offers particularly problematic consequences. Whereas in the past, civil rights filibusters stagnated the Senate as a whole, recently, given a reorientation in Congress' work environment and the resulting impracticality (and improbability) of leadership use of a one-track system, filibusters against civil rights have a debilitating impact that is now largely confined to the civil rights legislative effort itself. Not all measures under consideration in the Senate are negatively affected by civil rights obstruction, as in the past. As of recent proceedings, only civil rights measures are stalled. This procedural marginalization of racial policy proposals means, arguably, that it is more difficult to enact civil rights legislation in recent years as compared to earlier decades. These proposals now compete with other major legislative proposals for space on crowded policy agendas, but without the benefit of the usual political pressures against procedural obstructionism. Advocates must now work harder to muster uncommitteds' support beforehand. This likely serves to discourage pursuit of strong bills and perhaps even explains these recent proposals' weakness at the outset of proceedings. At the very least, taken together, these factors make for a much more demanding civil rights policy process.

Presidential Vetoes and Veto Threats

New to and further compounding the logistical complexities of contemporary civil rights lawmaking is the advent of presidential vetoes and veto threats against civil rights. Proponents of recent civil rights bills have had to grapple with veto threats from both the Reagan and Bush administrations. For example, with respect to the 1988 Grove City bill, Reagan remarked it was "a bill whose vague and sweeping language threatens to subject nearly every facet of American life . . . to intrusive regulation by Federal agencies and courts."[28] Republican Senators Hatch and Thurmond each conveyed the president's intent to veto the bill. Hatch said of the bill: "The simple fact is that unless we address legitimate concerns . . . it will certainly be vetoed by the President, and that veto will be sustained."[29] Thurmond stated in regards to a Republican compromise amendment offered: "The White House has sent word down. . . . [I]f this amendment is not adopted, the President will not sign this bill."[30] Reagan subsequently vetoed the 1988 Grove City bill. The prospect of a presidential veto of the 1988 housing bill was conveyed by the bill's chief advocate, Senator Kennedy, during remarks he made while outlining the compromise substitute agreed upon. He indicated the Reagan administration's support of the bill was strictly conditioned on the changes made by the substitute and that the administration would not support the bill if any additions or revisions were added to the substitute.

In 1991 as well, supporters faced a veto threat. Bush had earlier vetoed a bill very similar to that under consideration in 1991 and passed by both houses in 1990. The veto was sustained by 34 votes. The likelihood of a 1991 veto was evident. Hatch, who carried the flag for the administration relative to the 1991 proposal, stated after an agreement was reached: "If we did not have this type of compromise and this type of resolution and these types of word changes, I have to tell you this bill would have been just as hard fought as it had been over the last two years. It would have been vetoed."[31]

The effect of the Reagan-Bush vetoes and veto threats upon congressional civil rights policymaking was twofold. First, presidential vetoes generally amount to a form of obstruction in much the same way as procedural blockages do. Vetoes, at the very least, stall official enactment of legislation adopted in Congress. Veto threats are legislative obstacles, even if temporary. Thus, the Reagan-Bush veto politics essentially added to the procedural obstruction that confronted the bills within the Senate. Furthermore, and more importantly, the recent veto politics have effectively imposed supermajority requirements upon congressional civil rights advocates insofar as a two-thirds majority vote in both chambers is needed to override a presidential veto. Thus, the extraordinary majority requirements that inhered in the sixties civil rights proceedings, a requirement that had been significantly reduced by the 1975 change in the cloture rule, from two-thirds to three-fifths, was, in effect, revived in recent years in connection with the veto threats.

In short, well into the eighties and nineties, making civil rights law remained an especially onerous parliamentary task.

CONTEMPORARY CIVIL RIGHTS POLICY OUTCOMES

The political conflict that traditionally surrounds race has also affected the substance of recent civil rights proposals. Even today, and perhaps even more so than in the past, the divisive nature of racial politics bears directly upon the strength of civil rights laws. As in the past, the role race plays in contouring policy provisions is mediated through its bargainability. Civil rights advocates' need for supermajority support exists even following the infamous sixties and seventies eras due to continued procedural obstruction and veto threats. Again, the practical consequence of this need for more votes is that advocates have had to turn to Republican moderates to secure any kind of legislative victory. And, as in the past, advocates confront a formidable bargaining challenge in their attempts to win these votes and, thus, secure the necessary supermajority. Because of the great scrutiny that racial dissension adds to civil rights proceedings, Republican moderates have been unwilling to endorse even the modest proposals of the eighties and nineties without them being streamlined in ways that are commensurate with Republican ideals.

Due to the bargaining constraints engendered by racial politics, the already-modest proposals of the eighties and nineties have had to undergo even further weakening reformulations in order to become law. In their original form, the recent proposals have constituted, at best, attempts to salvage the policy gains of earlier decades. Thanks to the Nixon-Reagan-Bush Supreme Court, which has actively exercised the doctrine of judicial restraint in passing upon civil rights laws, race reform advocates have faced the task of restoring the sixties and seventies civil rights legislation back to its original force. Foremost among these legislative initiatives is that of ensuring that minority groups can effectively leverage the court enforcement remedies provided in these earlier laws and that of ensuring that the federal funds provided through these anti-discrimination laws are not used to support discrimination. In the end, nonetheless, because of the policy changes forced by negotiations with moderates, substantively little has been accomplished by way of the eighties and nineties proceedings.

Negotiating Race in Contemporary American Politics

As explained above, the supermajority support imperative of civil rights proceedings continues to inhere. In recent debates, the now common threat of internal procedural obstruction has been compounded by external obstruction in the form of presidential threats and vetoes. More specifically, advocates needed supermajority support during the 1982 and 1991 debates to invoke cloture. The three-fifths support required had already been met at the outset. In 1982 and 1991, supporters claimed at least sixty-five members from the outset, while opponents claimed eight and five members in the 1982 and 1991 debates, respectively. While this left roughly twenty-seven and thirty members essentially "on the fence" with regard to the bills, this fact in itself was relatively insignificant as a practical matter. Supporters did not need these additional members in order to succeed in invoking cloture. Nor were additional votes needed in 1992 as supporters claimed at least sixty votes at the outset of those proceedings as well.

Supporters did not, however, have a sufficient number of votes to override an impending presidential veto; and it was this need for additional support that served as the main catalyst for the ensuing policy negotiations. Advocates had to meet the two-thirds support requirement imposed by veto threats in order to ensure the bills would become law. And, because this supermajority support was lacking, the votes of uncommitted senators in each of the debates had to be won over. Given there were twenty-seven senators on the fence with respect to the 1982 bill, compared to a total of thirty-one, twenty-two, and thirty in the 1988 Grove City, 1988 housing, and 1991 bills, respectively, advocates needed at least two more votes to override a potential 1982 veto, thirteen votes to secure the 1988 Grove City bill, and two in relation to the 1991 bill.

Beyond the support need, also important for understanding the conditions shaping contemporary congressional civil rights negotiations is that the bulk of the additional votes that have been sought are those of Republican party members. Republicans continue to make up the majority of would-be supporters. During the 1982 debate, at least 82 percent (or 22) of the uncommitted senators were Republican, at least 55 percent (or 17) were during the 1991 debate, and at least three-fourths or twenty-six of the thirty-four in 1992 were Republican. As for the 1988 debates, 68 percent (or 15) of the senators on the fence during the Grove City proceedings were Republican and 70 percent (or 21) were during the housing proceedings.

Many of the same concerns voiced by Republican moderates in earlier decades have been pertinent during the eighties and nineties proceedings as well, but with a new twist. As in the past, meaningful policy differences separate these uncommitted senators from advocates, differences supplied largely by uncommitteds' conservative ideological bent relative to the federal government's role in civil rights. Very much in line with their now traditional policy reservations, they do not endorse the notion of an activist federal government. A new spin on Republican ideology as espoused by these uncommitteds, however, is their particularly strong objection to race-conscious policy proposals as well. So that, combined with their anti-government sentiment is a special distaste for policies that encompass ostensibly advantageous racial classifications for the purpose of leveling the playing field between minorities and whites. Such proposals are, for uncommitted moderates, as much at odds with their basic partisan principles as those providing for a sizeable federal role in enforcement.

Let us look in closer detail at how these varying perspectives have played out in each of the eighties and nineties debates. In application, moderates' contemporary policy reservations have centered upon scope and enforcement provisions. Thus, it is on these portions of the bills that moderates and civil rights advocates have disagreed most. In 1982, advocates' main objective was to overturn a Supreme Court ruling in *Mobile v. Bolden* (1980), a ruling believed to have undermined the voting rights protections established in the original Voting Rights Act of 1965 and its extensions. *Mobile*, advocates argued, made it difficult for minorities to challenge racially discriminatory districting plans because it required them to prove that the plans' authors were motivated by discriminatory intent at the time the plans were adopted. Supporters wanted to require courts to consider discriminatory impact as evidence of discrimination, rather than discriminatory intent alone.

Moderates, however, were concerned about forcing courts or states to enforce racial proportionality in districting. While they shared the view that the discriminatory intent test was a difficult one to meet, they rejected the implication that racially disproportionate representation constituted a prima facie case of voting discrimination. Crafting a "results test" that did not implicitly endorse or require affirmative racial gerrymandering was, for moderates, the most viable approach to reversing the potentially negative impact of *Mobile*. Senator Robert Dole, spokesperson for many of the moderate senators, believed the bill should be fashioned to "maintain the integrity of the results test while at the same time alleviating fears about proportional representation."[32]

Also, during the 1988 Grove City proceedings supporters' disagreement with Republican uncommitteds was about how best to structure the bill's impact. Advocates' goal here was to overturn another Supreme Court decision, this time the *Grove City v. Bell* (1984) ruling. They believed the *Grove City* holding permitted institutions receiving federal funds to discriminate on the basis of race. The Court held that the federal funds cutoff provisions in Title VI of the 1964 civil rights act[33] could only be applied against the specific program found to have discriminated and not the entire institution. Civil rights advocates sought in 1988 to re-establish what they believed was the long-standing legal precedent for application of Title VI, namely, institution-wide coverage. Their main point of disagreement with moderates had to do with government enforcement, but in an unusual way.

Moderates wanted to ensure that Title VI would not be construed so as to require religious institutions to perform abortions in order to be in compliance with federal prohibitions on gender discrimination. Abortion concerns first came to fore in 1985 in connection with a U.S. Catholic Conference memo suggesting the proposed bill could force Catholic hospitals to perform abortions or face the loss of federal assistance.[34] Supporters initially dismissed the abortion objections as a ploy to further restrict abortion rights by way of the civil rights debate. But, Senator John Danforth, who spoke for the group of moderates, supported the basic goals of the legislation, but insisted the bill might inadvertently expand abortion rights.

The 1988 housing proceedings also hinged on disagreement relative to government enforcement issues. Sponsors of the 1988 housing proposal were continuing a nearly two-decade-old effort to bolster the 1968 fair housing law, which, they believed, lacked a sufficiently strong enforcement mechanism. In its original form the 1968 housing bill entrusted federal courts, rather than the Department of Housing and Urban Development (HUD), with the authority to enforce nondiscrimination in housing. For this reason, advocates believed that the 1968 act "proved to be an empty promise because the legislation lacked an effective enforcement mechanism" and that the 1988 proposal would "put real teeth into the fair housing laws by giving HUD real enforcement authority."[35] HUD, under the advocates' proposal, would have cease-and-desist powers—powers to make a finding of housing discrimination, assign penalties, and enforce the penalties assigned.

Moderates rejected the plan to empower HUD with cease-and-desist authority relative to housing discrimination complaints. They believed this was a power more appropriately exercised by federal courts, rather than an administrative agency. Senator Orrin Hatch, speaking for a sizeable number of moderates, agreed that the 1968 bill's "enforcement mechanism has never been adequate," but later explained: "One of my greatest concerns with the legislation . . . involved the proposed administrative process, which would have placed all claims before an administrative law judge, without the possibility of de novo Federal district court review, thereby denying the parties their constitutionally protected right to a jury trial."[36]

Moreover, the divergence between supporters and moderates during the 1991 debate centered around affirmative action as well. In an effort to reverse a series of Supreme Court decisions handed down between 1986 and 1989, the advocates' original 1991 proposal contained provisions that would have bolstered the legal weight of evidence of racially unequal outcomes in employment discrimination cases. Advocates believed that the Court's combined rulings in nine cases[37] severely restricted the legal rights and court remedies made available to minorities in various federal civil rights and employment laws. Of the nine decisions, the Court's 1989 *Wards Cove Packing Co. v. Atonio* ruling was of greatest concern. Thus, the 1991 bill that was eventually adopted began by stating its primary purpose was that of restoring the meaning of certain key legal concepts as they existed prior to *Wards*. More specifically, where *Wards* held that workers challenging an employment practice that had a racially discriminatory impact must prove the practice did not have a legitimate business purpose, advocates wanted to shift to employers the burden of proving the legality of racial discriminatory outcomes caused by their employment practices.

Moderates expressed reservations about the bill's potential imposition of affirmative action requirements. Their specific focus was on how the bill treated employers' justifications for use of employment practices shown to have a racially discriminatory impact. For them, especially critical was defining a clear "business necessity" standard that outlined the acceptable reasons for maintaining a practice that had been shown to yield disproportionate outcomes, but that did not inadvertently force the use of quotas. Republican Senator John Chaffee remarked: "the business necessity issue has been by far the stickiest wicket in this whole 2-year debate."[38] The specific goal was to restore the legal standards enunciated by the Court before *Wards* in a 1971 decision, *Griggs v. Duke Power*, but without imposing quota requirements.

The objective in 1992 was to extend those portions of the Voting Rights Act (VRA) of 1965 that provide special protections for non-English-speaking voters. Specifically, advocates wanted to extend the bilingual requirements of the VRA of 1965 until the year 2007, when the main enforcement provisions of the bill (Sections 4 and 5) would expire. The 1992 bill was "particularly designed for the Hispanic, Asian-American and Native American communities,"[39] according to one of the principal co-sponsors of the bill, Senator Paul Simon. Under the 1982 extension of the original voting rights act, the federal requirement that states provide bilingual voting materials and assistance was set to expire on August 6, 1992. Thus, the thrust of the 1992 effort was to extend the federal bilingual voting requirements an additional fifteen years.

Additionally, advocates sought to expand the geographic coverage of the provisions, so that a larger number of jurisdictions were brought under the bill. The 1982 extension and its antecedents imposed the bilingual requirements only on those areas in which non-English-speaking citizens made up 5 percent of the voting age population and in states caught under the coverage formula in Sections 4 and 5 of the voting rights act. The effect of the 1982 law's scope, as such, was to exclude many jurisdictions in which there were large numbers of non-English-speaking citizens, but not enough to trigger coverage, such as Los Angeles, San Francisco, Chicago, and Philadelphia.[40] Thus, advocates wanted in 1992 to include also those areas with at least 10,000 citizens who were members of a single language minority and/or were limited-English proficient.

A sizeable number of moderate senators were concerned about the costs imposed upon states by the federal bilingual voting requirements. Much of the preceding discussion in this book highlights a limited federal role as a core element of Republican ideology. "New federalism" is also part and parcel of contemporary Republicanism. The 1995 Republican Contract with America embraced the concept of devolution, which in concrete terms connotes a limited federal government. More specifically, the contract imposed certain restrictions on the use of unfunded federal mandates. As such, moderates' concerns in connection with the 1992 bill essentially foreshadowed the crystallization of unfunded mandates as one manifestation of the traditional Republican antithesis toward big national government.

Moreover, in each of the eighties and nineties proceedings, moderates essentially held out until the bills were fashioned to fit their preferences. In fact, the 1982 bill had languished in the Republican-controlled Judiciary Committee roughly five months precisely because of deadlock over the racial proportionality issue. Dole explained that the committee agreed to report the bill only after the changes had been made and that, without those changes, "there was some doubt that the bill would be reported out."[41] During both 1988 proceedings, it was evident moderates would not support either of the proposals without changes. Danforth stated during the 1988 Grove City proceedings that he refused to "cram abortion down the throats of hospitals and colleges and universities that have the deepest religious and moral abhorrence at this practice."[42] The 1988 housing proceedings marked the end of a twenty-year struggle that made unmistakably clear moderates' unwillingness to support any form of administrative enforcement. In fact, HUD enforcement provisions had been scrapped as a condition for their support of cloture on the original 1968 housing bill. Twelve years later a similar provision was defeated in a nine-day filibuster led by a group of Republican senators. Senator Orrin Hatch said of the concessions eventually made during the 1988 proceedings: "These changes in enforcement provisions of the bill are important and they were primarily responsible in obtaining the broad support that this measure now enjoys, including my own."[43] He added that the revised bill deserved "affirmative consideration" because it was "a far cry from what it was back in 1979 and 1980 when that particular matter was fought and I had to lead the fight against the bill."[44]

Moderates were equally unwilling in 1991 to support the restoration bill without the revisions they desired. Just a year prior, a bill closely resembling the original version of the 1991 bill was defeated by a veto of President George Bush. That veto was sustained in the Senate by thirty-four votes. Many of the same senators who had helped to defeat the 1990 version were among those demanding revision of the 1991 bill and, according to Senator Hatch, were again prepared to sustain a veto.[45] Of the thirteen civil rights laws adopted in Congress during the modern civil rights period, moreover, the 1992 bill appears to be the only bill to have secured moderate votes in the absence of major policy concessions. On the surface, although roll call vote analysis indicates there was some substantive disagreement between supporters and moderates, there is little evidence to suggest these differences were critical enough to inhibit the development of supermajority support once proceedings were underway.

Civil Rights Policy Concessions and Provisions of the Eighties and Nineties

Ultimately, the concessions to which advocates have had to agree in order to secure moderates' decisive votes have, in effect, made contemporary civil rights laws even more constitutionally redundant than ever. The bills, which started out as relatively weak proposals, were weakened still further during policy negotiations. The changes that had been made to the bills to accommodate moderates' concerns were changes that, collectively, have proven debilitating. The compromise reached in 1982 retained the language adopted in the House. That version rejected the intent standard as the sole means of establishing a violation under the bill. The agreement also added a new subsection, described by Dole as having "delineated with more specificity the legal standards to be applied under the 'results' test in order to address the proportional representation issue."[46] According to this new subsection, the determinative factor for courts was to be whether the political processes are equally open to minority and nonminority groups alike. The compromise agreement was adopted by the full committee on May 4, 1982, and recommended to the floor where it was adopted on June 18, 1982.

As enacted, the bill, entitled the Voting Rights Act Amendments of 1982, consisted of five parts. In the first part, the preclearance requirement contained in Section five of the original act was amended so that a covered state could bail out of the preclearance requirements in advance of the applicable expiration date if it demonstrated to the District of Columbia Court that it had met six criteria outlined elsewhere in the bill. Part Two of the bill provided that a violation of Section 2 of the original act, which prohibited discriminatory voting qualifications and prerequisites, could be established if "based on the totality of circumstances, it is shown that the political processes leading to nomination or election" are not equally open in that minorities have "less opportunity" than others to participate in the political process and elect representatives of their choice. It pointed out, however, that the bill did not establish a right for minorities to have proportionate representation. This portion of the bill also extended Sections 4 and 5 of the enforcement provisions an additional twenty-five years. Part three of the bill, however, extended the protections for language minorities added to the Voting Rights Act of 1975 only ten years, rather than twenty-five. The final portion of the bill provided for voter assistance to disabled persons.

The 1988 Grove City concessions too were directly tailored to meet moderates' concerns. Senator Danforth sponsored an amendment that he said would neutralize abortion vis-à-vis the bill, that is, abortion rights would be neither expanded nor restricted by it. The Danforth amendment was adopted in a 56 to 39 vote.[47] In its final form, the bill, entitled the Civil Rights Restoration Act of 1987, comprised nine sections. I will briefly describe the five most important ones here. Section 2 contained the following statement: "Congress finds that certain aspects of recent decisions and opinions of the Supreme Court have unduly narrowed or cast doubt upon the application of four laws." Sections 3, 4, 5, and 6 defined the term "program or activity" as used in federal laws applied by courts to include "all of the operations" of an institution receiving federal financial assistance or engaged in education, health care, housing, social services, or parks and recreation.

Section 8 stipulated the act did not require hospitals or other institutions receiving federal funding to perform or pay for an abortion, and Section 3 provided that no penalty could be imposed on any person for seeking or receiving abortion services.

Revisions made to the 1988 housing proposal were also geared to resolve disagreement between moderates and supporters. Kennedy explained he and Senator Specter drafted a proposal following committee hearings on the bill and "made revisions in the bill to respond to some of the questions [raised] in those hearings."[48] The Kennedy-Specter compromise substitute effectively provided for mixed enforcement of the bill, rather than a strictly administrative or judicial method of enforcement. The compromise was incorporated into the House bill that eventually became the vehicle for action in the Senate. Kennedy explained: "The legislation which eventually passed the House was generally very similar to the measure we had reported to the full committee in the Senate."[49]

Upon enactment, the 1988 bill, officially entitled the Fair Housing Amendments Act of 1988, comprised fifteen sections, the two most important being Sections 6 and 8. Section 6 prohibited discrimination in real estate–related transactions, such as loan purchasing and appraising and it extended new protections to aged persons. Section 8, entitled "Enforcement Changes," contained the bulk of the bill's major provisions and spelled out a number of things. First, victims of housing discrimination could file a complaint with the Department of Housing and Urban Development, which could then issue a charge if its investigation warranted one. Once a charge has been filed, then either party involved can choose to have the charge decided upon by an administrative law judge appointed by HUD or to have the case decided in a civil court. If all parties elect to have the case heard by an administrative law judge, then the judge is to decide the case and order appropriate relief. If either party elects to have the matter decided by a civil court, then the secretary of HUD is to refer the matter to the attorney general, who, in turn, is to file suit in court. The bill also provided that individuals may file suit in federal or state court on their own and that the attorney general may initiate court action.

Changes made to the 1991 bill were huge concessions to Republican moderates. Meetings between Senators Kennedy and Danforth and various White House officials resulted in a compromise version of the bill that was formally presented in the Senate on October 24, 1991. Its two most important components were offered very early in the debate by Senators Chaffee, Durenberger, Hatfield, and several others, as early as September 24, 1991. They required specificity with regard to discrimination allegations, namely, a plaintiff's allegations had to be based on a showing of discriminatory impact on the part of a specific employment practice, rather than an employer's overall operation. They provided also that challenged practices that yielded a discriminatory impact were legal as long as they were proven to be "job related for the position in question and consistent with business necessity." The agreement was adopted in a voice vote of the floor on October 30, 1991.

Where the Supreme Court's *Wards* decision had held that workers challenging an employment practice that had a discriminatory impact must prove the practice did not have a legitimate business purpose, Section 105 of the 1991 law shifted somewhat the burden of proof. Specifically, it provided discrimination was proven if (1) workers proved it has a discriminatory impact; and (2) the employer failed to show the challenged practice was job related and consistent with business necessity; or (3) the challenging workers proved an alternative practice accomplished the same purposes, but without causing a disparate impact.

With respect to the 1992 bill, advocates were not forced to make policy concessions in order to secure the votes of moderates once proceedings were underway. The weakening amendments that were put forth and supported by a sizeable number of moderates were defeated. Senator Alan Simpson proposed an amendment that would have provided federal funding for bilingual voter services. The amendment was defeated both in committee and at the floor. At the floor, it was rejected in a 35 to 60 vote. A second amendment proposed by Simpson that would have extended the language requirements for five years, in place of the fifteen-year extension provided for in the House bill, was defeated by a 32 to 63 vote. Still, the bill, upon passage, commanded supermajority support.

Despite this, an alternative explanation may also be plausible. The bill's chief sponsors included a number of moderates. The bill was originally introduced with sponsors on both sides, including Democratic senators Paul Simon, Dennis DeConcini, Edward Kennedy, Daniel Inouye, Tom Daschle, Alan Cranston, Jeff Bingman, Howard Metzenbaum, Alan Dixon, and Tim Wirth and Republican senators Orrin Hatch, Arlen Specter, John McCain, and Dave Durenberger. Given its origins as a bipartisan legislative proposal and, more, its support by a conservative senator such as Orrin Hatch, it is possible and perhaps likely that the bill was modified in advance of the start of official Senate legislative proceedings on it.

Upon enactment, the 1992 bill comprised only two sections, one of which simply provided for the bill's entitlement as the Voting Rights Language Assistance Act of 1992. The main provisions of the bill contained in Section 2 provided a number of things. First, it reinstated until August 6, 2007, the prohibition on English-only voting materials. It also provided that the prohibition would apply to states and political subdivisions in which 5 percent and/or at least 10,000 citizens of voting age did not speak English or were limited-English proficient. Finally, it provided that "voting materials" meant registration or voting notices, forms, instructions, assistance, or other materials or information relating to the electoral process, including ballots.

The Impact of Contemporary Civil Rights Laws

On the whole, the primary weakness of the civil rights enactments of the eighties and nineties is that they continue enforcement of nondiscrimination primarily through the courts. This mode of enforcement goes a long way toward minimizing the potential and real-life impact of civil rights laws in a number of ways. Given conservative justices' preponderant share of recent lower and appellate federal court appointments, combined with the conservative majority on the Supreme Court, the laws' virtually exclusive reliance on the federal court system renders enormous consequences. It, in effect, not only makes it unlikely the laws will bring about major reforms, but actually jeopardizes the legal viability of the legislative bases for such reforms. Second, these laws, inasmuch as they are re-writes of earlier bills, fail to address or tackle "second generation" civil rights policy issues, such as inner-city deterioration, the urban underclass, and so forth. Given these drawbacks in recent civil rights laws, the socioeconomic racial gap remains and, in some respects, is actually worsening.

The source of these problematic outcomes can be traced directly to the policy concessions of recent debates. Specifically, because the 1982 law does not alter the venue for protecting voting rights, enforcement of voting rights remains very much a court-centered process. Challenges to election law changes and the appointment of federal registrars still have to be funneled through a federal court. Perhaps the only significant consequence of the 1982 law is to direct (or re-direct) courts to a somewhat more liberal standard of interpreting the federal voting rights laws. The 1988 Grove City bill too has added no new administrative features to the civil rights enforcement apparatus, and has left intact the largely court-dependent approach. Its real-life impact is simply that of helping to maintain existing opportunities of minorities via federally funded programs. Similarly, the effect of the 1988 housing compromise is, in essence, a continuation of the slow pace of equal housing enforcement that inhers in other civil rights laws. Leaving the choice of an administrative or judicial hearing to either party is, for all practical purposes, a replica of the judicial approach embraced by other civil rights bills and is widely regarded by advocates as a major restraint on the bill's capacity to create meaningful housing opportunities for blacks and other minorities. As for the 1991 enactment, the "business necessity" compromise is, by its very nature, a judicial tool—yet another court-dependent approach to securing equal rights for minorities. Thus, it does not alter, but merely adds to, the judicial enforcement apparatus incorporated in previous civil rights laws. Passage of the Language Assistance Act of 1992 does virtually nothing in the way of expanding civil rights as it is primarily an extension of the bilingual requirements incorporated into the original Voting Rights Act of 1965 as amended in 1975 and 1982. As such, the 1992 bill, like its post-sixties predecessors, breaks no new grounds, creates no new rights, and does not delve into the more entrenched elements of the race problem.

CHAPTER SUMMARY

In summary, by the eighties and nineties, the politics of race overlapped chiefly with partisan politics. Republicans' objections to affirmative action and an extensive federal civil rights role generally became a central component of their party's battle cry. The Reagan and Bush administrations propelled race to the very forefront of national party politics by utilizing affirmative action as a virtual litmus test in the nominations and appointment processes, by politicizing deregulation specifically in relation to civil rights enforcement, and, more importantly, by essentially shifting the tone in government as far as race reform was concerned. Thanks to their efforts and emphasis, race has undoubtedly become one of the issues that serves to define what it is to be a Republican versus a Democrat.

As the saliency and divisiveness of race has shifted to the partisan arena, the makeup and nature of obstructionism against civil rights legislative proposals has shifted as well. The southern contingent of the coalition blocking civil rights is a thing of the past. Gone too is civil rights opponents' claim to a sizeable number of senators. But, offsetting the dwindling numbers of obstructionists in the Senate is the threat of presidential vetoes. Combined, the internal and external contemporary obstruction of civil rights has imposed extraordinary procedural demands on advocates, as did earlier filibuster efforts. Different in the eighties and nineties is the confinement of filibuster tactics to lengthy speechmaking and refusals to vote, and, as a result, the bulk of unconventional civil rights policymaking has hinged around cloture.

Critically, what also has not changed relative to civil rights policymaking during this period is the tendency toward weak laws. In fact, on this score, what was true of the earlier years is even more true of the eighties and nineties. Whereas the sixties legislation had at least established new laws, contemporary policy efforts have merely preserved the sixties laws. And, even as Congress has attempted to do merely this, it has acquiesced to moderate demands. As in the past, the contemporary internal decisionmaking outcomes relative to race—that is, the demands, their impact on policy, and the process that initially stimulates these demands—continue to be shaped by race's destabilizing effect in the external environment.

6

An Overview: Race, Process, and Policy

Race has been and remains one of the most divisive and salient issues in American politics. It is this distinction that has, in effect, rendered race-related policy proposals unsuitable for the standard legislative process. It has also constrained reformers' ability to secure passage of strong civil rights laws. In short, because of the enormous discord it engenders, race cannot be governed through conventional decisionmaking apparatuses. Nor can these structures yield policies capable of altering persistent race-related educational, employment, and housing inequalities. The preceding chapters have analyzed trends in civil rights politics and policymaking that demonstrate what is, in essence, a fundamental incompatibility between race and conventional governance structures.

This chapter presents a more systematic analysis of the politics of race and their effect upon civil rights lawmaking during the modern civil rights period. It summarizes much of what has already been explained, but utilizes a mostly quantitative, longitudinal analysis to illustrate the book's main arguments. The first section presents an overview of the changes in the regional and partisan conflicts that have lain at the center of racial politics. It also assesses the political significance of these divisions over time. The impact of racial politics upon the parliamentary aspects of civil rights policymaking is discussed in the second section. Finally, the last section examines the substantive policy impact of racial politics. There the question of just how the dissension engendered by race has come to bear upon the content of civil rights legislative proposals is addressed.

THE POLITICS OF RACE

Polarization has been a critical facet of racial politics throughout the modern civil rights period. Although the nature of racial conflict has changed, the basic fact that the politics of race are, in essence, the politics of division has not. During the post-Reconstruction years through the sixties, race overlapped with deep regional and partisan cleavages. By the seventies, however, the line dividing the South and the non-South began to dissipate and eventually disappears. In the wake of this change emerged an intensified conflict within the national party system that centered to a significant degree upon the race problem in the eighties and later. Added to racial politics' basic conflictual nature is their greater political saliency. Racial divisions have not only persisted over time in varying forms, but these divisions themselves have been of pivotal importance within the broader arena of American politics. What follows is a closer look at the core elements of racial political conflict.

Racial Division

Regional Division

Initially, much of the public discord surrounding race revolved around the South's racial stance and its distinction from that of other regions in the country. That region's racial caste system stood out as one of the more troubling aspect of the race problem as manifested during the years leading up to the seventies. The specifically southern dimensions of the race problem can be seen in a number of ways, including public opinion surveys; various measures of the racial status quo; and the locus and focus of civil rights advocacy. Combined, the factual evidence on each of these items underscores the existence of deep regional conflict over race during the early years of civil rights politics. During the latter portion of the modern civil rights period, however, through these same lenses, we observe something of a regional reorientation around the race problem so that it is no longer one that is defined largely in terms of the South versus the North. Thus, the race problem and its politics no longer manifest in regional cleavages.

Surveys of white racial attitudes and opinions reveal the South's distinctive opposition to racial progressivism during the early years of the modern civil rights period. National Election Studies (NES) surveys and Gallup polls measure opposition to various aspects of race reform that were especially relevant during the late fifties and sixties period. These data show opposition is consistently higher among southern whites, initially. The South reacted negatively to the Supreme Court's desegregation decisions and especially the Court's landmark *Brown v. Board of Education* (1954) ruling, which overturned the separate-but-equal doctrine. Figure 6.1 reveals southern

Figure 6.1
**Segregation: Percentage in Favor of Racial Segregation by Race and Region,
1961–1978**

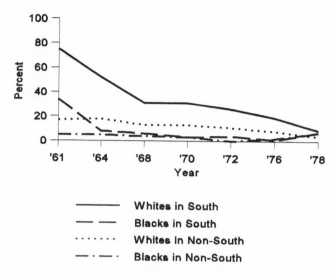

Whites in South

Blacks in South

Whites in Non-South

Blacks in Non-South

Source: Gallup, 1961; NES, 1964–1978. See Appendix C for details.

whites were initially far more likely than their nonsouthern counterparts to
favor segregation. According to a 1961 Gallup survey poll, fully 75 percent
of southern whites supported segregation, compared to only 17 percent of
whites outside the region. A 21 percent drop in their opposition occurred,
however, between 1964 and 1968, according to an NES survey asking
whether respondents favored desegregation. Starting in 1968, a steady decline began, culminating in a 9 percent pro-segregation support level among
southern whites by 1978, compared to a 4 percent rate among non-southern
whites. On the more thorny issue of open housing, southerners had also
taken a decidedly anti–civil rights stance during the first half of the modern
civil rights period. As shown in Figure 6.2, throughout the 1964 to 1990
period, southern whites register greater opposition than the remaining three
groups shown. But an NES survey asking respondents if they felt blacks
should "have the right to live wherever they could afford to just like anybody
else" indicates there was greater southern opposition to equal housing during the sixties than later. A General Social Survey (GSS) poll that asked
respondents if they would vote for a law prohibiting racial discrimination in
the selling of homes also shows a decline in southern opposition beginning
in the mid-seventies and continuing through 1990. In contrast to the NES
data, however, GSS data show initial opposition in the South to be as high
as 77 percent in 1976 and still at 55 percent in 1990, compared to some-

Figure 6.2
Housing: Percentage Opposed to Open Housing by Race and Region, 1964–1990

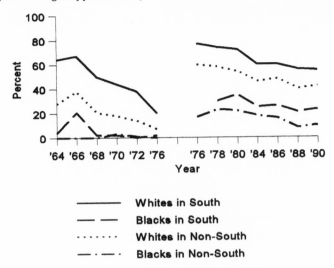

Source: NES, 1964–1976; GSS, 1976–1990. See Appendix C for details.

what less, 60 percent, among non-southern whites in 1976 and 44 percent in 1990.

Finally, southern attitudes concerning the election process are especially telling with regard to the region's stance on racial progressivism. They suggest very clearly that southerners' disposition toward civil rights was closely tied to and, arguably, driven by a racial animus. Much of southern legislators' arguments against civil rights reform invoked states' rights ideology, advanced charges of regional discrimination, and generally rejected such reforms on the premise that they were unnecessary. That there was, nonetheless, an arguably racist mindset behind the region's stance is indicated in Figure 6.3. The data shown reflect the percentage of persons who indicated in both GSS and Gallup surveys that their opposition to certain candidates in presidential elections would be based on racial considerations, that is, they would vote against a black candidate even if he or she were qualified and nominated by the respondents' party. Throughout the 1959 to 1990 period, southern whites demonstrated a much greater propensity to oppose black candidacies for race-related reasons than any of the groups shown. According to Gallup poll data, initially, three-fourths of southern whites would essentially discriminate in voting. However, as of 1963, a slight drop in their opposition occurred and an even more substantial drop took place between 1963 and 1967. According to the GSS data, between 1974 and 1990, a somewhat steady decline took place in their opposition, except between 1986 and 1988 when there was a small increase of roughly 5 percent.

Figure 6.3
Elections: Percentage Would Not Support Qualified Black Presidential Party
Nominee by Race and Region, 1959–1990

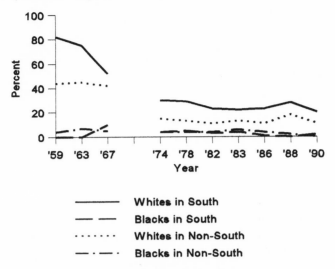

Source: Gallup, 1959–1967; GSS, 1974–1990. See Appendix C for details.

On the whole, these survey data reveal that, over time, the South became less likely to oppose race reform. Even beyond the seventies, the region remains somewhat more conservative on race than the rest of the country. However, its distinctive stance on race substantially dissipates later.

Other measures that gauge the politics of race in the South illuminate changes in the broader sociopolitical and socioeconomic structure of the South as it pertained to race. More specifically, analysis of these measures shows that, initially, the race problem was concentrated in the South, which meant the South had the most to "lose" in the push for reform. But, later, the region makes significant progress in this regard. The two areas to which race reformers and southern opponents alike devoted much attention throughout the modern civil rights period are school segregation and voting. Trends in each of these fields show that, at the outset, blacks in the South fared much worse than their non-southern counterparts. Later, however, they experience significant progress as racial disparities in education and political participation in the South more closely mirror those outside the region. At the same time that the South makes notable strides, the pace of reform in other areas begins to slow and/or regress. In effect, the race problem becomes less a problem specifically of the South and more a problem with national dimensions.

School segregation is initially pervasive in the South. Table 6.1 shows that in 1968 the overwhelming percentage of southern blacks are concentrated

Table 6.1
Extreme Racial Segregation in Public Schools for U.S. and Five Regions: Blacks Attending 99–100 Percent Minority Schools, 1968–1988, Selected Years

	1968	1974	1980	1988
U.S. Total	53.5	24.7	21.5	19.3
South	74.8	13.9	12.4	11.4
Northeast	22.6	27.8	31.5	31.9
Midwest	35.3	34.6	25.4	27.8
Border	46.0	36.8	27.2	25.0
West	26.6	23.8	22.2	17.3

Source: Orfield and Monfort (1992)

in 99–100 percent minority schools, even fourteen years after the *Brown* decision. Given the South's history of de jure discrimination and its intransigence to the *Brown* ruling, this should come as no surprise. By the mid-seventies, however, the South becomes the least likely of all regions to maintain extremely segregated school systems. Meanwhile, as Table 6.2 reveals, before the seventies, the South made little progress toward the desegregation goal; but, over time, it makes greater strides in this area than any of the other regions. In essence, on what was, arguably, the most pivotal issue of civil rights politics, school segregation, the South initially stood out as the most likely "beneficiary"of civil rights reform efforts. But, by the seventies, it became the least likely to be affected by such efforts. In yet another area of reform, the South's transformation is evident. Black political participation is virtually nonexistent throughout much of the post-Reconstruction era. Thanks to extensive disenfranchisement efforts on the part of southern state officials, combined with sheer violence and intimidation, the number of blacks registered to vote as of 1960 was extremely low. Following passage of the Voting Rights Act of 1965, by 1990, southern black registration had improved dramatically. A regional comparison of voter registration among blacks and whites reveals a progressive trend toward greater inclusion in the South. In particular, as shown in Table 6.3, the racial voting gap in the South gradually closed, while the gap outside the South doubled between 1966 and 1990. And, as of 1990, blacks and whites were more equal in the South by this measure than those outside the region.

A final key indicator of regional conflict relative to race is the placement and concerns of black protest politics. At the outset of the civil rights movement, most of the demonstrations either occurred in southern states and/or concerned specifically southern issues, namely segregation. Shown in Figure 6.4 is the regional location in which civil rights demonstrations took

Table 6.2
School Desegregation in Five Regions: Percentage of Blacks in Majority White
Schools, 1968–1988, Selected Years

REGION	1968	1972	1976	1988	% Change
South	19.1	45.1	42.9	43.5	+24.4
Border	28.4	39.9	40.8	40.4	+12.0
Midwest	22.7	29.7	30.5	29.9	+ 7.2
Northeast	33.2	27.5	20.1	22.7	-10.5
West	27.8	32.6	33.2	32.9	+ 5.1

Source: Orfield and Monfort (1992). "% Change" column calculated by author.

place between 1955 and 1970. Until 1960, the vast majority of demonstrations occurred in the South, with roughly 80 percent of civil rights demonstrations in the country occurring specifically in the former Confederate
states. However, within two years, this number began to decline and by
1964 dropped to 48 percent. As of 1968, the vast majority of movement
activity, fully 91 percent, unfolded outside the South. In addition to shifting
the location of civil rights demonstrations, race reformers also became more
concerned with issues other than segregation and, therefore, issues that were
less "southern" in nature. Doug McAdam's analysis of protest movement
activity demonstrates that between 1955 and 1960 roughly 84 percent of
demonstrations targeted racial segregation, but by 1964, this number declined to less than half.

Taken together, these trends—the decline in southern opposition to race
reform, the decline in racial inequality in the region, and the decline in civil
rights protest activity in the South—all point toward a diminution of regional conflict relative to race. The contentiousness of race was initially defined to a great extent in regional terms; later, however, this changes and
we observe the passing of regional demarcations relative to racial politics.

Partisan Division

In addition to regional conflict, moreover, the politics of race have also
encompassed substantial partisan conflict. The two major national parties
have disagreed sharply over racial issues. And, whereas the regional conflict
attendant to race eventually diminishes, the partisan division over race does
not. Instead, it deepens over time. At the center of the partisan racial division is the question of how best to redress the race problem and, more
specifically, the most appropriate role of the federal government vis-à-vis
race reform. Republicans have consistently embraced a conservative racial
ideology, one that is borne out of the party's traditional conservatism toward
individualism, laissez-faire economics, and limited government. In practice,

Table 6.3
Estimated Racial Gap in Voter Registration Rates in South and Non-South,
1960–1990, Selected Years (in percentages)

Year	Racial Gap in South	Racial Gap in Non-South
1960	32.5	NA
1966	19.4	3.4
1970	5.0	8.2
1976	4.7	13.7
1980	16.6	3.4
1986	9.2	-3.2
1990	1.5	7.5

Source: Various sources. See Appendix D for details.

this ideology has produced a stance among Republican legislators that dictates opposition to a proactive federal civil rights role. Democratic legislators, on the other hand, are far more likely by the sixties than are Republicans to advocate an active federal role in the field of civil rights. They are also more likely to specifically advocate adoption of progressive federal civil rights laws in not only voting, but education, employment, and housing as well. Democrats have more consistently supported also administrative, rather than court, enforcement of the rights proffered in federal civil rights laws. And, although recent presidential politics indicate a move toward the center within the Democratic party, this, juxtaposed to the Republican party's sharp turn to the right, does not detract from the status quo of racial politics. The party divide over race remains a definitive element of racial conflict.

Partisan racial conflict can be seen in a number of ways. Many of the same measures used to demonstrate the regional split over race are useful also for gauging party differences concerning race. Overall, they show Republicans are consistently less supportive of racial progress than are Democrats. Depicted in Figure 6.5 is support for desegregation by party. As of 1964, the two parties were not very far apart as both showed relatively little support for this item. From 1964 to 1976, the gap between the two widened. Following 1976, Republican support declined.

Also on measures of open housing support, the parties' stances are somewhat distinguishable. The NES data shown in Figure 6.6 indicate that the parties' positions closely mirrored one another from the mid-sixties to the mid-seventies. The NES survey asked respondents whether they believed "Negroes have a right to live wherever they can afford to, just like anybody

Figure 6.4
Location of Civil Rights Demonstrations, 1955–1970

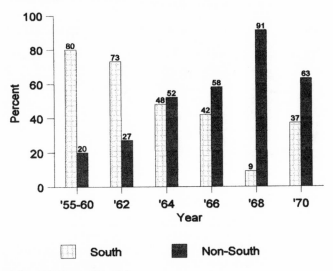

Source: McAdam (1982), pp. 152, 190

else." The GSS data, however, suggest a wider rift on the housing issue, one that maintains from the mid-seventies to 1990. The GSS survey specifically asked respondents to indicate their support for a fair housing law. The responses suggest that Democrats, on average, have shown greater support for housing desegregation than Republicans. There is some increase in Republican support over time; however, it is quite apart from that of the Democrats for much of the 1976 to 1990 period. As the discussion to follow will indicate, the difference in outcomes between the NES and GSS surveys may reflect, to some degree, differences concerning the role of government in housing matters, more so than housing rights. Still, the point here is that the two parties have consistently aligned themselves differently around most racial matters.

The one area in which Republicans and Democrats differ least is elections. While southerners and non-southerners differed sharply on this particular measure, suggesting an explicitly racial animus, Democrats and Republicans do not. Shown in Figure 6.7 are data measuring respondents' willingness to vote for a qualified, party-nominated black presidential candidate. According to Gallup data, in 1959, Republicans were ahead of Democrats, on this measure, but only slightly. For much of the period, Republicans' propensity to vote for a black candidate was much the same as that of Democrats. This suggests more broadly the existence of comparable party support for racial equality at least in the political arena.

Figure 6.5
Desegregation: Percentage in Support of Racial Desegregation by Party,
1961–1978

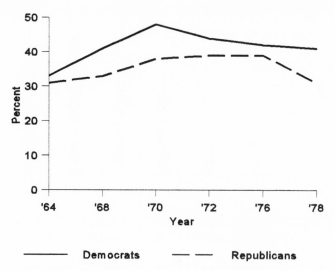

Source: GSS, 1961; NES, 1964–1978. See Appendix C for details.

Racial Saliency

Of fundamental importance to fully understanding racial politics is the fact that the regional and partisan cleavages that have underlain racial politics have themselves carried much weight within the larger political system—that is, the dissension that lies at the heart of racial politics is also a central feature of American politics. Race has and continues to figure prominently within the overall American political landscape. In particular, where the South of old is concerned, Gunnar Myrdal aptly described that region's earlier concerns relative to civil rights as tantamount to a "Negro phobia." Few issues commanded the attention and fervor that race commanded in the South. Indeed, given the structural locus of the U.S. black population, it was virtually inevitable race would figure largely in that region's politics for years. The majority of blacks in the United States resided in the eleven-state South until 1970. As shown in Table 6.4, during the earlier portion of the modern civil rights period, at least 60 percent of blacks residing in the United States as of 1950 resided in the former Confederacy and at least 52 percent did as of 1960. Although a substantial portion continued to reside in the South later, by 1970, the number living in the South had declined to less than half of the overall U.S. black population, remaining at 45 percent during the eighties and into 1990. Similarly, blacks initially claimed a fairly large share of the South's population, but held a smaller

Figure 6.6
Housing: Percentage in Support of Open Housing by Party, 1964–1990

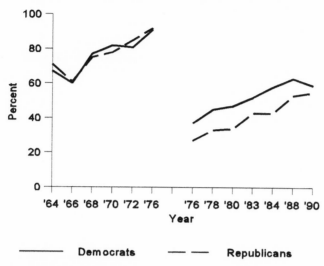

Source: NES, 1964–1976; GSS, 1976–1990. See Appendix C for details.

share later. Together, these data essentially tell us that, initially, given the regional residential patterns of the black population, their concerns would be more prominent in the South where they resided in larger numbers than elsewhere. Later, as the concentration of the black population diminished in the South, so does the political weight of racial issues in that region's politics.

The political clout of racial issues is evident at the national level as well. Much of America's politics unfold within or at least tangential to the political party system. Parties exist in elections, in government, and among the electorate. Much of the public's political participation; interest group politics; public policy agenda setting, formulation and implementation; public office campaigning; and government organization take place within the context of partisan politics. American national politics are, above all else, partisan politics. Thus, issues of great importance within the national party system are, by the same token, issues important for the national polity as as whole. Therefore, we can reliably look to the party system to gauge the national political significance of race. What we observe in this regard is that race has and continues to carry a great deal of political weight within the party system and thus, within the American political system generally.[1] Both Republicans and Democrats alike have placed a high premium on their respective racial ideologies, stances, and policies. Though divided substantively, the two have been in accord at least with respect to the amount of attention they believe racial issues should be accorded.

Race is part and parcel of what distinguishes a Republican from a Dem-

Figure 6.7
Elections: Percentage Who Would Support Qualified Black Presidential Party
Nominee by Party, 1959–1990

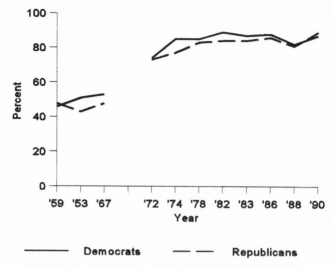

Source: Gallup, 1959–1967; GSS, 1972–1990. See Appendix C for details.

ocrat. Just as its perception of the role of government in society is a core element of Republican ideology, so too is its explicitly racial conservatism that is a byproduct of the party's beliefs about limited government. Consequently, contemporary Republicans have vigorously touted their party's beliefs about the role of government vis-à-vis race. Starting with Barry Goldwater's intense focus on race in the 1964 presidential election and continuing through the Reagan and Bush administrations' preoccupation with affirmative action, race has become a pivotal issue for the Republican party. It is equally important for Democrats too as they have carried the banner for racial justice.

Evidence of racial saliency within the party system is seen in the emphasis each party's national platform has placed on civil rights. National party platforms are useful for assessing party stance because they are each party's official statement of principles and ideology. A platform is also a mission statement as it lays out the major policies to be proposed and opposed by the party. Finally, platforms represent consensus within the party. Inasmuch as planks are drafted, included, and revised with various intra-party factions and interests in mind, they reflect both the attainable and substantive consensus within the party on a given issue. A platform succinctly symbolizes the party as a whole. Above all else, national platforms constitute each party's attempt to distinguish itself from its competitors.

Certain platforms are more telling in this regard than others. This is true

Table 6.4
Black Residential Population for South and Non-South, 1950–1990,
Selected Years (in percentages)

YEAR	BLACKS
1950	60%
1960	52
1970	45
1980	45
1990	45

Source: U.S. Bureau of the Census Reports, 1950–1990. See Appendix B for details.

in the case of platforms adopted during critical presidential election years, specifically those years in which party control of the presidency changes hands. Such shifts in control do not emerge in a vacuum, with no prior warning. Instead, they are symptomatic of more fundamental political changes within the system, not the least of which is some weakening of the ruling party's stronghold among the electorate. Because such a weakening is often due to a downturn in the economy or the emergence of some other kind of social, economic, and/or political destabilization, parties are often well aware beforehand of the resulting political vulnerability or strength that they inherit from such shifts. Thus, both work harder at communicating their respective capacity to redress the existing problems and they do so, moreover, largely by way of distinguishing themselves from one another.

As a consequence, it is these occasions of shifts in control of the presidency that provide a bird's-eye view of each party's character and, importantly, its priorities. Party control of the presidency has changed hands at least five times during the modern civil rights era. These include Democrat John F. Kennedy's win over Republican Richard Nixon in 1960; Nixon's win over Democratic Hubert Humphrey in 1968; Democratic Jimmy Carter's win over Republican Gerald Ford in 1976; Republican Ronald Reagan's win over Carter in 1980; and Democrat Bill Clinton's win over Republican George Bush in 1992. In each case, we observe Republicans and Democrats working especially hard during national party conventions to define their policy positions in a way that sets them apart from one another. Thus, in each case, we can see the amount of importance each party placed upon racial issues as against other domestic policy issues.

One objective approach to comparing the prioritization of race by both parties over time is to measure the points in the parties' platforms at which each turns to race. If race is addressed relatively early on in the platform, this would suggest greater prioritization of race, rather than less. If, on the other hand, race is mentioned toward the end of the platform or not mentioned at all, then it is safe to say that race is not very important to each party or the party system generally. An analysis of party platforms for the five presidential election years mentioned earlier indicates that race was a high priority of both parties.[2]

More specifically, an examination of the point at which the platforms first mention race, racism, discrimination, equality of opportunity, civil rights, minorities, and so forth shows that, consistently, race is addressed at the very beginning of each platform. For each of these five election years, with the exception of the 1960 Democratic platform, some aspect of civil rights is discussed in the section specifically designated as the preamble of the platform. In those platforms in which there are no preamble designations as such, race is mentioned in the first of the major sections comprised by the platform—that is, where, for example, a platform is divided into six major sections, race is typically discussed in the first of these six sections. Given that the average platform comprises 6.3 sections,[3] each party's concern for race, in effect, supersedes its concern for roughly 85 percent of domestic policy issues and problems. This serves as evidence that race is among the party system's top priorities.

In summary, the most critical characteristics of the politics of race during the modern civil rights period are that (1) it is extremely divisive and (2) the dissension it engenders is itself important within the overall context of American politics. Race is both a highly conflictual and, at the same time, highly visible political issue. The nature and substance of the racial polarization is transformed over time, so that it is less centered around regional differences and subsumed to a greater extent into the national party system's political framework. However, its fundamental antagonistic nature remains relatively consistent throughout the sixties and seventies and into the eighties and nineties.

CIVIL RIGHTS PROCESS AND PROCEDURES

Due to the persistent political conflict surrounding race, civil rights lawmaking is abnormal policymaking in its most unmistakable form. The logistical complexities inherent in the modern civil rights legislative process have almost always far exceeded those of the normal policy process. In particular, the parliamentary procedures used to secure passage of race-related proposals are often those least used in Senate legislating and also the most demanding. As compared to the normal process, the civil rights process typically exacts greater skill, greater energy, greater coordination, and, most importantly, greater support from policy advocates.

The reason race reform advocates are confronted with an alternative process that encompasses higher procedural requirements has to do with the political antagonisms generated by race. Race is among the handful of issues that prompts opposition coalitions to invoke powerful prerogatives provided in the formal rules. In the ordinary course of legislative proceedings, such prerogatives are seldom used due to the restraint dictated by institutional norms and traditions and also by the standard bargaining modes. However, when racial issues are presented in legislative proceedings, it provokes extreme opposition of the kind that cannot be dissuaded from utilizing obstructionist procedures. Civil rights opposition is commonly intense, and enough so as to warrant defiance of institutional norms and invocation of the written rules.

Due to the intense opposition engendered by race and, more directly, the obstructionist strategies employed by such opposition, civil rights advocates during the sixties had to develop a procedural strategy encompassing a wide range of rules-based and nonrules-based tactics. Virtually all alternative committee routes were considered and/or tried. At the floor, the rules were strictly enforced, various countermotions were submitted, and a recess schedule was followed, among other things. Several informal tactics had to be used as well, including publication of an informational newsletter and numerous, meticulously scheduled planning sessions. In addition, team coordination, a one-track system, schedule adjustments, and even rule reform were considered and/or tried in one or more of the debates. Finally, several cloture motions were pursued. The particular features of civil rights formal process have changed in a number of ways, but the basic formula of abnormalcy and greater demands have not. What follows is a detailed overview of the various ways in which the civil rights process compares to that of the normal process. It begins with a discussion of civil rights opposition and obstruction.

Civil Rights Opposition

Civil rights opposition in the Senate has often come in the form of procedural obstruction, and it this circumstance that fundamentally drives the abnormalcy of legislative civil rights process. Rather than working against passage of legislative civil rights laws through traditional mechanisms such as deliberation and persuasion, weakening amendments, and voting, opponents of civil rights have turned to rarely used parliamentary tools to try to defeat the laws. Initially, it was the contingent of senators representing the former Confederate states who made up the bulk of the obstructionist coalition. Later, the southern wing's contribution to the obstruction effort diminishes substantially. In fact, the overall number of senators engaged in active obstruction of civil rights dwindles significantly. The coalition that remains active in the post-seventies proceedings is a mostly Republican group of senators. As indicated in Table 6.5, Republican obstructionists' numbers may be too small to attribute contemporary civil rights obstruction

Table 6.5
Regional-Political Makeup of Obstruction Coalition: Southerners, Republicans, and Southern Republicans, 1957–1991 (in percentages and by numbers)

	'57	'60	'64	'65	'68	'70	'72	'75	'82	'88	'88	'91	'92
S	100	100	78	95	83	89	77	85	50	0	0	20	17
	(17)	(18)	(21)	(19)	(19)	(16)	(13)	(11)	(4)	(0)	(0)	(1)	(2)
NS	0	0	22	5	17	11	23	15	50	0	0	80	83
	(0)	(0)	(6)	(1)	(4)	(2)	(4)	(2)	(4)	(0)	(0)	(4)	(4)
R	0	0	22	5	26	17	35	46	88	0	0	100	100
	(0)	(0)	(6)	(1)	(6)	(3)	(6)	(6)	(7)	(0)	(0)	(5)	(6)
SR	0	0	4	5	9	11	12	31	38	0	0	20	33
	(0)	(0)	(1)	(1)	(2)	(2)	(2)	(4)	(3)	(0)	(0)	(1)	(2)
T	100	100	100	100	100	100	100	100	100	0	0	100	100
	(17)	(18)	(27)	(20)	(23)	(18)	(17)	(13)	(8)	(0)	(0)	(5)	(6)

Note: "S" refers to southerners; "NS" refers to non-southerners; "R" refers to Republicans; "SR" refers to southern Republicans; and "T" refers to total.

Source: Compiled by author. See Appendix D for details.

wholly to partisan causes, but what is unmistakably clear is that southerners no longer feel compelled to actively impede consideration of civil rights proposals put forth in the Senate. This change can be tied directly to the demise of regionally based racial conflict.

Obstruction of Civil Rights Legislative Proposals

Although the makeup of the civil rights opposition camp has changed over time, the group's reliance on parliamentary tactics has not. Opposition coalitions have constructed procedural barriers in virtually every major civil rights proceeding between 1957 and 1992. One or more of the major stages of the formal policy process has been blocked by opponents either through the use of extended floor discussion, excessive amendment activity, repeated quorum call demands, dilatory motions and points of order, and/or committee chairman powers. Occasionally opponents' strategy has been coordinated through the use of team floor coverage and planning and this has served to bolster the formidableness of their blockages.

Routes of Passage

Alternative routes have almost always been pursued and devised by advocates of civil rights as a means of bypassing opponents' procedural impediments and have demanded much more than is ordinarily required for legislative success in the Senate. For example, they require advocates to expend more time and energy in committee and at the floor in order to keep the targeted proposals afloat. This adds to the physical burden of civil rights lawmaking and it impacts on senators' schedules and commitments generally. Unconventional routes often require a greater familiarity with and experience in utilizing the formal rules in order to thwart opposition attempts to displace and further stall civil rights bills. Many of these routes involve cumbersome, multistep procedures that proffer even more opportunities for obstruction. Finally, cloture, which enormously increases the support and, thus, bargaining imperative of civil rights proceedings, has been a centerpiece of civil rights lawmaking. On the whole, throughout the modern civil rights period, civil rights lawmaking is consistently a more arduous task than conventional lawmaking.

Several quantitative indicators often used to gauge, in essence, how hard Congress is working enable us to systematically compare the demands of the civil rights process against those of the normal policy process. Specifically, we can compare the number of days; debate pages; amendment activity; roll call votes; quorum calls; and cloture votes and petitions involved in each type of process.

First, the amount of time consumed by floor debate in civil rights proceedings versus that of average Senate proceedings is an important indication of the level of active involvement each side of a policy struggle chooses to invest in its efforts, and, relatedly, how much each is obligated to invest. Time at the floor also reflects how much a given proceeding impinges upon individual senators' personal schedules. Consequently, more time, rather than less, at the floor would suggest that legislators, especially policy advocates, are required to invest more. Figure 6.8 shows the number of days the floor spent on the average Senate bill and how much went toward civil rights decisionmaking. In each case, civil rights proceedings consumed much more time than the average floor proceedings. The variation between the amount of time between civil rights and average Senate proceedings was much greater during the earlier debates than the later ones. Starting in the eighties, by this measure, civil rights proceedings began to somewhat approximate normal proceedings. However, throughout, civil rights policymaking required more time input at the floor than was normally the case.

The number of debate pages occupied by congressional floor proceedings also offers a glimpse into how civil rights process compares to the standard Senate process. At the very least, the number of debate pages speaks to the amount of debate and discussion that actually occurs at the floor. The bulk

Figure 6.8
Number of Days for Civil Rights Debates v. Average Senate Debate, 1957–1991

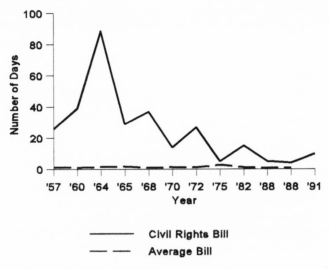

Source: Compiled by author. See Appendix E for details.

of pages in the *Congressional Record* consist of senators' speeches and interchanges. Thus, more debate pages would suggest more dialogue and deliberation and vice versa. As shown in Figure 6.9, what we find in comparing the debate pages of civil rights proceedings to those of the average Senate proceeding is the former consistently outpaces the latter during the pre-seventies years. Interestingly, however, certain of the post-seventies civil rights debates consumed fewer debate pages than did most other Senate proceedings. While on the surface this would suggest accession to normalcy, it would only be with respect to debate. Still, the decline in debate pages alone hardly detracts from the overall backdrop of unconventional lawmaking that is suggested by the remaining measures of Senate and civil rights proceedings.

Amendment activity is another useful indicator of the demands inherent in legislative proceedings. Each submission of an amendment triggers a series of additional parliamentary activities, including debate, floor vote(s), and coalition building. An amendment is the kind of formal parliamentary motion that could potentially affect the substance of a bill. Thus, in order to control the potential policy damage that could flow from amendment activity, advocates must deliver not only a regular presence at the floor, but they must also supply policy majorities when and as necessary. More amendment activity, rather than less, suggests the imposition of relatively greater procedural and political pressures upon the advocacy coalition. There are no readily available quantitative data that would allow a systematic comparison

Figure 6.9
**Pages of *Congressional Record* Consumed by Civil Rights Debates v. Average
Senate Debate, 1957–1991**

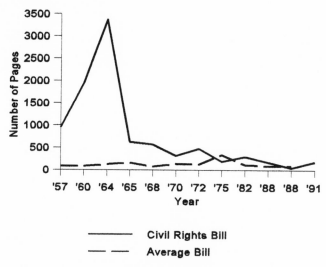

Source: Compiled by author. See Appendix E for details.

of proceedings on the basis of amendment activity. However, it is insightful
that more than 500 amendments were pending at the close of the 1964
civil rights debate and between sixty and eighty were during the remaining
sixties debates. By the time of the 1990s debate, only two were considered
at the floor.

Roll call votes serve as a third important measure of how policy debates
compare to one another, procedurally. Whereas voice and standing votes
consume less time and involve fewer risks, roll call votes are just the opposite. Roll call votes, whereby the clerk calls the name of each senator who
must then appear at the floor and respond, require more time to be completed. Also, because roll call votes record the positions taken by senators
on procedural, amendment, and other legislative matters, such votes involve
higher political stakes than nonrecorded votes. There are certain political
risks involved in taking an official, public position on a matter. The immediate consequence of this is to increase the importance of the coalition
building in which a bill's advocates are engaged. The coalition-building imperative on roll call votes is more challenging. More roll call votes, rather
than less, therefore, drive up the procedural, political, and coalition-building
demands of a given proceeding. Figure 6.10 reflects the number of roll call
votes conducted during the average Senate proceeding and the number involved in civil rights debates. Consistently, civil rights debates encompass a
larger number of roll call votes than do other major policy debates. Over

Figure 6.10
Roll Call Votes Held during Civil Rights Debates v. Average Senate Debate,
1957–1991

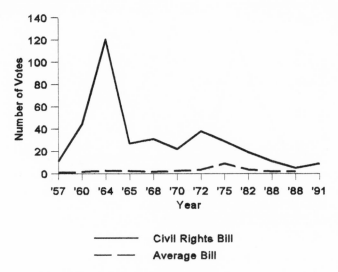

Source: Compiled by author. See Appendix E for details.

time, as with the other measures discussed so far, the level of roll call vote activity diminishes, most notably by the eighties; however, even then it remains above that of the normal policy process.

Quorum calls have a dual practical meaning. On the one hand, they can be important leadership tools for coordinating and facilitating decisionmaking at the floor. They are often used by the leadership to alert senators to an impending floor vote, to signal a change in speakers, to interject a break in floor proceedings to allow for bargaining and cloakroom discussion, and so forth. On the other hand, in the hands of an intense opposition coalition, quorum calls can be a powerful tool for frustrating and wearing down advocates of a targeted bill. Because they require senators' presence at the floor in much the same way as a roll call vote does, repeated quorum calls can prove especially taxing on senators' physical stamina. This is especially true if the quorum calls are untimely, that is, they are made during the early or later hours of the day.

A second, more worrisome potential impact of quorum calls is this: if a majority of senators fail to appear at the floor and respond to their names being called, then an adjournment can be forced. Adjournment opens up an incredible array of opportunities for opponents to further delay, perhaps indefinitely, proceedings. Finally, on the whole, obstructionists stand to benefit from a failed quorum call while advocates stand to lose from one. Thus, quorum calls primarily impose on advocates the burden of both ensuring

Figure 6.11
Quorum Calls Made during Civil Rights Debates v. Average Senate Debate,
1957–1991

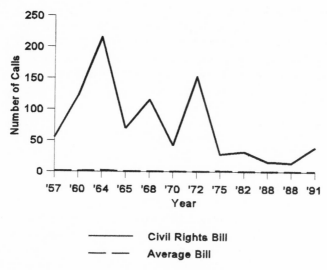

Source: Compiled by author. See Appendix E for details.

that a majority of senators is always on hand and near the chamber as needed and coordinating the logistics of delivering that majority as and when necessary. For the most part, irrespective of the interests of the quorum "caller," once made, quorum calls entail much. The greater the number of quorum calls made during a proceeding, the greater the burden advocates must carry. Shown in Figure 6.11 is the number of quorum calls involved in the average Senate proceeding and in civil rights proceedings in particular. Throughout the period shown, civil rights debates encompassed a much larger number of quorum calls than were involved in most Senate debates. By the eighties civil rights quorum call activity diminished substantially. Still, by this measure, throughout the eighties and up until 1992, the burden of civil rights proceedings exceeded the usual burden of policymaking.

Cloture votes are the most frequently used indicator of abnormal policymaking. While most analysts recognize that it is not an exclusive indicator, as there are other ways of pinpointing abnormalcy, virtually all agree that it most poignantly signals a departure from the norm. The cloture procedure, provided for in Rule 22 of the Senate's standing rules, essentially provides for debate cutoff. It is the Senate's recourse to its own valued, but potentially debilitating, tradition of unlimited debate. It is, more specifically, a means by which advocates can forthrightly confront and defeat opposition obstruction at the floor. This is the primary reason why cloture votes serve as a red flag for obstruction and alternative process. At the same time that cloture is a ready indication of a policy proceeding's departure from the norm, the procedure itself entails relatively higher skill and support requirements than most procedures. At least sixteen senators must endorse a petition for a cloture motion. As of 1975, at least three-fifths of senators must vote in favor of the motion. Previously, two-thirds support was required. Cloture requires, in essence, supermajority support. Also, various strict rules dictate how debate and proceedings are to be conducted once cloture is invoked—rules advocates must be aware of in order to obtain the full benefit of cloture.

Beyond the skill and support requirements that cloture imposes on advocates, there are also certain political constraints advocates must face when attempting to invoke cloture. Advocates face great odds in persuading senators to support a cloture motion. The norm of reciprocity dictates that senators vote to undermine the debate privileges of other senators only sparingly. A vote by Senator X against Senator Y's right to engage in extended debate today could be a vote against Senator X's right to do so tomorrow. There is great reverence in the Senate for the right of unlimited debate. It lies at the heart of the Senate's deliberative capacity and is the hallmark of its tradition of individualism. As a consequence, proponents of a bill targeted by obstruction must not only work to win a supermajority vote, but they must also overcome the constraints of a tradition that preliminarily stacks the odds against securing cloture support. A cloture vote signals not only an inordinate procedural burden, but also a formidable political burden.

Civil rights proceedings claim a greater proportion of Senate cloture votes than any other policy area. Of the approximately 220 cloture petitions and votes that have occurred in the Senate through 1992, fully twenty-eight of these involved a civil rights measure. In fact, civil rights bills are infamous for their share of cloture votes. Most analysts point to the sixties civil rights legislation when drawing out this distinction. The fact is, however, civil rights "cloturitis" continues well beyond the sixties. Cloture is a virtual staple feature of civil rights policymaking throughout the modern civil rights era. Of the thirteen civil rights laws that are the focus of this analysis, at least eleven (or 85%) of the proceedings on these laws involved one or more cloture votes. Multiple cloture votes are still another distinctive characteristic of civil rights decisionmaking. The 1972 civil rights debate alone involved three separate cloture votes, the 1968 debate involved fully four, and at least two were involved in the 1975 debate.

The proportion of civil rights laws for which cloture was used far surpasses the percentage of Senate bills generally that call for cloture. Figure 6.12 depicts an extremely conservative comparison of these measures. It demonstrates clearly that only a tiny portion of Senate bills are subject to a cloture vote or petition, while the overwhelming proportion of civil rights bills have involved cloture. The bar depicting Senate filibusters reflects the total number of cloture votes and petitions filed in an entire decade as a percentage of all of the major public bills adopted in the Senate during the

Figure 6.12
Estimated Percentage of Senate and Civil Rights Bills "Clotured," 1950–1980, Selected Years

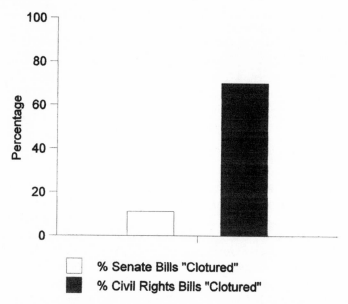

☐ **% Senate Bills "Clotured"**
■ **% Civil Rights Bills "Clotured"**

Source: Compiled by author using the *Congressional Record* "Daily Digest" series and Democratic Study Group (1994)

first year only of each of the following decades: the fifties, sixties, seventies, and eighties. The civil rights bar depicts the total number of civil rights cloture votes and petitions against the major civil rights bills that have been enacted into law. This number excludes successive cloture votes on a single bill, so that, although the 1968 open housing proceedings involved four separate cloture votes, these votes are captured here as one.

What this examination of cloture use against civil rights essentially tells us is that enacting a civil rights law requires the building of not just majority support, but more, supermajority support. Of course, the political implications of this fact are varied and enormous. Beyond this, the analysis of "civil rights cloturitis" poignantly demonstrates the persistent abnormalcy of civil rights lawmaking.

CIVIL RIGHTS POLICY OUTCOMES

Racial issues' controversiality within the larger arena has had a direct bearing upon the substantive elements of decisionmaking within legislative institutions. The intense political conflict tied to race has negatively affected the content of laws considered and adopted in Congress. Just as racial dis-

Table 6.6
Need for Support: Votes Required Minus Votes Acquired

	`57	`60	`64	`65	`68	`70	`72	`75	`82	`88	`88	`91	`92
Votes Required to Defeat Filibuster	64	67	67	67	67	67	67	60	60	60	60	60	60
Votes Required to Defeat Veto	na	na	na	na	na	na	na	na	67	67	67	67	na
Votes Acquired	53	49	57	61	59	63	55	55	65	54	75	65	60
Votes Needed to Defeat Filibuster	11	18	10	6	8	4	12	5	0	na	na	0	0
Votes Needed to Defeat Veto	na	na	na	na	na	na	na	na	2	13	+8	2	7

Source: Compiled by author. See Appendix A for details on how coalitions are configured.

cord has generated abnormal procedural processes, it has also led to what amounts to "abnormal" policymaking. The policy influence of racial politics is transmitted through several factors. First is the need for additional votes to secure movement of civil rights bills beyond procedural obstacles. Second is advocates' reliance on conservative Republican senators for the additional votes needed. Third is these senators' insistence on major policy concessions as a condition for their support. Lastly, it is the heightened scrutiny attendant to racial issues that has rendered alternative modes of bargaining ineffective as means of securing additional votes.

Negotiating Race

The basic driving force behind the abnormal policy compromises that typify civil rights lawmaking is the limited bargainability of race. The extraordinary support requirements of the unconventional process faced by advocates have forced them to seek out more votes. Indicated in Table 6.6 is the number of votes already acquired and the number needed by advocates. In virtually every case, more support has to be won over, either to confront internal obstruction or to deal with the external threat of a presidential veto.

In practice, getting the extra votes required to effectively deal with civil rights obstruction has almost always meant turning to mostly Republican uncommitteds. And, as demonstrated in the previous chapters, the majority of senators who have made up the "uncommitted" coalition are Republican. At the floor and/or in committee, the mostly Republican group of uncommitted senators either voted with the opposition on key procedural and/or amendment votes, provided some indications they would do so, or simply withheld their support of civil rights bills on key votes. Consequently, in both on- and off-floor policy negotiations, uncommitted Republican senators were a central concern of supporters. Shown in Table 6.7 is the pro-

Table 6.7
Republicans' Share of "Uncommitted" Coalition

Debate Year	Total Number of Uncommitteds	Republican Percentage Share of Uncommitteds
1957	26	39%
1960	33	64%
1964	16	69%
1965	19	90%
1968	18	67%
1970	19	79%
1972	28	64%
1975	31	45%
1982	27	82%
1988 (Grove City)	31	68%
1988 (Housing)	22	70%
1991	30	55%
1992	34	77%

Source: Compiled by author. See Appendix A for details.

portion of uncommitteds who were Republican. More to the point, winning their active support went hand in hand with accommodating their racially conservative Republican ideals. Critically, given the high visibility of racial issues, these uncommitteds have almost always been unwilling to engage in politics-as-usual in return for their indispensable votes. The relatively greater exposure that attends race and, thus, civil rights policy negotiations, in effect, inhibits the feasibility of common negotiating tools such as side payments and logrolling. Where racial policy negotiations are concerned, side payments and logrolling are relatively ineffective. As a result, compromise has proven the only viable means for securing the supermajority votes required of the abnormal policy process. More to the point, uncommitted legislators have demanded substantive revisions to civil rights proposals as a condition for their indispensable support.

Given that Republicanism serves as the main ideological cue for the majority of these as-yet uncommitted senators, the revisions they have stipulated comport with the basic principles of Republican ideology, namely, small government, laissez-faire economics, and individualism. As applied to

civil rights, these principles dictate virtually the opposite of what race reformers have sought. Inherent in federal civil rights advocacy is a call for an
active federal government role in the protection of civil rights, government
expansion of socioeconomic opportunities, and, recently, advantageous racial preferences. Civil rights is, in essence, regulatory policy. It tells states
and other private and public entities what they must, can, and cannot do—
all primarily under the authority of the federal government. Republicanism
is fundamentally at odds with government regulation, especially at the federal level and in areas traditionally seen as private or state domain, such as
education, housing, and so forth. This point of departure has proven key as
it has directly shaped policy negotiations with advocates and, ultimately, the
content of civil rights laws.

Republicans have been consistently more conservative on measures involving assessments of the federal government's role. The survey data in
Figures 6.5, 6.6, and 6.7, discussed earlier, measure responses to general
questions about nondiscrimination and equal rights. While those data show
a gap, the data in Figures 6.13, 6.14, and 6.15 reveal even more substantial
disagreement between the two parties. Critically, the data shown in these
figures measure responses to questions that specifically reference the role of
the federal government. And each set reveals a much sharper rift within the
party system on questions pertaining to the government's role than on those
concerning essentially legal and political rights. Depicted in Figure 6.13 are
survey data responses to the following question: "Do you think the government in Washington should see to it that white and black children go to
the same schools?" Clearly, the parties are not very far apart initially with
regard to their views of federal intervention in schools. Over time, however,
they grow further apart. Starting in 1964 and continuing through 1990,
Republicans are much more apt to reject the notion of a justifiable federal
role in school desegregation.

In Figure 6.14 are responses to the question: "Should the government in
Washington see to it that black people get fair treatment in jobs?" These
data also reveal a rift between the two parties, but one that is more stable
over time than that concerning school segregation. Republicans are consistently less likely than Democrats to endorse a federal role in the workplace.

The most telling indication of partisan differences over the federal government's role in civil rights is the trend in attitudes toward government
aid that is revealed in Figure 6.15. Shown are respondents' support for the
idea that "the government in Washington should make every possible effort
to improve the social and economic position of blacks and other minority
groups." Republican support on this particular item is lower than that on
any other item. Clearly, Republicans are far less likely than Democrats to
support government intervention on behalf of minorities generally.

Figure 6.13
Federal Government and Schools: Percentage Feels Federal Government Should Ensure School Desegregation by Party, 1960–1990

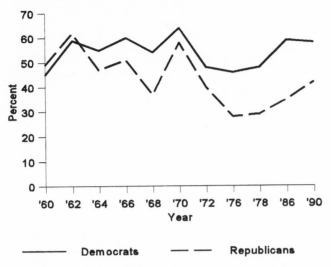

Source: NES, 1960–1990. See Appendix C for details.

Civil Rights Policy Concessions and Provisions

The policy concessions made by advocates in order to win over Republican votes, moreover, have been particularly debilitating. Civil rights compromises can be appropriately described as abnormal. Under normal circumstances compromise yields a moderating effect upon a bill's provisions, as advocates must concede on one or more aspects of a proposed bill. And, under ordinary circumstances it is the enforcement provisions that compromise most affects, given it is easier to build consensus on matters of principle than on a specific approach. Ordinarily, however, policy compromise does not strip a proposed bill of its most essential components—that is, seldom do policy negotiations erode and/or eliminate the very provisions that distinguish the bill's prohibitions and proclamations from already-existent rights. Bargains that have this effect may be appropriately characterized as outside of the norm.

This is precisely where civil rights compromises lie, outside of the norm. Almost consistently, civil rights advocates have been forced to abandon the core elements of the civil rights legislative proposals put forth over the past four decades. As shown in Table 6.8, it is precisely those provisions that are designed to add force to the constitutional guarantee of equal treatment that are sacrificed for the sake of Republican support. Shown are the bills that initially establish or address rights. Excluded are the extensions or re-

Figure 6.14
**Federal Government and Jobs: Percentage Feels Federal Government Should
Ensure Fair Treatment in Jobs by Party, 1964–1988**

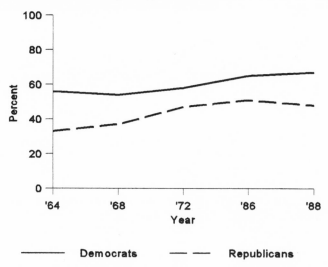

Source: NES, 1964–1988. See Appendix C for details.

visions of the original legislation. What remains of major civil rights proposals when they emerge from policy negotiations is the bare bones of
advocates' original plan for reform. Advocates' overriding goal was to subject the problem of racial discrimination to congressional control. By way
of administrative enforcement, Congress would have had at its disposal several immediate means of redressing the race problem, such as its broad governing powers, its oversight authority, its budget authorizations and
appropriations process, and its investigations authority. Proponents of the
bills have had to settle, instead, for what is essentially a piecemeal, litigative
approach to dismantling racial inequality.

As enacted, each of the major federal civil rights laws is reliant chiefly on
the federal court system for enforcement. There are no administrative remedies guaranteed to minorities under civil rights laws, except in voting.
There are no administrative apparatuses in place to enforce compliance and/
or assign penalties relative to racial discrimination, except by way of the
court system. Specifically, under each of the seven voting rights laws passed
during the modern civil rights era (namely, the 1957, 1960, 1965, 1970,
1975, 1982, and 1992 bills), the U.S. attorney general is empowered to
litigate on behalf of alleged victims of voter discrimination and to suspend
the use of devices in covered states. Under the 1964 and 1991 bills and
also the 1988 restoration act, the U.S. attorney general is authorized to file
suit in federal court on behalf of alleged victims of school discrimination.

Figure 6.15
Government Aid: Percentage Feels Federal Government Should Try to Improve Position of Blacks and Other Minorities by Party, 1970–1990

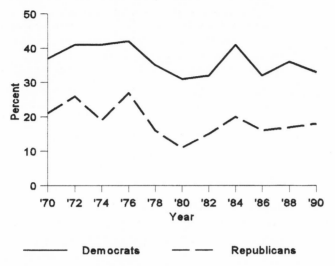

Source: NES, 1970–1990. See Appendix C for details.

Under the 1972 bill, the Equal Employment Opportunity Commission (EEOC) is authorized to initiate federal court civil suits if it identifies a pattern of employment discrimination. Under the 1968 and 1988 housing bills, the Department of Housing and Urban Development (HUD) is empowered to initiate legal proceedings in a federal court. Only in the unlikely case that those charged under the bill agree to HUD enforcement is the administrative remedy available and, as such, it is a conditional administrative remedy at best.

In effect, civil rights compromises have reduced advocates' proposals to little more than cosmetic legislative reforms that are constitutionally redundant. The federal civil rights laws that have been enacted prohibit discrimination on the basis of race and, thus, extend the right of equal treatment. But, so does the U.S. Constitution. The Fourteenth Amendment reads: "No state shall . . . deny to any person within its jurisdiction the equal protection of the laws." Roughly half of the civil rights laws guarantee equal voting rights. Yet, the Fifteenth Amendment already provides this: "The right of citizens of the United States to vote shall not be denied . . . on account of race, color, or previous condition of servitude." In essence, civil rights laws bestow rights already prescribed in the Constitution. They proscribe the same kinds of behavior, namely, discrimination, that is proscribed by the Constitution. Even as these bills delineate with more specificity than the

Table 6.8
Civil Rights Policy Concessions: Advocates' Original Major Goals and Policy Concessions in Landmark Legislation

Year of Passage	Advocates' Original Key Goals	Policy Concessions
1957 Voting	Authorize U.S. attorney general to seek civil rights protection orders.	Deleted authorization for U.S. attorney general to seek civil rights protection orders.
1960 Voting	Authorize use of presidentially appointed registrars to enlist voters.	Deleted authorization for presidentially appointed voter registrars.
1964 General	Establish wide coverage of the bill. Give U.S. attorney general wide discretion in filing discrimination suits.	Restricted bill's coverage. Restricted U.S. attorney general's authority to sue.
1965 Voting	Provide for administrative registrars. Establish administrative ban on the use of poll taxes.	Included only a statement of Congress' disapproval of poll tax use.
1968 Housing	Authorize HUD enforcement. Establish wide coverage of the bill.	Deleted HUD enforcement. Restricted bill's coverage.
1972 Employment	Authorize EEOC enforcement. Extend bill's coverage.	Deleted EEOC enforcement.
1988 Housing	Authorize HUD enforcement.	Provided option of court enforcement to defendants.

Source: Compiled by author.

Constitution the particular areas in which racial discrimination is prohibited, they do not go far beyond the general constitutional prohibition.

Though Congress is empowered to make laws that are "necessary and proper" to effectuate constitutional guarantees, in the case of civil rights, it has done little to effectuate the guarantee of equality. Instead, on this score, Congress repeats much of what is already contained in the Constitution. As noted earlier, federal civil rights laws entrust enforcement of their key anti-discrimination provisions to the federal court system. But, so does the U.S. Constitution. Article III empowers the Supreme Court and lower federal courts to decide cases and controversies involving constitutional rights. So, in this respect also, Congress adds little to what is already established in the Constitution. Under the threat of defeat by opponents and the demands of moderates, advocates have been forced to abandon the more effective administrative-centered approach to enforcement. And, in doing so, Congress has consistently reduced civil rights legislative proposals to little more than echoes of the century-old promise of equality contained in the U.S. Constitution.

The Impact of Civil Rights Laws

Existing federal civil rights laws have wrought little tangible racial change. More specifically, they have had minimal impact on the real-life circumstance of blacks—the primary intended beneficiaries of these laws. Many of the troublesome racial disparities between blacks and whites that had existed before passage of these laws, disparities that, in fact, prompted pursuit of their enactment, remain largely intact. The one area in which we do observe notable progress is voting, but even here we can question the practical significance of the reform achieved. On the whole, a near half-century of civil rights politics and policymaking has failed to make blacks substantially better off, in concrete terms, than they were before the advent of civil rights law.

The facts regarding racial change are unmistakably clear. Statistical measures of the racial status quo as it was prior to the enactment of federal civil rights legislation and those measuring the existing status quo reveal a consistent trend of racial inequality, except in relation to voting. The "before and after" of civil rights lawmaking are not notably distinguishable. Federal civil rights policy has failed to substantially reduce, let alone eliminate, sizeable inequities in life opportunities. In particular, trends in educational attainment, employment status and occupation, median income, poverty, and homeownership all demonstrate very clearly that these more entrenched elements of the race problem have survived the modern civil rights "revolution" of reform. In two areas, blacks have begun to move toward parity as previously steep differences have begun to diminish. In most others, however, the gap between blacks and whites relative to opportunity and outcomes has not improved significantly. And, in still others blacks' status relative to whites' has worsened. Let us look at the specifics of the "before and after" picture.

Political participation among blacks is now more comparable to that of whites. During the early years of the modern civil rights period, blacks' involvement in the electoral process was virtually nonexistent in the South, where most blacks resided. However, since the seventies the black vote has become a meaningful force in local mayoral elections and remains significant at the national presidential level as well. Importantly, black voter participation, nationally, is more equal to that of whites. Interestingly, as Table 6.9 shows, part of the reason blacks and whites are more equal relative to voting is that whites are far less likely to vote now than they were in the past. Still, while demobilization is a trend that is observed across virtually all racial and

Table 6.9
Voter Turnout: Percentage Reported Voting* by Race for U.S., 1964 and 1996

	1964	1996	Change
Black	58.5**	50.6	-7.9
White	70.7	56.0	-14.7
B-W Gap	12.2	5.4	-6.8

*Of total persons of voting age.
**Includes other races.

Source: Census Bureau, Voting and Registration (1996)

ethnic groups, black political participation has declined at a slower pace than has that of whites.

Nonetheless, blacks' greater political equality is, arguably, inconsequential in light of certain other factors. The most important of these is the original goal of voter participation. Early civil rights advocates and, to some extent, contemporary proponents as well have emphasized the importance of voting as a means to an end—that is, voting was and is recognized as a door of opportunity toward more tangible gains. Advocates believed then and now that giving blacks a louder voice in elections would yield more government policy responsiveness, which, in turn, would produce a more equitable distribution of socioeconomic benefits. As I will demonstrate shortly, black political power has not yielded the desired outcomes. Therefore, we can question just how meaningful the achievement of greater voter equality is, given its basic purpose.

The black educational progress that has been achieved is of limited practical significance. On the one hand, the high school completion rate among blacks has improved substantially since 1950. Between 1950 and 1997, as shown in Table 6.10, blacks have moved from an 8.1 rate to a much greater (74.9) rate of completing twelve years of schooling. As well, black achievement on this measure has moved at a faster pace than that of whites. Black high school completion is now comparable, though not equal, to that of whites.

On the more important measures of educational attainment, namely, college completion rates, blacks fare poorly in comparison to whites. Given the preponderant share of service-oriented jobs in the labor market and the higher skill and educational requirements of these jobs, the practical worth of blacks' progress at the high school level is minimal. In order to effectively capitalize upon many of the existing employment opportunities in the American labor market, especially the higher-paying jobs, a college degree or, at the very least, technological training and background is virtually indispensable. And, as Table 6.10 shows, it is at this level of education that blacks

Table 6.10
Educational Attainment: High School* and College** Completion Rate by Race, 1950 and 1997 (in percentages)

	High School Completion Rate		College Completion Rate	
	1950	1997	1950	1997
Black	8.1***	74.9	2.2***	13.3
White	21.4	83.0	6.4	24.6
B-W Ratio	2.6	1.0	2.9	1.8

*Percentage persons 25+ completed 4 years of high school or more
**Percentage persons 25+ completed 4 years of college or more
***Actual category: "Non-white"

Source: Calculated by author from data contained in U.S. Bureau of the Census, *Statistical Abstract of the U.S. 1960,* Table 137 (1960), and ibid., *Statistical Abstract of the U.S. 1998,* Table 260 (1998)

continue to be at a disadvantage. Admittedly, black college completion rates have improved substantially since 1950. However, whereas in the past blacks were almost three times less likely than whites to complete college, they are still almost two times less likely to obtain a college degree. In the workplace, too, blacks continue to lag behind whites. As demonstrated in earlier chapters, blacks were concentrated in blue-collar jobs during the sixties and seventies. As of 1997, the majority of blacks (roughly 48.5%) continue to be employed in blue-collar jobs, whereas the majority of white workers (roughly 58.7%) are employed in white-collar jobs (see Table 6.11). Similarly, blacks are less likely than whites to be employed in managerial and professional jobs. This fact has enormous implications relative to the experience of blacks in the workplace, both in terms of advancement opportunity, independence, and marketability.

Shown in Table 6.12 is an even more telling portrait of progress relative to black employment status. In comparing the pre–civil rights laws years to the post–civil rights laws years, we find that blacks are even more likely than whites now to be unemployed than they were in the past. As of 1955, blacks were 2.2 times more likely than whites to be unemployed. As of 1997, blacks were 2.4 times more likely to be unemployed. The increase in the rate of unemployment among blacks is substantially higher than that of whites. The unemployment rate among blacks has increased 1.3 percentage points, while that of whites has increased only 0.3 percentage points. This faster pace of black unemployment points toward an even more dim future.

As in the fifties, in the nineties too blacks earned only half of the income whites did. As shown in Table 6.13, as of 1950, the black-white ratio with respect to median family income was 0.54, while in 1996, it was 0.59. In

Table 6.11
Occupational Employment of Blacks and General Populace, 1997
(in percentages)

	Black	White
Managerial and Professional Specialty	19.7	29.1
Technical, Sales, and Administrative Support	28.8	29.6
Service Occupation	22.1	13.5
Precision Production, Craft and Repair	8.2	10.1
Operators, Fabricators, and Laborers	19.9	14.2

Note: Column totals equal less than 100% due to rounding errors.

Source: U.S. Bureau of the Census, *Statistical Abstract of the U.S. 1998,* Tables 646 and 672 (1998)

effect, almost fifty years of civil rights lawmaking has produced a gain of only .05 with respect to the black-white income ratio. Further, the ramifications of lower income are substantial. Financial income has a ripple effect. It dictates housing patterns, which, in turn, have been shown to drive school quality, which, in turn, affects employability. In addition to income, the total wealth acquired by blacks is also substantially lower than that of whites. While lower income negatively affects purchasing power, fewer assets compound income constraints by limiting also borrowing power. In short, financially, blacks are no better off now than they were in the years preceding the modern civil rights period.

While income measures reflect financial status, poverty rates are an indication of financial disadvantage specifically. And, over an almost forty-year period, black impoverishment remains substantial both in absolute and relative terms. Table 6.14 shows that as of 1959 more than half of blacks lived below the poverty line. By 1996, this number had declined. Still, almost one-third of blacks continue to live in poverty, compared to about one in ten whites. More specifically, blacks are initially three times more likely than whites to be impoverished and, later, are still far more likely than whites (2.5 times) to be impoverished. An important note to add to this discussion of the statistical trends in poverty is that being poor in contemporary American society means something quite different than it meant in the past. Financial impoverishment is often accompanied now by certain other social disadvantages, namely, ghettoization, high drug dependency, high teenage

Table 6.12
Unemployment Rate by Race, 1955 and 1997 (in percentages)

	1955	1997	Change
Black	8.7*	10.0	+1.3
White	3.9	4.2	+0.3
B-W Ratio	2.2	2.4	-0.2

*Includes "Negro and other"

Source: U.S. Bureau of the Census, *Statistical Abstract of the U.S. 1970*, Table 321, and ibid.,
    Statistical Abstract of the U.S. 1998, Table 646

pregnancy rate, high numbers of single-parent households, high crime rate, and so forth. The suggestion here is not that all of today's black poor exhibit these behavioral pathologies; rather, the point is that contemporary poverty is often attended by other negative trends.

Homeownership, perhaps the most poignant symbol of arrival at the "American dream," is also a less likely prospect among blacks than it is for the U.S. population as a whole. Shown in Table 6.15 are homeownership rates for blacks and the general populace in 1950 and 1990. Clearly, blacks are less likely to own their own home than most others. This is true of then and now. Black homeownership rates have increased since 1950, however, less than half of blacks own homes, while almost two-thirds of the population at large does. The gap between the two groups is virtually the same in 1990 as it was in 1950. In fact, it has grown by a tiny percentage. Additionally, black progress on this measure is outpaced by that of the population at large, given an 8.9 percent increase for blacks, compared to a 9.2 percent increase for the general population. This suggests the likelihood of inequality in the housing market not only continuing, but perhaps increasing in years to come.

On the whole, it could be argued that, given the persistence of socioeconomic inequality, federal civil rights policy efforts of the past and of recent years have failed. This is because advocates, especially the proponents of earlier civil rights laws, wanted to redress the race problem as manifest in objective measures of inequality, particularly those in the South. And even though segregation was the critical concern at the outset, even during the sixties, segregation was only part of the overall set of concerns. The chief goal of congressional civil rights advocates has been that of outlawing racial discrimination for the purpose of ensuring racially equal opportunity. Proponents of civil rights, in floor speeches, committee reports, and other forums, have repeatedly made reference to what they regard as troubling racial disparities in elections, schools, employment, and housing. Indeed, as noted earlier, the initial emphasis on voting rights was intended to spark racial

Table 6.13
Income: Median Family Income by Race, 1950 and 1996 (in current dollars)

	1950	1996
Black	1,869*	26,552
White	3,445	44,756
B-W Ratio	.54	.59

*Includes "other"

Source: U.S. Bureau of the Census, *Statistical Abstract of the U.S. 1970*, Table 486, and ibid.,
     Statistical Abstract of the U.S. 1998, Table 746

progress in other areas. The aim of civil rights policy reform has been to reduce stark racial inequalities across the board. And, in this respect, federal civil rights policy has failed.

It would be a gross overstatement, nonetheless, to characterize federal civil rights laws as complete and total failures. The fact is, the laws favorably altered the political climate relative to racial progressivism. Civil rights laws have, in effect, shifted morality and "political correctness" to the side of civil rights reform. The question of whether blacks are entitled to equal opportunity, without regard to race, has been largely settled by existing civil rights law. Physical signs of disadvantaging racial classification or any other for that matter are considered intolerable, thanks to changes in American law wrought by civil rights policy. Generally, there is a heightened sensitivity to and regard for the cause of racial inequality due to the federal legislative enactments. In this respect, the accomplishments of civil rights policy are substantial. Yet and still, they are largely symbolic.

CHAPTER SUMMARY

In conclusion, when we examine the substance of racial politics, we find that, over the years, it has come to revolve less around regional cleavages and more around partisan discord. Nonetheless, race has proven to be a particularly contentious issue. Another consistent feature of racial politics is that the polarization it gives rise to has unfolded at the forefront of American politics during much of the modern civil rights period. And, precisely because race has typically been a highly salient and divisive issue, it has always stimulated breakdowns in the normal process and, thereby, emergence of unorthodox policy processes. The extent of the obstructions that have led to the breakdowns has diminished, as the extraordinary filibusters of the sixties and earlier are unparalleled. But, despite the scaled-down nature of contemporary civil rights obstruction, enacting civil rights legislation remains a particularly onerous task. Making civil rights law is a bigger chal-

Table 6.14
Poverty: Percentage below Poverty Level by Race for U.S., 1959 and 1996

	1959	1996
Black	55.1*	28.4
White	18.1	11.2
B-W Ratio	3.0	2.5

*Includes "other"

Source: U.S. Bureau of the Census, *Statistical Abstract of the U.S. 1970*, Table 502, and ibid.,
    Statistical Abstract of the U.S. 1998, Table 756

Table 6.15
**Homeownership Rate for Blacks and General U.S. Populace, 1950 and 1990
(in percentages)**

	1950	1990
Black	34.5	43.4
U.S.	55.0	64.2
Gap	20.5	20.8

Source: U.S. Bureau of the Census Web Site, 1999

lenge than is making most public laws. To meet the challenge of
unconventional procedural routes, civil rights policy advocates have always
depended on the aid of moderates. And, in adding their indispensable support to the civil rights cause, moderates have always demanded that advocates abandon what is, in effect, their basic policy goals. The result is that
little has changed with regard to the inequality between black and white
Americans. Existing civil rights laws, essentially, buttress the guarantee of
equal treatment conferred by the U.S. Constitution. But, what these laws
have failed to do is make the constitutional guarantee a reality.

In the absence of institutional structures that lend themselves to manipulation by minority opposition groups, it is quite possible that tangible civil
rights policy accomplishments can be realized. What this analysis has made
clear, however, is that under existing institutional arrangements, the explosive nature of racial politics has effectively rendered the race problem an
ungovernable one.

Appendix A: Methodology for Identifying Policy Coalitions in Senate Civil Rights Proceedings

Senators who took part in blocking civil rights proposals through the use of formal procedures are classified as "obstructionists." A two-step method was used to identify obstructionists. First, I identified all senators who were either recorded as voting "nay" on the question of final passage of the bill; announced as paired against the bill on the question of final passage; or, if absent, announced as likely to vote against passage. Then, by way of corroborating the number identified in this first step, I compared it to the number indicated by certain debate remarks as well as other recorded votes. That is, I cross-checked the number of obstructionists identified through reliance on the final roll call votes against the number identified by floor remarks. It is more challenging to identify those actively blocking the 1991 and 1992 bills. This is because the "holds" placed against the bill are carried out by the leadership on behalf of senators and because the leadership traditionally does not divulge the senator(s) for whom the hold is being carried out. Still, analysis of committee votes, floor roll call votes, and debate remarks provide some useful clues of the likely objectors.

"Uncommitteds" are those who, although supportive of the goals of the basic bill, did not provide their full and complete support to the civil rights legislative efforts at the outset, but had differences with proponents on the original proposals, other pending modifications, or some other facet of the proceedings. Typically these senators offered moderate support of the bill either by backing the more conservative version of the bill and/or its provisions and/or by voting against supporters more often than not. These were senators who more than just dissented on one or two votes, but who had major problems with the bills. Uncommitteds were identified by way of a three-step process. First, a set of key amendment votes was compiled, which included all roll call votes on amendments on which there was a significant split among the membership, specifically, in which both the "yea-voting" and "nay-voting" sides claimed around 40 percent of the pool of voting senators, indicating substantial disagreement. Excluded from the set of key amendment votes were second- and third-round votes held on single amendments—that is, in those instances in which there was one or more reconsideration votes on the same amendment, I counted only the first vote on the amendment as a key amendment vote. Excluded also were standing and voice votes on amendments.

The next step of identifying uncommitteds involved identifying which amendments constituted weakening amendments and which did not. Weakening amendments are basically those that would likely dilute the potential impact of the bill, either by limiting its scope or enforcement, or those that go against the grain of the bill's advocacy, either by adding extraneous, nongermane provisions or by decreasing the bill's chances of being adopted. In those instances in which the language of the amendment did not clearly indicate whether or not it was of a weakening nature, I relied upon the comments and votes of the bill's most liberal spokesmen as well as its most outspoken opponents as an indication of the predominant perception in the Senate vis-à-vis the nature of the amendment. The final step of identifying moderates involved selecting those senators who voted for weakening amendments in at least 60 percent of the key amendment votes. A senator who voted for weaker amendments at least two out of three times would be considered an uncommitted.

During the 1988 housing debate and the 1992 debate, I departed downward from the 40 percent floor vote standard. In 1982, the two key votes selected claimed only 22 percent and 12.5 percent on the "opposing" side. In 1992, there were only two floor amendment votes. Both were selected. Then, in identifying uncommitteds in 1982 and 1992, I selected those senators who voted for the weakening amendment in one out of the two key votes because there were only two votes that came close to meeting the "key vote" standard used in this study. This departure does not weaken the claims regarding uncommitteds during this particular debate because the point of the methodology is to measure who is aligned with supporters most of the time versus who is voting against supporters most of the time. Where there are only two votes, one out of two votes can be safely judged as "most of the time."

Supporters are those who voted in favor of the bill on key votes, final passage, and the majority of the remaining votes. They were initially identified through a process of elimination. Basically, all those remaining after the identification of obstructionists and moderates were classified as supporters. The number of supporters arrived at was checked against (1) debate remarks on both sides of the bill, advocates and opponents; (2) several of the procedural and substantive votes held in connection with the bill; and also (3) the vote on final passage.

Appendix B: Sources and Methodology for Compilation of Population Data

Population data were derived from the following U.S. Bureau of the Census sources: for 1950, 1960, and 1970, U.S. Bureau of the Census, *Statistical Abstract of the United States 1971*, 92d edition (Washington, D.C.: U.S. GPO, 1971); for 1980: U.S. Bureau of the Census, *Statistical Abstract of the United States 1981*, l02d edition (Washington, D.C.: U.S. GPO, 1981); and for 1990: U.S. Bureau of the Census, *Statistical Abstract of the United States 1993*, 113th edition (Washington, D.C.: U.S. GPO, 1993).

In each population table and graph, the South is configured to include the eleven former Confederate states. The "non-South" includes the remaining 39 states and the District of Columbia. For the non-South, however, I derived the figures on whites, blacks, and "others" by calculating the difference between the number of persons in the South and the number of persons in the United State as a whole. Data on racial and ethnic groups other than blacks and whites are available in the bureau's population reports, but are not reported here, nor are these data included in the population tables and graphs. However, "others" are included in the regional totals. The result of including "others" in the calculation of totals is that the proportion of whites and blacks will not equal 100 percent. Although, according to the data reported here, for the years 1950 and 1960, blacks and whites composed 100 percent of the South's population; this is due in part to the fact that "others" made up less than 1 percent of the population in certain states, but mostly because of rounding. Finally, for 1950, 1960, and 1970, because the Census Bureau reports did not report state totals, the "South Total" was calculated by summing "other" for individual states, then adding this figure to the total number of whites and blacks for each state.

Appendix C: Sources of
Survey Data

Survey data were obtained from three survey series: the National Elections Studies (NES), conducted through the Center for Political Studies at the University of Michigan; the General Social Survey (GSS), administered through the University of Chicago National Opinion Research Center; and the Gallup Poll, produced by the American Institute of Public Opinion. The following sources were used as a guide in selecting specific polls from the NES, GSS, and Gallup survey series, respectively: Warren E. Miller and the National Election Studies, *American National Election Studies Cumulative Data File, 1952–1990* (Ann Arbor: University of Michigan, Center for Political Studies, 1991); James Davies and Tom Smith, *General Social Surveys, Cumulative Codebook, 1972–1991* (Chicago: National Opinion Research Center, George Gallup 1991); *Gallup Poll: Public Opinion, 1935–1971* (New York: Random House, 1972).

In selecting survey questions and responses from these sources, I was guided foremost by (1) the goal of assessing patterns of change in public opinion vis-à-vis racial issues during the period from 1960 to 1990 and (2) that of comparing racial opinions by race, region, and party. For each survey series, there was some slight variation in the wording of the questions from one interview wave to the next. In each case, I selected the wording used most frequently during the period 1960 to 1990.

The vast majority of responses to the selected survey questions were collapsed and recoded differently than they appear in the codebooks and indexes. All of the "No Answer" and "Don't Know" responses were eliminated. In coding racial groups, "other" was excluded, as was "independent" in the coding of the political parties. Additionally, geographic areas were coded so that the "South" includes the eleven former Confederate states, namely, Alabama, Arkansas, Florida, Georgia, Louisiana, Mississippi, North Carolina, South Carolina, Tennessee, Texas, and Virginia. The "non-South" includes all other states. The figures reported here have been rounded to the nearest whole number so that some discrepancies may be attributed to rounding errors.

Given the variety of sources from which these data are derived, some minimal problems of comparability between the data sets and their approach to measuring opinions are no doubt present. This most likely affects this analysis' depiction of respondents' absolute stance from year to year on the various racial subjects discussed. But, primary emphasis in the analysis is not placed upon the absolute stance of the regional, racial, and political groups examined, although there are references to their absolute stance. Instead, the gist of the discussion focuses upon how these groups compare to one another and, more importantly, changes in the groups' attitudes over time. Potentially problematic also are the small black samples. However, the bulk of this analysis necessarily centers upon the attitudes of the majority population rather than that of blacks. A more precise measurement of modern black opinions is made available through the University of Michigan's *National Black Election Study*.

Appendix D: Sources and Methodology for Compilation of Voting Data

Data for the South for 1960 were derived from the Census Bureau's *Statistical Abstract 1980*. The 1962 and 1964 data are taken from Pat Watters and Reese Cleghorn's *Climbing Jacob's Ladder*. The 1966 data are derived from the Census Bureau's *Statistical Abstract 1980* and Watters and Cleghorn's *Climbing*. Actual registration numbers for 1966 were taken from the Census Bureau's *Abstract*, while Voting Age Population (VAP) figures were taken from Watters and Cleghorn to generate registration rates.

Southern voter data for 1970 were derived from two sources, the 1980 Census Bureau's *Abstract* (Table 849, p. 514) and the Subcommittee on Constitutional Rights, Committee on the Judiciary, U.S. Senate, *Hearings on the Extension of the Voting Rights Act of 1965*, 94th Congress, 1st Session (Washington, D.C.: U.S. GPO, 1975), Exhibit 18, p. 698. Actual registration numbers were taken from the Census Bureau's *Abstract*, while VAP figures were taken from the subcommittee report to generate registration rates. Registration rates and voting age population data for 1970 were available only for seven of the eleven selected southern states. Voter data for the remaining four states, Arkansas, Florida, Tennessee, and Texas were derived as follows: I calculated the average percentage change in registration rates between 1966 and 1970 for the remaining seven southern states for blacks (+3.9%) and whites (−4.9%). I applied this rate of growth to the 1966 rate of the four missing states to estimate their 1970 registration rates. I then used this estimated registration rate and data on the number of registered voters available in the sources to estimate the number of eligible voters.

Data on the South for 1976 were taken from the 1980 *Statistical Abstract*. Finally, the Census Bureau's population series on presidential elections year voting was used to obtain southern data for 1980, 1982, 1986, 1988, and 1990. See the discussion below for more. State data for the eleven states for years 1974 and 1978 are not available.

I combined data from the Census Bureau's series of reports on national presidential elections with the above-compiled data for the South to generate a picture of the southern and non-southern electorates. Not until 1980 did the Census Bureau provide racial breakdowns of voter data for each of the fifty states and the District of Columbia. And, the Census Bureau's regional data do not correspond with this analysis' regional focus because of differences in how "regions" have been configured. So, to develop the regional comparison, I took the total number of registered persons for the United States as a whole and subtracted from this the total number of registered persons for the South to obtain the total number of registered persons for the non-South. I also took the difference between the total number of eligible voters for the United States as a whole and the South as defined here to estimate the total number of eligible voters or "voting age population" for the non-South. Finally, I used the resulting VAP and registration figures for the non-South to generate a registration rate for the non-South. Figures on the racial makeup of southern and non-southern constituencies were obtained by totaling only the number of whites and blacks registered to vote and then calculating the percentage of whites and blacks in the registered voters population total.

Data on the U.S. voter population as a whole were obtained from a series of Census Bureau reports. Data on the non-southern electorate for the years 1960 and 1962 are not available because the Census Bureau did not begin publishing its series on presidential elections until 1964. And, for 1964, only data on actual participation, that is, the number and rate of persons who actually voted are available. For the respective years 1966, 1970, 1976, 1980, 1986, 1988, and 1990, they are as follows: Bureau of the Census, *Voting and Registration in the Election of November 1966*, (Current Population Reports, Population Characteristics, Series P-20, No. 174 (Washington, D.C.: U.S. GPO, 1968), Table 2, p. 12; idem, *Voting and Registration in the Election of November 1970*, Series P-20, No. 228 (Washington, D.C.: U.S. GPO, 1971), Table 2, p. 14; idem, *Voting and Registration in the Election of November 1976*, Series P-20, No. 322 (Washington, D.C.: U.S. GPO, 1978), Table 2, p. 16; idem, *Voting and Registration in the Election of November 1980*, Series P-20, No. 370 (Washington, D.C.: U.S. GPO, 1982), Table 2, p. 14; idem, *Voting and Registration in the Election of November 1986*, Series P-20, No. 414 (Washington, D.C.: U.S. GPO, 1988), Table 2, p. 16; idem, *Voting and Registration in the Election of November 1988*, Series P-20, No. 440 (Washington, D.C.: U.S. GPO, 1989), Table 4, p. 36; and idem, *Voting and Registration in the Election of November 1990*, Series P-20, No. 453 (Washington, D.C.: U.S. GPO, 1991), Table 2, p. 18.

Appendix E: Sources and Methodology for Compilation of Data on Senate Proceedings

CIVIL RIGHTS PROCEEDINGS

The data on civil rights proceedings were derived from selected volumes of the *Congressional Record*. For each bill, my review of the *Record* began with the first reading of the bill and continued through to final passage. Starting with the 1965 bill, I relied heavily on the "History of Bills and Resolutions Index" of the *Record* as a guide for locating civil rights debate and procedures that preceded continuous consideration of the bills. This is because the period of time over which the later civil rights proceedings stretched was significantly greater than that attendant to earlier debates. This increased the burden of relying solely on a page-by-page reading of the *Congressional Record* volumes for information on the bills.

In compiling the civil rights proceedings data, I began by establishing what constituted civil rights "debate." I then proceeded to select the remaining procedural factors (such as time, pages, quorum calls, etc.) on the basis of whether or not they appear in the context of civil rights debate. As used here, civil rights "debate" encompasses all official, active consideration of civil rights bills at the floor. It includes primarily the actual floor discussion of either the bills or procedures affecting the bills by two or more persons, but also that which follows the *Record*'s official civil rights headings, for example, "The Senate Resumes Consideration of the Civil Rights Bill . . . ," and the presiding officer's laying of the bill before the Senate for consideration. In most instances, the headings are an accurate precursor of the debate that follows and, in those instances where they are not, seldomly was more than one or two pages counted. For the 1960 bill, included also was debate that followed the "Leasing of a Portion of Fort Crowder, MO" heading.

Excluded from "debate" are speeches included under the "Extension of Remarks" and "Additional Statements" sections of the *Record*; individual speeches delivered when the Senate as a whole was not considering the bill, for example, during the morning hour, unless there was some interchange between at least two persons; and extraneous speeches only peripherally related to the civil rights bills, such as speeches concerning race riots, violence in the North, southern culture, and so forth. These excluded items do not constitute active, official consideration of the bill by the floor of the Senate.

The selected days are those on which some debate of civil rights bills occurred, however minimal. As a result, unlike many analyses of civil rights debates and other congressional debates, it is not restricted to those days on which there was continuous debate of the bill. The "pages" data include all those pages of the *Congressional Record* on which civil rights debate as defined here is contained. Information on the bills enacted from 1957 to 1982 was obtained from the hardback editions of the *Record* while information on those enacted between 1988 and 1991 was obtained from the paperback editions. Floor speeches in the Senate are occasionally printed to include supporting documents and records not necessarily read at the floor. The inclusion of pages containing these supporting documents may inflate the page figures somewhat. However, because, as explained before, speeches delivered as part of civil rights debate at the floor, but only peripherally related to the legislating being considered, were excluded, some balance in the tabulation of pages has been achieved here.

The data on quorum calls encompasses all quorum calls, live and not live, recorded on the civil rights pages as defined above. Those calls that occurred both before and after headings or actual discussion are included as they are likely related to civil rights debate and or scheduling of debate. Included in the tabulation of yea-and-nay votes on civil rights are all floor votes on amendments, procedures, and final passage for which the Senate clerk called the roll and there is a record of how individual senators voted. "Recess" as used in the analysis refers to the number of days on which the Senate ended its daily session on a motion to recess rather than to adjourn. It does not refer to the total number of recesses, which would include recesses taken in the middle of a daily session as well as those at the conclusion of a daily session. For 1960, when the Senate met around the clock, in calculating the total number of recesses, each 24-hour period was counted as one recess.

AVERAGE SENATE PROCEEDINGS

The data on what I refer to as "average" Senate proceedings are derived from the *Congressional Record*'s "Resume of Congressional Activity" contained in the "Daily Digest" for each year in which a civil rights debate took place. The "Digest" provides a kind of summary of each session of Congress. For this analysis, the average number of days, hours, pages, quorum calls, and yea-and-nay votes expended on Senate bills was calculated by using as a base the total number of public bills originating in the Senate and subsequently adopted by the whole Congress and enacted into law. Specifically, the total number of Senate public bills enacted into law was divided by the total number of days, hours, pages, calls, and votes for the Senate for each of the sessions in which a civil rights bills was enacted.

Private bills, joint resolutions, and concurrent resolutions are excluded from the compilation. Although these measures make up a larger percentage of the bills considered in the Senate, whereas public bills, which serve as the basis for this analysis, comprise only a small percentage of the total measures introduced, reliance on the latter is a more accurate gauge of the average Senate proceedings because most of the Senate's time is spent on larger, public bills. Were the private bills and resolutions included, the result would likely be an even greater difference between civil rights proceedings and the average Senate proceeding.

"Average Senate days" represent the total number of calendar days on which the Senate was in session. "Quorum calls" include the total number of quorum calls made in the Senate for the entire session. The "Digest" does not provide a separate listing of which calls are live and which are not. The tabulation of yea-and-nay votes reflects the average number of yea-and-nay votes on Senate public bills eventually enacted into law. There are three types of votes in the Senate: voice, standing (or division), and roll call. In the case of a voice vote, the volume of senators' verbal response to the question determines the outcome of the vote. In the case of a standing vote, a headcount takes place. In the case of a roll call vote, the names of senators are called individually by the Senate clerk and their response is listed as part of the *Record*. The source used here for general congressional votes, the "Daily Digest" of the *Record*, counts as yea-and-nay votes in the Senate all votes for which there is a "record" or a roll call.

Notes

INTRODUCTION

1. See Walter J. Oleszek, *Congressional Procedures and the Policy Process* (Washington, D.C.: Congressional Quarterly, Inc., 1996); Steven S. Smith, *Call to Order: Floor Politics in the House and Senate* (Washington, D.C.: The Brookings Institution, 1989); Barbara Sinclair, *The Transformation of the U.S. Senate* (Baltimore: Johns Hopkins University Press, 1989); and Sarah A. Binder and Steven S. Smith, *Politics or Principle?: Filibustering in the United States Senate* (Washington, D.C.: Brookings Institution Press, 1997). See also Daniel Berman, *A Bill Becomes Law: The Civil Rights Act of 1960* (New York: Macmillan Co., 1962); Randall Ripley, *Congress: Process and Policy* (New York: W. W. Norton & Company, 1983); and Raymond Wolfinger, "Filibusters: Majority Rule, Presidential Leadership and Norms," in *Readings on Congress*, ed. Raymond Wolfinger (Englewood Cliffs, NJ: Prentice-Hall, Inc., 1971).

2. Howard Schuman, "Senate Rules and the Civil Rights Bill: A Case Study," *American Political Science Review*, Volume LI, Number 4, December 1957, p. 955.

3. Lewis Froman, *The Congressional Process: Strategies, Rules and Procedures* (Boston: Little, Brown and Company, 1967); Ripley, *Congress: Process and Policy*; and Oleszek, *Congressional Procedures and the Policy Process*.

4. See Barbara Sinclair, *Unorthodox Lawmaking: New Legislative Processes in the U.S. Congress* (Washington, D.C.: Congressional Quarterly, Inc., 1997).

5. See Charles E. Lindblom, *The Policy-Making Process* (Englewood Cliffs, NJ: Prentice-Hall, 1968); and Michael T. Hayes, *Incrementalism and Public Policy* (New York: Longman, 1992).

6. See Lucius Barker and Mack Jones, *African Americans and the American Political System* (Englewood Cliffs, NJ: Prentice Hall, 1994); Charles Bullock and Charles

M. Lamb, *Implementation of Civil Rights Policy* (Monterey, CA: Brooks/Cole Publishing Company, 1984): Hugh Davis Graham, *The Civil Rights Era: Origins and Development of National Policy, 1960–1972* (New York: Oxford University Press, 1990). See also J. W. Anderson, *Eisenhower, Brownell, and the Congress* (Tuscaloosa: University of Alabama Press, 1964); and James L. Sundquist, *Politics and Policy: The Eisenhower, Kennedy, and Johnson Years* (Washington, D.C.: Brookings Institution, 1968).

7. Hanes Walton, Jr., *When the Marching Stopped: The Politics of Civil Rights Regulatory Agencies* (New York: State University of New York Press, 1988).

8. Edward Carmines and James Stimson, *Issue Evolution: Race and the Transformation of American Politics* (Princeton, NJ: Princeton University Press, 1989).

9. I have compiled elsewhere a more in-depth description of southern obstruction, one that draws upon a number of key data sources, ranging from personal papers of the more active opposition and advocacy senators to a page-by-page review of the *Congressional Record*. See Nina M. Moore, "Motive, Opportunity and Issue Politics: A Case Study of Senate Rules and Civil Rights Policymaking, 1957–1991" (Ph.D. diss., University of Chicago, 1998).

CHAPTER 1

1. See Lewis Froman, *The Congressional Process: Strategies, Rules and Procedures* (Boston: Little, Brown and Company, 1967); Randall Ripley, *Congress: Process and Policy* (New York: W. W. Norton & Company, 1983); Steven Smith, *Call to Order: Floor Politics in the House and Senate* (Washington, D.C.: The Brookings Institution, 1989); Walter J. Oleszek, *Congressional Procedures and the Policy Process* (Washington, D.C.: Congressional Quarterly, Inc., 1996); and Barbara Sinclair, *Unorthodox Lawmaking: New Legislative Processes in the U.S. Congress* (Washington, D.C.: Congressional Quarterly, Inc., 1997).

2. The parliamentary rules discussed here concern the formal standing rules that are listed in editions of the *Senate Manual*. Specifically, I rely throughout the book on the following sources in detailing the provisions and development of the Senate's standing rules: Committee on Rules and Administration, U.S. Senate, *Senate Manual*, 85th Congress, 1st Session, Senate Document No. 19 (Washington, D.C.: U.S. GPO, 1957), which contains the rules as they existed in 1957; Committee on Rules and Administration, U.S. Senate, *Standing Rules of the Senate* (Washington, D.C.: U.S. GPO, 1979), which contains Senate rules as they existed prior to the 1979 general revision and details changes made in the rules between 1957 and 1979; Committee on Rules and Administration, U.S. Senate, *Senate Manual*, 96th Congress, 1st Session, Senate Document No. 96–1 (Washington, D.C.: U.S. GPO, 1979), which reflects changes/renumerations accomplished by the 1979 revision; and Committee on Rules and Administration, U.S. Senate, *Senate Manual*, 102d Congress, 1st Session, Senate Document 102–01 (Washington, D.C.: U.S. GPO, 1992), which contains the rules as they existed in 1991 and details also changes made in the rules following the 1979 general revision through 1991. For a thorough discussion of the remaining precedents and informal rules, see Floyd M. Riddick and Alan S. Fruman, *Riddick's Senate Procedure*, 101st Congress, 2d Session, Senate Document 101–28 (Washington, D.C.: U.S. GPO, 1992).

3. Over half of the rules listed in the 1991 *Senate Manual* do not address formal legislating, but focus instead on Senate committee structure, restrictions on Senate conduct, and so forth.

4. For much of Senate history, the entire set of parliamentary rules has averaged roughly thirty in number, with the 1991 *Senate Manual* listing a total of forty-three. Senate precedents, which help to fill in the gaps of the formal rules, number in the tens of thousands. Technically, however, they do not carry the weight that the actual standing rules do. They are not necessarily as binding.

5. For an original exposition of Senate norms, see Donald Matthews, *U.S. Senators and Their World* (New York: Vintage Books, 1960). For a discussion of the contemporary force of norms, see David W. Rohde, Norman Ornstein, and Robert Peabody, "Political Change and Legislative Norms in the U.S., 1957–1984," in *Studies of Congress*, ed. Glenn Parker (Washington, D.C.: Congressional Quarterly Press, 1985); and Richard Fenno, "The Senate through the Looking Glass: The Debate over Television," in *The Changing World of the U.S. Senate*, ed. John R. Hibbing and John G. Peters (Berkeley: University of California at Berkeley IGS Press, 1990).

6. See, for example, Barry Weingast, "A Rational Choice Perspective on Congressional Norms," *American Journal of Political Science*, May 23, 1979.

7. Unanimous consent can be granted on virtually every matter, except a request to suspend the provisions of Rule 12, which governs the manner in which floor votes are to be conducted.

8. For more on the history of Rule 22, see Richard Beeman, "Unlimited Debate in the Senate: The First Phase," *Political Science Quarterly*, Volume LXXXIII, Number 3, September 1968.

9. 1991 *Senate Manual*, Sections 14.2 and 14.3, p. 12.

10. Oleszek, *Congressional Procedures and the Policy Process*, p. 96.

11. 1991 *Senate Manual*, Section 8.1, p. 8.

12. As of 1917, two-thirds of senators actually present on the floor and voting were needed. As of 1949, two-thirds of all Senate members were needed. In 1959, the rule was changed again to require two-thirds of voting members. Finally, in 1975, the rule was amended to reflect the current three-fifths of membership requirement. In addition to the support requirements are many others, the most important of which are the caps on post-cloture debate. A 1986 rule change limited the Senate as a whole to considering a matter on which cloture has been invoked to "no more than thirty hours." As of 1979, the limit had been 100 hours. Previously, there was no cap on Senate consideration, only a one-hour limit per senator.

13. See, for example, Sinclair, *Unorthodox Lawmaking*. See also Sarah A. Binder and Steven S. Smith, *Politics or Principle?: Filibustering in the United States Senate* (Washington, D.C.: Brookings Institution Press, 1997).

14. See, for example, Oleszek, *Congressional Procedures and the Policy Process*, 1989 and 1996; Ross K. Baker, *House and Senate*, 2d ed. (New York: W. W. Norton & Company, Inc., 1995); and Joseph Bessette, *Mild Voice of Reason* (Chicago: University of Chicago Press, 1994).

15. See Charles E. Lindblom, *The Policy-Making Process* (Englewood Cliffs, NJ: Prentice Hall, 1968); and Michael Hayes, *Incrementalism and Public Policy* (New York: Longman, 1992), for further elaboration of this theme.

16. For more on reelection as the goal of legislators and constituent concerns as steppingstones toward achievement of that goal, see Morris Fiorina, *Congress: Key-*

stone of the Washington Establishment (New Haven: Yale University Press, 1989); and Morris Fiorina and David Rohde, eds., *Home Style and Washington Work* (Ann Arbor, MI: University of Michigan Press, 1989).

17. For a more complete look at the argument that legislators operate chiefly in line with the perception of electoral costs, see Morris Fiorina, *Representatives, Roll Calls, and Constituencies* (Lexington, MA: Lexington Books, 1974).

CHAPTER 2

1. C. Van Woodward, *The Strange Career of Jim Crow* (New York: Oxford University Press, 1957), pp. 8, 81–82, 87.

2. For more, see Richard Bardolph, *The Civil Rights Record: Black Americans and the Law, 1849–1970* (New York: Thomas Y. Crowell Company, 1970).

3. For additional details, see Peter M. Bergman, *The Chronological History of the Negro in America* (New York: Harper & Row, 1969).

4. For details, see ibid.

5. See Nancy Weiss, *Farewell to the Party of Lincoln* (Princeton, NJ: Princeton University Press, 1983), pp. 4–5.

6. For more background on the administration's development of the Civil Rights Act of 1957, see: J. W. Anderson, *Eisenhower, Brownell, and the Congress* (Tuscaloosa: University of Alabama Press, 1964).

7. *Congressional Quarterly 1957* (Washington, D.C.: Congressional Research Service, 1957), p. 562.

8. *Congressional Quarterly 1960* (Washington, D.C.: Congressional Research Service.

9. Gunnar Myrdal, *An American Dilemma* (New York: Harper & Brothers Publishers, 1944), pp. 430–431.

10. Ibid., p. 431.

11. Doug McAdam, *Political Process and the Development of Black Insurgency, 1930–1970* (Chicago: University of Chicago Press, 1982), p. 79.

12. U.S. Bureau of the Census, Census Population Report Series (Washington, D.C.: U.S. GPO, Various Years).

13. See Weiss, *Farewell to the Party*, p. 206, Table IX.2, for specific figures on the presidential vote in black districts in 1946.

14. Edward Carmines and James Stimson, *Issue Evolution: Race and the Transformation of American Politics* (Princeton, NJ: Princeton University Press, 1989), p. 46.

15. This discussion of party platforms relies on Donald Bruce Johnson and Kirk H. Porter's *National Party Platforms, 1840–1971* (Chicago: University of Illinois Press, 1973).

16. *Congressional Record*, 86th Congress, 2d Session, Volume 106, Part 3, p. 3702.

17. Congressional Research Service, *Congressional Quarterly Almanac 1957* (Washington, D.C.: U.S. GPO, 1957), p. 189.

18. *The Atlantic Monthly*, undated, Michael Mansfield Papers, University of Montana Library, Missoula, Montana.

19. See remarks of Senator Paul Douglas, *Congressional Record*, 85th Congress, 1st Session, Volume 103, Part 7, pp. 9793–9794.

20. Ibid., p. 9780.
21. Daniel M. Berman, *A Bill Becomes Law: The Civil Rights Act of 1960* (New York: Macmillan Co., 1962), p. 31.
22. *Congressional Record*, 86th Congress, 2d Session, Volume 106, Part 2, p. 2470.
23. The vote also displaced the Senate version of the bill, which was eventually passed by the Senate as the Stella School Bill after the civil rights bill was passed.
24. See remarks of Senator Lyndon Johnson, *Congressional Record*, 86th Congress, 2d Session, Volume 106, Part 3, p. 3178.
25. Letter from Senators Douglas and Humphrey, October 19, 1956, Mansfield Papers.
26. Statement of Jacob Javits, June 17, 1957, Jacob Javits Papers, State University of New York Library at Stony Brook Library, Stony Brook, New York.
27. The following explanation of the 1957 rules change effort rules on Howard Schuman's discussion of the rules in "Senate Rules and the Civil Rights Bill: A Case Study," *American Political Science Review*, Volume LI, Number 4, December 1957, pp. 267–268.
28. *Congressional Quarterly Weekly*, January 11, 1957 (Washington, D.C.: Congressional Research Service, 1957), p. 39.
29. See remarks of Senator Jacob Javits, June 27, 1957, Javits Papers.
30. *Congressional Record*, 86th Congress, 2d Session, Volume 106, Part 3, p. 3919.
31. During the interim there were three breaks. The first was a fifteen-minute recess on March 2, 1960, and the second a 42-and-a-half-hour weekend recess from Saturday evening to Monday afternoon. The third was a three-minute adjournment from roughly 4:02 A.M. to 4:05 A.M. on the morning of March 8.
32. *Congressional Record*, 2d Session, Volume 106, Part 4, p. 4440.
33. See Appendix A for a description of the methodology used to distinguish coalitions.
34. *Congressional Record*, 85th Congress, 1st Session, Volume 103, Part 8, p. 11004.
35. See remarks of Senator Wayne Morse, *Congressional Record*, 86th Congress, 2d Session, Volume 106, Part 2, p. 2486.
36. U.S. Commission on Civil Rights, *Biennial Report 1959* (Washington, D.C.: U.S. GPO, 1959).
37. *Congressional Record*, 85th Congress, 1st Session, Volume 103, Part 9, p. 15172.

CHAPTER 3

1. *Congressional Record*, 88th Congress, 2d Session, Volume 110, Part 4, March 13, 1964, p. 5329.
2. U.S. Commission on Civil Rights, *1961 Commission on Civil Rights Report*, Book 1, *Voting* (Washington, D.C.: U.S. GPO, 1961), p. 21.
3. The discussion of southern history to follow draws partly upon the chronological histories compiled in the following sources: Peter Bergman, *The Chronological History of the Negro in America* (New York: Harper & Row, 1969); Harry A. Ploski

and James Williams, eds., *The Negro Almanac*, 4th ed. (New York: John Wiley & Sons, 1983); Richard Bardolph, *The Civil Rights Record: Black Americans and the Law, 1849–1970* (New York: Thomas Y. Crowell Company, 1970); and other sources as noted.

4. Bardolph, *The Civil Rights Record*.

5. C. Vann Woodward, *The Strange Career of Jim Crow* (New York: Oxford University Press, 1957).

6. For more details, see U.S. Bureau of the Census, *Census of the Population 1960*, Volume I, *Characteristics of the Population*, Part 1, *United States Summary* (Washington, D.C.: U.S. GPO, 1963), p. 1–243, Table 103.

7. U.S. Department of Labor, *Manpower Report of the President* (Washington, D.C.: U.S. GPO, March 1970), p. 42.

8. Gerald D. Jaynes and Robin M. Williams, Jr., eds., *A Common Destiny: Blacks and American Society* (Washington, D.C.: National Academy Press, 1989), pp. 78–79, Table 2–5.

9. Taken from a reprint of passages from the speech contained in Peter B. Levy, ed., *Documentary History of the Modern Civil Rights Movement* (New York: Greenwood Press, 1992), pp. 122–124.

10. Taken from a reprint of John Lewis' speech contained in Levy, *Documentary History*, p. 122.

11. David Garrow in *Protest at Selma: Martin Luther King, Jr. and the Voting Rights Act of 1965* (New Haven: Yale University Press, 1978) points to the central role of television and the news media in dramatizing the events of the movement and, thereby, enhancing the national spotlight on the South.

12. For further discussion of this point, see James Sundquist, *Politics and Policy: The Eisenhower, Kennedy, and Johnson Years* (Washington, D.C.: Brookings Institution, 1968), p. 253.

13. For more, see Carl M. Brauer, *John F. Kennedy and the Second Reconstruction* (New York: Columbia University Press, 1977).

14. For more discussion on this point, see ibid.

15. Ibid., p. 23.

16. Sundquist, *Politics and Policy*, p. 254.

17. Barry Goldwater, *The Conscience of a Conservative* (New York: MacFadden Books, 1960), p. 38.

18. Ibid., p. 35.

19. Kenneth O'Reilly, *Nixon's Piano: Presidents and Racial Politics from Washington to Clinton* (New York: The Free Press, 1995).

20. See "1964 Republican" table in "Convention Ballots" section of Congressional Quarterly, Inc., *National Party Conventions*.

21. James L. Sundquist, *Dynamics of the Party System: Alignment and Realignment of Political Parties in the United States* (Washington, D.C.: Brookings Institution, 1973), p. 345.

22. Congressional Research Services, *Congressional Quarterly Almanac, 1973* (Washington, D.C.: U.S. GPO, 1973), p. 82.

23. See Appendix C for survey data sources.

24. For discussion of Gallup poll data, see Doug McAdam's *Political Process and the Development of Black Insurgency, 1930–1970* (Chicago: University of Chicago Press, 1982). For NES data sources, see Appendix C.

25. *Congressional Record*, 88th Congress, 2d Session, Volume 110, Part 3, February 26, 1964, p. 3702.

26. Memo to Senator Mansfield from Staff, October 20, 1963, Michael Mansfield Papers, University of Montana Library, Missoula, Montana.

27. Before the tabling vote, Mansfield made two attempts to get Senate approval of an agreement that would have had the House bill referred with instructions and reported back with or without amendments by March 4, 1964. *Congressional Record*, 88th Congress, 2d Session, Volume 110, Part 3, February 27, 1964, p. 3830.

28. Minutes of meeting with Senators Mansfield, Humphrey, and others, February 28, 1964, Mansfield Papers.

29. *Congressional Record*, 88th Congress, 2d Session, Volume 110, Part 4, p. 4357.

30. Text of radio address recorded by Senator Allen Ellender, February 22, 1964, Mansfield Papers.

31. Minutes of meeting with Senator Russell, February 19, 1964, Mansfield Papers.

32. Memo to Mansfield from Staff, March 9, 1964, Mansfield Papers.

33. Ibid.

34. Ibid.

35. *Congressional Record*, 88th Congress, 2d Session, Volume 110, Part 10, June 16, 1964, p. 13946; and Minutes of meeting on civil rights, February 19, 1964, Mansfield Papers.

36. Letter to various senators from Mansfield, March 3, 1964, Mansfield Papers.

37. *Congressional Record*, 89th Congress, 1st Session, Volume 111, Part 7, May 4, 1965, p. 9342.

38. See Appendix E for discussion of methodology used to identify policy coalitions in Senate civil rights proceedings.

39. "The Civil Rights Bill: Some Observations by Senator Everett McKinley Dirksen," February 26, 1964, Everett Dirksen Papers, Dirksen Congressional Leadership Center, Pekin, Illinois.

40. *Congressional Record*, 88th Congress, 2d Session, Volume 110, Part 4, March 16, 1964, p. 5335.

41. Dirksen Senate speech, September 6, 1966, Dirksen Papers.

42. *Congressional Record*, 88th Congress, 2d Session, Volume 110, Part 9, March 26, 1964, p. 11935.

43. *Congressional Record*, 90th Congress, 2d Session, Volume 114, Part 4, March 1, 1968, p. 4848.

44. Senate Committee Report 162, p. 32. Committee on the Judiciary, U.S. Senate, *Voting Rights Legislation*, Report 162, Part 3, 89th Congress, 1st Session (Washington, D.C.: U.S. GPO), p. 32.

CHAPTER 4

1. For more discussion on this subject, see Thomas Cavanagh, *The Impact of the Black Electorate* (Washington, D.C.: Joint Center for Political Studies, 1984), and also U.S. Commission on Civil Rights, *Voting Rights Act: Unfulfilled Goals* (Washington, D.C.: U.S. GPO, 1981).

2. U.S. Commission on Civil Rights, *Political Participation* (Washington, D.C.: U.S. GPO, 1968), p. viii. The following discussion draws on chapters 2–3 of the USCCR's 1968 report referenced here.

3. The USCCR' s 1968 report notes these included various barriers to registration, such as changing the time and place of registration without public notice, purging the voter registers, and requiring registrants to re-register. Barriers to actual voting remained, such as changing without notice the polling place, providing insufficient aid to illiterate voters, and inhibiting absentee voting. And, finally barriers to candidacy continued, such as excessive filing fees, erroneous information concerning qualifying requirements, miscounting of votes, and so forth.

4. See U.S. Commission on Civil Rights, *The Voting Rights Act Ten Years After* (Washington, D.C.: U.S. GPO, 1975).

5. Ibid., p. 1.

6. U.S. Commission on Civil Rights, *Political Participation*, p. 14.

7. Harry A. Ploski and James Williams, eds., *The Negro Almanac: A Reference Work on the Afro-American* (New York: John Wiley & Sons, 1983).

8. The 1960 data include males only (14+ years), while the 1970 data include all persons (16+ years). So, at least some of the change could be attributed to the positive effect that including black women in the portrait would yield. Also, the 1970 Census Report and later reports did not include an "Occupation Not Reported" category as did the 1960 Census Report.

9. U.S. Bureau of the Census, *The Social and Economic Status of the Black Population in the United States: An Historical View, 1790–1978*, Current Population Reports, Special Studies Series P-23, No. 80 (Washington, D.C.: U.S. GPO, 1979).

10. For more evidence of this, review the chronological record provided in Ploski and Williams, *The Negro Almanac*.

11. Also, protest activities led by traditional civil rights leaders/activists and characterized as "civil rights" activities were no longer strictly racial in overtone—that is, other issues less directly related to race than segregation began to be targeted by movement events. This is most evident in Dr. King's April 1967 anti-war demonstration involving some 100,000 participants.

12. U.S. Commission on Civil Rights, *Political Participation*, 1968 Report, p. 1.

13. The following discussion of Hubert Humphrey draws from Nelson Polsby's *Humphrey or Nixon* (Washington, D.C.: Public Affairs Press, 1968).

14. Ibid., p. 12.

15. Congressional Quarterly, Inc., *National Party Conventions, 1831–1976* (Washington, D.C.: Congressional Quarterly, Inc., 1979).

16. A. James Reichley, *Conservatives in an Age of Change: The Nixon and Ford Administrations* (Washington, D.C.: Brookings Institution, 1981), p. 204.

17. *Congressional Quarterly 1979* (Washington, D.C.: Congressional Research Service, 1979), p. 107.

18. See Leon Panetta and Peter Gall's *Bring Us Together: The Nixon Team and the Civil Rights Retreat* (Philadelphia: J. B. Lippincott Company, 1971).

19. Reichley, *Conservatives in an Age of Change*, p. 192.

20. Ibid., p. 197. The proposed moratorium was challenged by constitutional experts across the country and a bill fashioned after the idea was defeated by a Democratic-led filibuster in the Senate.

21. Michael A. Genovese, *The Nixon Presidency* (Westport, CT: Greenwood Press, 1990), p. 85.

22. Charles Bullock and Charles M. Lamb, *Implementation of Civil Rights Policy* (Monterey, CA: Brooks/Cole Publishing Company, 1984), p. 94 et seq.

23. Greene, p. 88.

24. Ploski and Williams, *The Negro Almanac* (New York: John Wiley & Sons, 1983), p. 78.

25. *Congressional Quarterly 1976*, p. 72.

26. Ibid.

27. Ibid.

28. See M. Glenn Abernathy, Dilys M. Hill, and Phil Williams, eds., *The Carter Years: The President and Policy Making* (New York: St. Martin's Press, 1984), pp. 106–122, for discussion to follow.

29. Steven S. Shull, *The President and Civil Rights Policy* (New York: Greenwood Press, 1989), p. 97.

30. *Congressional Quarterly Almanac 1992* (Washington, D.C.: U.S. GPO, 1992), p. 324.

31. See remarks of Senator Ervin in *Congressional Record*, 91st Congress, 1st Session, Volume 115, Part 29, December 15, 1969, p. 39100.

32. Ibid., December 16, 1969, p. 39335.

33. Staff memo, undated, Michael Mansfield Papers, University of Montana Library, Missoula, Montana.

34. *Congressional Record*, 94th Congress, 1st Session, Volume 121, Part 18, July 18, 1975, p. 23599.

35. The second cloture motion was later vitiated on Monday, July 21, when the Senate adopted the first cloture motion.

36. Staff memo to Chairman Williams, February 1, 1972, Williams Papers, Rutgers University, New Brunswick, New Jersey.

37. See Appendix A for a discussion of the method used to configure and distinguish civil rights policy coalitions.

38. Senator Jacob Javits Press Release, June 6, 1968, Jacob Javits Papers, State University of New York Library at Stony Brook Library, Stony Brook, New York.

39. *Congressional Record*, 92d Congress, 2d Session, Volume 118, Part 1, January 20, 1972, p. 588.

40. *Congressional Record*, 94th Congress, 1st Session, Volume 121, Part 19, July 23, 1975, p. 24221.

41. See remarks of Senator Michael Mansfield, *Congressional Record*, 91st Congress, 2d Session, Volume 116, Part 5, March 12, 1970, p. 7160.

42. *Congressional Record*, 92nd Congress, 2d Session, Volume 118, Part 3, February 14, 1972, p. 3812.

43. Ibid., February 7, 1972, p. 2861.

44. *Congressional Record*, 94th Congress, 1st Session, Volume 121, Part 19, July 23, 1975, p. 24224.

45. Ibid., p. 24220.

46. Ibid., July 24, 1975, p. 24731.

47. *Congressional Record*, 91st Congress, 2d Session, Volume 116, Part 5, March 11, 1970, p. 6958.

48. An earlier Supreme Court decision had restricted the 1970 bill to federal elections only.

CHAPTER 5

1. William J. Wilson, *The Declining Significance of Race: Blacks and Changing American Institutions*, 2d ed. (Chicago: University of Chicago Press, 1980).

2. Joint Center for Political Studies, *National Roster of Black Elected Officials*, Volume 12 (Washington, D.C.: JCPS, 1982), Table 2; and ibid., 1990.

3. Katherine Tate, *From Protest to Politics: The New Black Voters in American Elections* (Cambridge: Harvard University Press, 1993).

4. For details, see Charles Lamb, "Education and Housing," in *The Reagan Administration and Human Rights*, ed. Tinsley E. Yarbrough (New York: Praeger Publishers, 1985).

5. Congressional Quarterly, Inc., *President Reagan* (Washington, D.C.: Congressional Quarterly, Inc., 1981).

6. Howard Ball and Kathanne Greene, "The Reagan Justice Department," in *The Reagan Administration and Human Rights*, ed. Tinsley E. Yarbrough (New York: Praeger Publishers, 1985), p. 5.

7. Ball and Greene, "Reagan Justice," p. 19.

8. Lamb, "Education," p. 85.

9. Stephen C. Halpern, "Title VI Enforcement," in *The Reagan Administration and Human Rights*, ed. Tinsley E. Yarbrough (New York: Praeger Publishers, 1985), pp. 139–140.

10. Ibid., p. 140.

11. For more on this discussion, see Ball and Greene, "Reagan Justice."

12. For more on this discussion, see ibid.

13. Charles Bullock III and Katherine Ingis Butler, "Voting Rights," in *The Reagan Administration and Human Rights*, ed. Tinsley E. Yarbrough (New York: Praeger Publishers, 1985), p. 34.

14. Robert J. Thompson, "The Commission on Civil Rights," *The Reagan Administration and Human Rights*, ed. Tinsley E. Yarbrough (New York: Praeger Publishers, 1985), p. 185.

15. Ball and Greene, "Reagan Justice," p. 22.

16. Michael Duffy and Dan Goodgame, *Marching in Place: The Status Quo Presidency of George Bush* (New York: Simon & Schuster, 1992), p. 65.

17. Ibid., p. 203.

18. See Lucius Barker and Mack Jones, *African Americans and the American Political System* (Englewood Cliffs, NJ: Prentice-Hall, 1994).

19. Duffy and Goodgame, *Marching in Place*, p. 102.

20. Barker and Jones, *African Americans*, p. 230.

21. Congressional Research Service, *Congressional Quarterly Almanac 1992* (Washington, D.C.: U.S. GPO, 1992), p. 54.

22. See Barker and Jones, *African Americans*, p. 230, Table 8–1.

23. *Congressional Record*, 97th Congress, 2d Session, Volume 128, Part 11, June 17, 1982, p. 14084.

24. Ibid.

25. *Congressional Record*, 97th Congress, 2nd Session, Volume 128, Part 10, June 9, 1982, p. 13166.

26. See remarks of Majority Leader Stevens, *Congressional Record*, 97th Congress, 2nd Session, Volume 128, Part 11, June 16, 1982.

27. For more discussion on the transformation in the Senate see Barbara Sinclair, *The Transformation of the U.S. Senate* (Baltimore: Johns Hopkins University Press, 1989). For more on the transformation in the House, see Steven S. Smith, *Call to Order: Floor Politics in the House and Senate* (Washington, D.C.: Brookings Institution, 1989).

28. *Congressional Record*, 100th Congress, 2d Session, Volume 134, No. 2, January 26, 1988, p. 78.

29. Ibid., p. 42.

30. *Congressional Record*, 100th Congress, 2d Session, Volume 134, No. 4, January 28, 1988, p. 242.

31. *Congressional Record*, 102d Congress, 1st Session, Volume 137, No. 155, October 25, 1991, p. 14238.

32. *Congressional Record*, 97th Congress, 2d Session, Volume 128, Part 11, June 17, 1982, p. 14132.

33. The case concerned four laws, including Title IX of the Education Amendments of 1972, the Rehabilitation Act of 1973, the Age Discrimination Act of 1975, as well as Title VI of the Civil Rights Act of 1964—all of which governed federal funding of various institutions.

34. Congressional Research Service, *Congressional Quarterly Almanac 1988* (Washington, D.C.: U.S. GPO, 1988).

35. See remarks of Senator Edward Kennedy, in *Congressional Record*, 100th Congress, 2d Session, Volume 134, No. 112, August 1, 1988, p. 10455.

36. *Congressional Record*, 100th Congress, 2d Session, Volume 134, No. 112, August 1, 1988, p. 10460.

37. The nine cases include: *Wards Cove v. Packing Co. v. Atonio* (1989); *Patterson v. McLean Credit Union* (1989); *Price Waterhouse v. Hopkins* (1989); *Martin v. Wilks* (1989); *Equal Employment Opportunity Commission v. Arabian American Oil Co.* (1991); *Lorance v. AT&T Technologies* (1989); *Crawford Fitting Co. v. J. T. Gibbons* (1987); *West Virginia University Hospitals v. Casey* (1991); and *Library of Congress v. Shaw* (1986).

38. *Congressional Record*, 102d Congress, 1st Session, Volume 137, No. 133, September 24, 1991, p. 13581.

39. *Congressional Record*, 102d Congress, 2d Session, August 6, 1992, p. 11743. Available at www.thomas.loc.gov.

40. *Congressional Quarterly Almanac 1992*, p. 330.

41. *Congressional Record*, 97th Congress, 2d Session, Volume 128, Part 11, June 17, 1982, p. 14132.

42. *Congressional Record*, 100th Congress, 2d Session, Volume 134, No. 3, January 27, 1988, p. 164.

43. *Congressional Record*, 100th Congress, 2d Session, Volume 134, No. 112, August 1, 1988, p. 10461.

44. *Congressional Record*, 100th Congress, 2d Session, Volume 134, No. 112, August 1, 1988, p. 10462.

45. See remarks of Senator Orrin Hatch in *Congressional Record*, 102d Congress, 1st Session, Volume 137, No. 155, October 15, 1991, p. 15238.

46. *Congressional Record*, 97th Congress, 2d Session, Volume 128, Part 11, June 17, 1982, p. 14132.

47. Danforth later voted with Reagan to sustain the veto.

48. *Congressional Record*, 100th Congress, 2d Session, Volume 134, No. 112, August 1, 1988, p. 10462.

49. *Congressional Record*, 100th Congress, 2d Session, Volume 134, No. 112, August 1, 1988, p. 10462.

CHAPTER 6

1. See Edward Carmines and James Stimson's discussion in *Issue Evolution: Race and the Transformation of American Politics* (Princeton, NJ: Princeton University Press, 1989) for a fuller discussion of racial saliency in party politics.

2. The analysis focuses only on the domestic portion of the platforms, excluding those portions dealing with foreign policy and/or national defense issues.

3. This calculation excludes the 1976 Republican platform section total, which numbers twenty-six, because it would exaggerate the average.

Bibliography

Abernathy, M. Glenn, Dilys M. Hill, and Phil Williams, eds. *The Carter Years: The President and Policy Making*. New York: St. Martin's Press, 1984.

Anderson, J. W. *Eisenhower, Brownell, and the Congress*. Tuscaloosa: University of Alabama Press, 1964.

Baker, Ross K. *House and Senate*. 2d ed. New York: W. W. Norton & Company, Inc., 1995.

Ball, Howard, and Kathanne Greene. "The Reagan Justice Department." In *The Reagan Administration and Human Rights*, ed. Tinsley E. Yarbrough. New York: Praeger Publishers, 1985.

Bardolph, Richard. *The Civil Rights Record: Black Americans and the Law, 1849–1970*. New York: Thomas Y. Crowell Company, 1970.

Barker, Lucius, and Mack Jones. *African Americans and the American Political System*. Englewood Cliffs, NJ: Prentice-Hall, 1994.

Beeman, Richard. "Unlimited Debate in the Senate: The First Phase." *Political Science Quarterly*, Volume LXXXIII, Number 3, September 1968.

Bergman, Peter M. *The Chronological History of the Negro in America*. New York: Harper & Row, 1969.

Berman, Daniel. *A Bill Becomes Law: The Civil Rights Act of 1960*. New York: Macmillan Co., 1962.

Bessette, Joseph. *Mild Voice of Reason*. Chicago: University of Chicago Press, 1994.

Binder, Sarah A., and Steven S. Smith. *Politics or Principle?: Filibustering in the United States Senate*. Washington, D.C.: Brookings Institution Press, 1997.

Bositis, David A. *Black Elected Officials: A Statistical Summary: 1993–1997*. Washington, D.C.: Joint Center for Political and Economic Studies, 1997.

Brauer, Carl M. *John F. Kennedy and the Second Reconstruction*. New York: Columbia University Press, 1977.

Bullock, Charles, III and Katherine Ingis Butler. "Voting Rights." In *The Reagan Administration and Human Rights*, ed. Tinsley E. Yarbrough. New York: Praeger Publishers, 1985.

Bullock, Charles, and Charles M. Lamb. *Implementation of Civil Rights Policy*. Monterey, CA: Brooks/Cole Publishing Company, 1984.

Carmines, Edward, and James Stimson. *Issue Evolution: Race and the Transformation of American Politics*. Princeton, NJ: Princeton University Press, 1989.

Cavanagh, Thomas. *The Impact of the Black Electorate*. Washington, D.C.: Joint Center for Political Studies, 1984.

Committee on the Judiciary, U.S. Senate. *Senate Committee Report 162*. Washington, D.C.: U.S. GPO, 1965.

———. Committee on Rules and Administration, U.S. Senate, *Senate Manual*, 85th Congress, 1st Session, Senate Document No. 19. Washington, D.C.: U.S. GPO, 1957.

———. *Senate Manual*, 96th Congress, 1st Session, Senate Document No. 96–1. Washington, D.C.: U.S. GPO, 1979.

———. *Standing Rules of the Senate*. Washington, D.C.: U.S. GPO, 1979.

———. *Senate Manual*, 102d Congress, 1st Session, Senate Document 102-01. Washington, D.C.: U.S. GPO, 1992.

Congressional Quarterly, Inc. *National Party Conventions, 1831–1976*. Washington, D.C.: Congressional Quarterly, Inc., 1979.

———. *President Reagan*. Washington, D.C.: Congressional Quarterly, Inc., 1981.

Congressional Research Service. *Congressional Quarterly Almanac, 1957–1991*. Washington, D.C.: U.S. GPO, 1957–1991. Selected Years.

Davies, James, and Tom Smith. *General Social Surveys, Cumulative Codebook, 1972–1991*. Chicago: National Opinion Research Center, 1991.

Democratic Study Group Report, U.S. House of Representatives. *Special Report: A Look at the Senate Filibuster*. Nos. 103–28. Washington, D.C.: U.S. GPO, June 13, 1994.

Duffy, Michael, and Dan Goodgame. *Marching in Place: The Status Quo Presidency of George Bush*. New York: Simon & Schuster, 1992.

Fenno, Richard. "The Senate through the Looking Glass: The Debate over Television." In *The Changing World of the U.S. Senate*, ed. John R. Hibbing and John G. Peters. Berkeley: University of California at Berkeley IGS Press, 1990.

Fiorina, Morris. *Representatives, Roll Calls, and Constituencies*. Lexington, MA: Lexington Books, 1974.

———. *Congress: Keystone of the Washington Establishment*. New Haven: Yale University Press, 1989.

Fiorina, Morris, and David Rohde, eds. *Home Style and Washington Work*. Ann Arbor, MI: University of Michigan Press, 1989.

Froman, Lewis. *The Congressional Process: Strategies, Rules and Procedures*. Boston: Little, Brown and Company, 1967.

Gallup, George. *Gallup Poll: Public Opinion, 1935–1971*. New York: Random House, 1972.

Garrow, David J. *Protest at Selma: Martin Luther King, Jr. and the Voting Rights Act of 1965*. New Haven: Yale University Press, 1978.

Genovese, Michael A. *The Nixon Presidency*. Westport, CT: Greenwood Press, 1990.

Goldwater, Barry. *The Conscience of a Conservative*. New York: MacFadden Books, 1960.

Graham, Hugh Davis. *The Civil Rights Era: Origins and Development of National Policy, 1960–1972*. New York: Oxford University Press, 1990.

Halpern, Stephen C. "Title VI Enforcement." In *The Reagan Administration and Human Rights*, ed. Tinsely E. Yarbrough. New York: Praeger Publishers, 1985.

Hayes, Michael T. *Incrementalism and Public Policy*. New York: Longman, 1992.

Horton, Carrell Peterson, and Jessie Carney Smith. *Statistical Record of Black America*. Detroit: Gale Research, 1991.

Jaynes, Gerald D., and Robin M. Williams, Jr., eds. *A Common Destiny: Blacks and American Society*. Washington, D.C.: National Academy Press, 1989.

Johnson, Donald Bruce, and Kirk H. Porter. *National Party Platforms, 1840–1971*. Chicago: University of Illinois Press, 1973.

Joint Center for Political Studies. *National Roster of Black Elected Officials*. Washington, D.C.: JCPS, various years.

Lamb, Charles. "Education and Housing." In *The Reagan Administration and Human Rights*, ed. Tinsely E. Yarbrough. New York: Praeger Publishers, 1985.

Levy, Peter B., ed. *Documentary History of the Modern Civil Rights Movement*. New York: Greenwood Press, 1992.

Lindblom, Charles E. *The Policy-Making Process*. Englewood Cliffs, NJ: Prentice-Hall, 1968.

Matthews, Donald. *U.S. Senators and Their World*. New York: Vintage Books, 1960.

McAdam, Doug. *Political Process and the Development of Black Insurgency, 1930–1970*. Chicago: University of Chicago Press, 1982.

Miller, Warren E., and the National Election Studies. *American National Election Studies Cumulative Data File, 1952–1990*. Ann Arbor: University of Michigan, Center for Political Studies, 1991.

Moore, Nina M. "Motive, Opportunity and Issue Politics: A Case Study of Senate Rules and Civil Rights Policymaking, 1957–1991." Ph.D. diss., University of Chicago, 1998.

Myrdal, Gunnar. *An American Dilemma*. New York: Harper & Brothers Publishers, 1944.

Oleszek, Walter J. *Congressional Procedures and the Policy Process*. Washington, D.C.: Congressional Quarterly, Inc., 1996.

Oleszek, Walter J. *Congressional Procedures and the Policy Process*. Washington, D.C.: Congressional Quarterly, Inc., 1989.

O'Reilly, Kenneth. *Nixon's Piano: Presidents and Racial Politics from Washington to Clinton*. New York: The Free Press, 1995.

Orfield, Gary and Franklin Monfort. *Status of School Desegregation: The Next Generation*. Alexandria, VA: National School Boards Association Council, 1992.

Panetta, Leon, and Peter Gall. *Bring Us Together: The Nixon Team and the Civil Rights Retreat*. Philadelphia: J. B. Lippincott Company, 1971.

Ploski, Harry A., and James Williams, eds. *The Negro Almanac: A Reference Work on the Afro-American*. New York: John Wiley & Sons, 1983.

Polsby, Nelson. *Humphrey or Nixon*. Washington, D.C.: Public Affairs Press, 1968.

Reichley, A. James. *Conservatives in an Age of Change: The Nixon and Ford Administrations*. Washington, D.C.: Brookings Institution, 1981.

Riddick, Floyd M., and Alan S. Fruman. *Riddick's Senate Procedure*. 101st Congress, 2d Session, Senate Document 101–28. Washington, D.C.: U.S. GPO, 1992.

Ripley, Randall. *Congress: Process and Policy*. New York: W. W. Norton & Company, 1983.

Rohde, David W., Norman Ornstein, and Robert Peabody. "Political Change and Legislative Norms in the U.S., 1957–1984." In *Studies of Congress*, ed. Glenn Parker. Washington, D.C.: Congressional Quarterly Press, 1985.

Schuman, Howard. "Senate Rules and the Civil Rights Bill: A Case Study." *American Political Science Review*, Volume LI, Number 4, December 1957.

Shull, Steven S. *The President and Civil Rights Policy*. New York: Greenwood Press, 1989.

Sinclair, Barbara. *The Transformation of the U.S. Senate*. Baltimore: Johns Hopkins University Press, 1989.

———. *Unorthodox Lawmaking: New Legislative Processes in the U.S. Congress*. Washington, D.C.: Congressional Quarterly, Inc., 1997.

Smith, Jesse Carney, and Carrell Peterson Horton. *Statistical Record of Black America*. Detroit, MI: Gale Research, 1997.

Smith, Steven S. *Call to Order: Floor Politics in the House and Senate*. Washington, D.C.: Brookings Institution, 1989.

Subcommittee on Constitutional Rights, Committee on the Judiciary, U.S. Senate. *Hearings on the Extension of the Voting Rights Act of 1965*. 94th Congress, 1st Session. Washington, D.C.: U.S. GPO, 1975.

Sundquist, James. *Politics and Policy: The Eisenhower, Kennedy, and Johnson Years*. Washington, D.C.: Brookings Institution, 1968.

———. *Dynamics of the Party System: Alignment and Realignment of Political Parties in the United States*. Washington, D.C.: Brookings Institution, 1973.

Tate, Katherine. *From Protest to Politics: The New Black Voters in American Elections*. Cambridge: Harvard University Press, 1993.

Thompson, Robert J. "The Commission on Civil Rights." In *The Reagan Administration and Human Rights*, ed. Tinsely E. Yarbrough. New York: Praeger Publishers, 1985.

U.S. Bureau of the Census. *Census of Housing 1960*. Volume 1, *States and Small Areas*, Part 1, United States Summary. Washington, D.C.: U.S. GPO, 1963.

———. *Census of the Population 1960*. Volume 1, *Characteristics of the Population*, Part 1, *United States Summary*. Washington, D.C.: U.S. GPO, 1963.

———. *Census of the Population 1970*. Volume 1, *Characteristics of the Population*, Part 1, *United States Summary*. Washington, D.C.: U.S. GPO, 1973.

———. *The Social and Economic Status of the Black Population in the United States: An Historical View, 1790–1978*. Current Population Reports, Special Studies Series P-23, No. 80. Washington, D.C.: U.S. GPO, 1979.

———. *Census of Housing 1980*. Washington, D.C.: U.S. GPO, 1983.

———. *Census of the Population 1980*. Washington, D.C.: U.S. GPO, 1983.

———. *Voting and Registration in the Election of November 1966, 1976, 1980, 1986, 1990, 1996*. Current Population Reports, P-20–504. Washington, D.C.: U.S. GPO, selected years 1966–1996.

———. *Statistical Abstract of the U.S. 1960, 1970, 1971, 1981, 1988, 1993, 1998*. Washington, D.C.: U.S. GPO, selected years 1960–1998.

———. *1961 Commission on Civil Rights Report*, Book 1, *Voting*. Washington, D.C.: U.S. GPO, 1961.

———. *Political Participation*. Washington, D.C.: U.S. GPO, 1968.

———. *The Voting Rights Act Ten Years After*. Washington, D.C.: U.S. GPO, 1975.

———. *Voting Rights Act: Unfulfilled Goals*. Washington, D.C.: U.S. GPO, 1981.

U.S. Commission on Civil Rights. *Biennial Report 1959*. Washington, D.C.: U.S. GPO, 1959.

U.S. Department of Labor. *Manpower Report of the President*. Washington, D.C.: U.S. GPO, March 1970.

U.S. National Advisory Commission on Civil Disorders. *Report of the National Advisory Commission on Civil Disorders*. Washington, D.C.: U.S. GPO, March 1968.

Walton, Hanes, Jr. *When the Marching Stopped: The Politics of Civil Rights Regulatory Agencies*. Albany, NY: State University of New York Press, 1988.

Watters, Pat, and Reese Cleghorn. *Climbing Jacob's Ladder: The Arrival of Negroes in Southern Politics*. New York: Harcourt, Brace & World, Inc., 1967.

Weingast, Barry. "A Rational Choice Perspective on Congressional Norms." *American Journal of Political Science*, May 23, 1979.

Weiss, Nancy. *Farewell to the Party of Lincoln*. Princeton, NJ: Princeton University Press, 1983.

Wilson, William J. *The Declining Significance of Race: Blacks and Changing American Institutions*. 2d ed. Chicago: University of Chicago Press, 1980.

Wolfinger, Raymond. "Filibusters: Majority Rule, Presidential Leadership and Norms." In *Readings on Congress*, ed. Raymond Wolfinger. Englewood Cliffs, NJ: Prentice-Hall, 1971.

Woodward, C. Van. *The Strange Career of Jim Crow*. New York: Oxford University Press, 1957.

Yarbrough, Tinsley E., ed. *The Reagan Administration and Human Rights*. New York: Praeger, 1985.

Index

About the Author

NINA M. MOORE is Assistant Professor of Political Science at Colgate University. Her research interests focus on American Political Institutions and the role of race in American politics.